Starlight Elixirs and Cosmic Vibrational Healing

Starlight Elixirs and Cosmic Vibrational Healing

Michael Smulkis & Fred Rubenfeld

SAFFRON WALDEN
THE C.W. DANIEL COMPANY LIMITED

Acknowledgement

This is to acknowledge all of those sentient entities without whose continuing patience support, love, and guidance this project would never have reached the state of completion it has. Much gratitude to all who have allowed us to participate in bringing this information and experience to humanity.

We would especially like to thank Deki Fox and Ted Denmark, and, of course, that energy, or vibration, we know as Hilarion.

First published in Great Britain in 1992
by the C.W. Daniel Company Limited
1 Church Path, Saffron Walden
Essex, CB10 1JP, England

ISBN 0 85207 258 9

Designed by Dale Dawson
Production in association with
Book Production Consultants, Cambridge

Typeset by Cambridge Photosetting Services
Printed and bound by St Edmundsbury Press, Bury St Edmunds, Suffolk.

Contents

Introduction
The Purpose of this Book

As humanity evolves, people begin to sense the possibility of being a part of galactic civilization, intergalactic awareness, deeper awareness of the nature of a living universe, and, more importantly, a living galaxy. This is an energy that is beyond the solar system, beyond individual consciousness, beyond the group called humanity. Individual experience can provide this awareness more deeply and in ways far different than by reading books about the stars or by learning about them by second-hand means. The meditation on a star or the utilization of a star elixir can experientially bring into a people a deeper awareness which connects them to this much higher realm of consciousness. This will be unique and special for each person.

All the time, being poured into humanity from so many beings all over this galaxy is the thought: "Join us. Find peace on your world. Grow in understanding so that we may share in your love, and you share in ours." This is not for the purpose of creating a willful change, but an invitation. Many people unconsciously recognize this invitation, and seek in some way to create in themselves an experience so that they will resolve the difficulty: "Where does this energy come from? Why do I feel drawn to the stars? What is their connection to me?" This deeper understanding of your consciousness as it connects to the galactic consciousness is coming to humanity to rectify the difficulties between people as they are attempting to understand their world.

When you take the point of view that you are to live in peace and harmony, that you are to share one world, that you are to be in coordination with Mother Earth, then you are in harmony with the principles of your galaxy that the beings who have survived far, far longer than humanity have accepted for themselves and benefitted from on many levels. As a race, you are unconsciously attempting to create these connections to these galactic ideals. When this is made a little clearer, brought to you in a different form, and shown to you experientially, there can be additional benefit. It is as if those beings who might overshadow the development of the star elixirs and meditation upon the stars recognize in many people this unconscious need, and if at all possible, they wish to fulfill this for people. With humanity's evolution and the evolution of the galaxy in receiving humanity, the preparation for what is to come can happen for people when they extend their vibrational understanding beyond that of the physical world and the subtle worlds into space, into the galaxy as they share it with many beings and many levels of intelligence beyond that which they have conscious knowledge of.

Foreword
by Jon C. Fox

Relaxing, I breathe deeply and imagine the breath moving in and out of my third eye, giving it the internal sounds of "hong...sau...hong...sau..." After about a minute, I say a prayer of protection aloud, calling in Almighty God, the Highest Christ, Babaji Krishna, Mother Mary, Hilarion, and Sathya Sai Baba. I relax each part of my body, allowing my breath to become rhythmic and even. I see myself in an empty movie theater—whatever appears on the screen, whatever sounds come from the speakers are okay. Then I say silently to myself, "I'm asking for Hilarion to come through now."

Instantly, I begin to feel a tingling up and down my spine, a slight pressure in the center of my head, and warm, gentle waves of love flowing through me. I faintly hear a voice (my own) saying "Yes! This is that energy, being, or vibration you call Hilarion!" I put my attention on continuing to relax all the parts of my body, and feel a drifting away, a pleasant yet energetic floating sensation.

As the channeling continues, I am vaguely aware of sounds, movement, images, yet in a dreamlike way, with a focus quite unlike my waking state. Emotions of great love or sadness pass through, very quickly. Sometimes there is a brief sense of emptiness, like a soft gray fog, then suddenly great light and intelligence. Then I hear "Om" sounds and it is over. I stretch, thank Hilarion, and get up.

Remembrance of these sessions sometimes occurs the next day, or after I have slept. Images of beautiful translucent beings of light, swirling galaxies of stars, a sort of cathedral in the clouds, or a clear quartz crystal city. There is also an experience of the friendship and joy of my relationship with Hilarion.

Although it is easier to relate to Hilarion as a single, male entity, Hilarion insists on being considered as a group. Over the years I have grown accustomed to this, and suggest you do the same. "They" are coming through several people right now, but perhaps because of my technical background and my ability to easily go into trance, they frequently provide specific technical information through me.

Since my early youth, I have been a builder, tinkerer, then later an electronics engineer. I love inventing devices, experimenting in science, machining metal, welding, and reading technical non-fiction. In 1982 I happened on research done in Canada on the inert gases (Helium, Neon, Argon, Krypton and Xenon). I replicated some of the experiments, and built some devices containing these gases (which come from our atmosphere, and which we are breathing right now). In 1983 I went to visit a psychic to ask about these devices, as they were scientific curiosities to me.

She channeled a personal "guide" who said she could not channel the technical information from Hilarion I wanted, and that I could! She asked if I wanted to learn how, and I told her I would. She came out of trance, hypnotized me, and five minutes later I was channeling for the first time. That was a turning point in this process which bridges my physical being and technical perspective with the intuitive, non-physical, and greatly expanded consciousness of Hilarion.

People often want to know what it is like to channel, and some want to do it themselves. I have seen many channels in the last few years, and I am impressed with the great variety of their experiences and techniques. If you have been attracted to this yourself, I suggest you try various ways of channeling, intuition, or meditation, but then strike off on your own. Don't try to compare or judge your channeling against that of others. A sense of surrender to and trust of the channeling energy as it comes through is important. More than anything else, this relationship you develop will be a journey of discovery, characterized by challenging surprises.

I am often asked how does one identify a "good" channeling, or how do we know which channels or spirit entities to trust. I think it is wise to apply the criteria Hilarion suggested when I first began, "By their fruits you shall know them." I recommend that people work with information in their own way, looking especially for any resonance in their hearts, and seeing if the concepts and ideas hold up over time. I put no credence on the personality of the channel or the name of the being channeled or the tone of voice or accent used. Nor do I find it important how the person channels (deep trance, conscious channeling, intuitive impressions). Nor do I look at how they came to do channeling in the first place. Rather, I ask if the experience was helpful to me, broadened my understanding, expanded my knowledge, opened up something new in me, or improved my relationships.

We are entering into a period of intense change on Earth. Increasing volcanic activity, depletion of the ozone layer, environmental pollution and societal problems of homelessness, violence, drug use and broken families are all around us. The problems of the environment or the problems of people around us are no longer "out there." Our need to find meaning and purpose for our existence includes a responsibility to sometimes go beyond the limitations of what is "known," and be willing to establish a new context. Channeling offers other perspectives for us, and many otherwise unknown alternatives that can be beneficial.

When I began channeling Hilarion, the phenomenon of channeling non-physical consciousness to assist us in our learning about the physical world did not enjoy as much acceptance. Today there are thousands of publications that represent the pioneering efforts of individuals who have made this intuitive leap. Challenging ourselves by daring to ask the apparently unanswerable questions has opened many new frontiers for humanity's journey in the cosmos.

This book you hold in your hand has a birth story and is part of an on-going discovery process that seeks to further define our relationships in the universe. Inspired by the book *Tapestry* (Hilarion channeled by Maurice B. Cooke, Marcus Books 1985, page 65), in a 1987 channeling, an astrologer/astronomer (Ted Denmark) asked Hilarion through me about the principles of meditating on the stars. Almost as an aside, Hilarion told him one could use a telescope to bring the light of a star into water, and some of the vibrational qualities of the star and its consciousness would go into the water. Years later, Ted began looking into this further, and with the tremendous support of Fred Rubenfeld, and the patience and persistent inquiries of Michael Smulkis, we began our project. As Michael used Ted's specially modified telescope to make the elixirs, I channeled Hilarion to answer questions about the stars and the principles involved. Fred provided the marketing and support needed to make these elixirs available to the world.

For thousands of years humans have gazed up at the stars, and always we have known they were far more than reflections of our own projections. The stars speak to us, to inspire and encourage our collective learning. Most significantly, they suggest a course to follow on our life's journey. Now, by using the starlight elixirs, we can also open ourselves to knowing and feeling their love for us. In this book, you will learn that each star has a personal history and expresses a consciousness with which you can have relationship. As we collectively prepare to meet these magnificent beings, I am excited by the timeliness of this project. I hope you can welcome their vibrations into your life, with the joy and love that I now welcome them into mine.

PART ONE

INTRODUCTION

Chapter 1

★☆☆☆☆☆☆☆☆☆

The Influence of the Stars

Recognize that hanging over all of your lives as an intimate but often unrecognized part are the stars. During your everyday life on Earth you pay little attention to your sky. And at night, though you may be aware of the stars, you usually do not focus on them. Nevertheless, their energies, radiance, love, and upliftment, pour into you at all times. These are energies of a multidimensional character which provide vibrational change on fundamental levels for all the people, animals, and plants of the Earth, as well as the Earth herself. Recognize that these are energies that you tap into unconsciously for the most part. So the process of becoming more aware of the stars, using them in various forms, and understanding their symbolism is one of an inner journey as well as an outer journey, for many of the things that they symbolize extend back through human consciousness for millennia and have influenced the development of symbols, legends, and the understanding of consciousness itself. Each star can provide energy, vibration, and a reflection of some aspect of yourself, which will assist you—should you seek out and request such help—in order to provide a new sense of your life, your purpose, and your coordination with other humans, plants, animals, and the Earth herself.

Although you can look at stars within the constellations within which they appear and recognize the constellations for their zodiacal significance or legendary or symbolic significance, recognize that the stars themselves offer unique energies that have in most cases, especially for the bright stars, a component found within you. Throughout history back into the beginnings of civilization on Earth, the relative brightness of the stars has been a constant. There are certainly relatively minor changes, but by and large, if you were to go back in time, though the stars would have moved a bit, they would look pretty much as they do today. So then you have this as a continuing influence throughout humanity's history, as if affecting the collective unconscious, a way of individual's superconscious and coordinated life form's energy being influenced by the same set of patterns throughout the centuries as anyone would gaze upon the stars and absorb their energy.

The brighter stars are the ones of maximum influence. Part of this is that some of these stars have a greater brightness towards Earth. This will eventually be understood once sufficient travel well outside your solar system has taken place. There is also the way in which stars of greater brightness have been chosen by several civilizations, not of those stars, to act as radiating bodies for the important ideas that have been described in the text. Some of these were influenced by a number of civilizations, some were influenced by the civilizations who call that star their home. But even beyond the brightest stars or even beyond those visible with telescopes, all of these energies are exerting an influence, and these influences are by and large beneficial. The stars are offering guidance, upliftment, insight, understanding, and in most cases, a shift in consciousness for those who would attune to them.

Recognize that the stars, being interconnected and communicating, do form as if an entity in and of themselves. This entity has its own unique characteristics—certain vortices or interference patterns of energy which you recognize as points of light. These points of light might be seen as equivalent to chakra, grid, or various other energy-center forms associated with people. In this way you can more easily attune your own vibration to receive the energies of the stars. Thus what is suggested in this book are techniques for this, and the energies to begin looking at.

The descriptions in this book are only a beginning. As you attune to a star in an elixir form or by meditating upon the star or simply by being aware of its energy as an important component in your life, you may then begin to open, to draw in new energies in yourself, and shift your perspective. The descriptions as given are not limits or limitations, but rather an invitation for you to explore in yourself the energies that begin to open and unfold in you. At this time, humanity is moving through a period of rapid change, much personal growth, and growth in larger areas of human function in the creation of new forms of government, new communities, and even new forms of families and relationships. Besides the continuing influence from past millennia of the stars vibrations, at this time there are additional energies now available from the civilizations associated with these stars that have a special interest in humanity's upliftment, understanding, and awakening. Over the next two decades, perhaps continuing until 2025, great amounts of additional energy from the stars will be available for many people. The stars will have a greater and greater influence, whether accepted consciously or not, on more and more people worldwide.

Imagine yourself in a beautiful place, able to shift context and see things from a different perspective, not chained by past events. It could be in the clouds of Earth, on a planet far away, in another galaxy, but it is a place in which you feel welcome. This place developed by your imagination is actually separate from time and space. The imagination is important in your life in ways that you do not yet fathom because it often points out to you how to accept and work with something in a different context. This allows you to have a more complete picture about it. Imagination is usually seen to be something separate from your reality, but in fact it often gives you this other point of view that is actually more complete.

The awareness of the life cycle of a star is fascinating to think about. So we ask you to think in terms of billions of years, and to think in terms of what a star would be wishing for. What would be involved in its life process? It is difficult for most people to imagine such beyond the sense of awe or magnificence or wonderment, and that is a good place to start. If you imagine yourself as a star, because you are light, you feel inherently connected to other stars, to the planets that you have created, to the civilizations that have worked with you, and to consciousness on all levels. In an awareness of this deeper sense of light in yourself, there can be the sense of outreaching, as if you are deeply connected on all dimensional levels to so much. This sense of connectedness then presents an interesting paradox: you feel this sense of connection, yet there are tremendous distances between the stars. In this way you can understand through your imagination the transcendence of space that a star experiences. In an awareness of the billions of years of the lifetime of a star, a sense of the transcendence of time can take place for you.

Indeed it is theorized by your physicists at this time that in the center of a star, gravity, time, and space are very different from the way you know them. This is because of the tremendous pressures and energies involved, but also because of the tremendous intelligence of this being. The being you call a star has such deep awareness and powerful creativity that is the source from which the significant changes at physical and other vibrational levels takes place.

It is good therefore to imagine yourself a star, to see yourself moving through a star, to imagine what it is like to have such patience, awareness of time, and connection to other stars, beings, and energies. But know also that there is besides imagination, a connection between you and your star, the Sun. Although powerful in its own way and connected to so many other celestial bodies, the Sun is able to appreciate you and know you in your own way. Even though you may be meditating on stars at night, you can allow in your imagination a connection to the Sun on the other side of the Earth. The Sun is able to connect to these other stars in powerful communication with them, and in this way a transference of energy to you can take place as well. It is as if you utilize your Sun to help you know your place in the universe.

There are many interesting things that can be said about stars, but the magnificence of such a being defies any encapsulation. What will be of far more benefit is the way in which people can discover this for themselves. By opening to the light of a star and being the star for a moment, they can know this in their own way by creating this understanding in themselves.

This is the basic message that is also to be imparted by the study and understanding of the stars. It is not simply an intellectual pursuit, it is not just for the purposes that are provided by each of the vibrations associated with the stars. It is to attune you to a natural way of being that is inherent to your very survival. The cells themselves are based on light. All growing things on your planet come from light. This light is utilized chemically, physically, and biologically, but most importantly in this way in which love is manifested as light from you. In your imagination, in your intuitive understanding, you can begin to recognize that the study of a star—the understanding of it, the playing with the knowledge and with the awareness—does more than give you a basic life force that transcends the other forces you are used to. This light is that which precedes the forces that creates such things as food, water, and air.

In this way in which the Sun is your friend, it sometimes sheds light that you do not understand or that may seem to be damaging under certain circumstances. It is as if the Sun is incomplete in some sense and requires your understanding and awareness of love. It is not only hoped that you will develop by working with elixirs, meditation on the stars, and other ways of working with and understanding the stars, but also that you will eventually give this understanding of love to the other beings of other civilized worlds, as well as to the stars themselves and to your Sun.

Because you have the ability to transcend space and time by your imagination, by your mind, you can make this journey between this place far away and the place where you are now. To a large extent, you have not put this to work in a practical, physical, manifestable sense on your Earth. Oh yes, you have certain enlightened ones who do this regularly. But by and large, you are restricted to various vehicles of a physical nature as modes of transportation. However, this is also an inkling of what is to come for humanity. There are essentially three methods of transportation that are utilized by organic beings such as yourself in this galaxy. You may eventually take on as part of your being the most beneficial, the highest, the most beautiful of these. This a way in which you simply disappear from one place and reappear in another. But it is not just by the forces of will or imagination; it is through magnetic, electrical, electromagnetic, and many other energies combined with one essential characteristic. This essential characteristic could be that of mental development, as in other civilizations. Yet here on Earth, this will most likely take place through a tremendous compassion combined with the light of the most powerful aspects of your Sun and of your Earth and of your soul center. As these become one, there is an instantaneous translation in space.

The Influence of the Stars

The stars have been there a long, long time. Many of them long before there was an Earth, some even before there was a Sun or anything remotely like it, some even before there was such as you understand as your galaxy. The stars are living beings with life cycles which move through long patterns lasting millions or even billions of years. These patterns have associated with them individual characteristics relating to various components, organic materials, various metals, certain gasses, and other things within the stars. In their own growth patterns, in their relationships to other stars, in the ways in which they have formed, these various components come together in order to provide what might be assumed in an anthropomorphic representation to be a personality of the star. This usually influences any civilization that grows up around or is nourished by that star, and this as a powerful influence continues. Those civilizations that are developed in a star system that is significantly impacted by the presence in their star of large quantities of a particular mineral, metal, or other substance of an unusual quality by comparison to other stars will also be transmitting to some extent those characteristics of that substance. The civilization itself is tempered to some extent by the substance.

The civilizations associated with the various stars have an important contribution to the vibrational aspects that will be received by Earth people. As the star is a living being, it is influenced by the civilization that grows up around it. Where multiple civilizations are involved, multiple characteristics will usually be transferred to the star. In the later development of such civilizations, direct manipulation and utilization of the energies of the stars takes place. The light of the star can be either modulated, or have added to it certain energetic components, all of which are transmitted with light acting as a carrier. Through their interaction with this energy, and their ability to transfer that which they have to Earth of a positive quality, they give the best of what they have at the highest level. These are the energies which will be of assistance to Earth people. These energies are not just transmitted to Earth, of course, but all over the galaxy and to other galaxies.

But it is important to understand that the energies from the stars are filtered by the aura of the Sun, which extends to the orbit of Pluto. This is done through the awareness of the beings working with humanity on higher dimensional levels so that what reaches Earth is specifically tailored for people.

This transcends the barrier of time. When stars are very far away, it takes a long time for the light from the star to reach you. But the same light that influenced the development of a civilization perhaps 1,000 years ago is always with that civilization. This is the same light that nurtured and affected the civilization. The components of various materials found within the star will usually also be found in abundance on the planets and within that civilization. The nature of the energy that those beings send to you is not trapped in time and space, and thus corresponds to the development of such a civilization as it is now. These energies are tempered by these materials, and therefore have a signature associated with the civilization and their use of these materials. This is why two stars that might be very similar in makeup might still have different qualities, though what you might accept as their signature would be the same.

What is that which you receive from the star? If you look at light and it is a particular color, then couldn't you simply make that color using various forms of filtration or laser production or whatever. No, it is not the light at all that does it. The light is a nice marker, a beacon, a place to attune ones consciousness. But it is the civilization, it is the energy of these beings at a level associated with thought, with your aetheric body, with your spiritual bodies, with the receiving of whatever it is that they have to share with you that can be of direct inspiration. This does transfer on an aetheric level and is not modulating the light. The light will carry some of your attention to this place and attune you and open you to the characteristics that these civilizations make available.

But remember the basic underlying concept: when you attune to the nature of the star, you are working with the energies associated with that star from the civilizations that worked with the star, and from the essential qualities of the star itself. These are what come into you. They are first stimulated within you by the light that falls into your eyes or the vibration from that light captured in various forms of liquid matter such as water or alcohol. In this attunement you are not attuning to the light itself.

When you are working with the starlight in the elixir form or in the meditative form, you are working with that light by only one step down. The vibrational characteristics that are stimulated within you by means of the light will affect the glandular systems of your body and shift your own ability to receive vibration. This is the way in which light works. After that it then becomes a matter of recognizing a vibration that is in kinship, harmony, or in certain unusual cases, in opposition to your own vibration. What is created here is a vibrational bridge that really works with your being, your essence, the part of you that transcends time and space. When you attune to this energy, you are releasing something deep within you which then focuses on a similar vibration, and that vibration is transferred. If the beings at the other end who are transferring this have some capacity that awakens something in you, this is going to happen because what happens in you is ready to happen, and their energy is just a trigger.

This civilization's awareness of you now and its interaction with you now is influencing your decisions and your life. You do not understand this because the civilizations of greatest impact are affecting Earth in the most positive and yet non-interfering way that they can. These beings of great light and spiritual assistance are the majority of those civilizations associated with the stars. Thus they do not impose their will, but they are able to share their energies in a way in which you may accept them better. In opening to the stars that have benefit, that are of assistance, you open to such an energy.

It is impossible to separate the interconnection between the civilization and the star. Humanity's technology within a few hundred years may be able to directly interact and affect the Sun. Those civilizations that have worked on a technological level long enough in such areas have also affected their stars. This sort of interaction is far too difficult to generalize about. But to note of all these possible effects, and work with the general tendencies of a star is usually sufficient.

When you deal with the larger groups of stars—galaxies, globular clusters, various unusual objects, and so on—you have the more difficult question with regards to consensus of energies from many civilizations. And here it is more the representation or signature of the stellar body that allows the individual to tune into this energy and work with it on many levels. This allows the individual more choice in attuning to any specific characteristic of that stellar body.

You do not have to understand all aspects of something to work with it. Being aware of it, opening to it, drawing it in, absorbing it where it appears to be of benefit is quite sufficient. Those who simply utilize the essence or meditate on a given star or work with the energies themselves may notice slightly unusual effects in themselves, ways in which they see and feel themselves differently. This then is the real truth, how this emerges for individuals; and not just the underlying concepts and ideas.

The development on Earth of the ability to see one's place in the cosmos is a natural evolution of the gem elixir and flower essence material. In working with the energies of the stars, people are shown unconsciously that they are capable of working with much more than simply information about the stars. This stimulates an important aspect in people.

Now due to various UFO abduction experiences and other things related to this that people are so concerned about, they might ask very real and important questions about the safety of tuning into these energies. Our answer to this is to tune into those energies that are appropriate. As has been pointed out by many channels and is understood by many in their hearts, the majority of the civilizations in the galaxy (which are most of the stars that you see when you look into the night sky), these are civilizations of benefit, or even in many cases neutrality. Many civilizations which have transcended relating to you as a peer are not constrained by third, fourth, fifth, sixth, or even seventh dimensions.

Many times these beings have understood by faster than light travel, by awareness of what this light is that pours through them, that they are not constrained by the speed of light. The scientist in you may say: "But that star is 2,000 light years away, how could its light possibly have anything to do with me when the light coming to me now is 2,000 light years old?" Even if it is a star that is very close, only a few light years away, still you would not have the sense of it being current. But thought transcends time and space. These beings and their thoughts can be instantly transmitted to you, just as yours are transmitted to them. The beings you recognize as beneficial or helpful, as for instance beings from the Pleiades, they are not depending upon their understanding of Earth from many centuries ago, nor are they even depending upon the transmission from Earth of television and radio of a few decades ago. They understand by thought, by awareness, by consciousness in the present moment; and so it is also that you can understand the energies of these stars in the same manner.

You may have to start understanding the stars with some aspects of the logical thinking process. When you have enough of these to have your foothold, to know where you are, to understand just basically what this is about, you can let go of this. Let the energies of these beings, of these elixirs, of these meditations be with you, and what you may discover is that there is a part long-dormant in you willing to wake up. This is why this information is being released now. We are not the only channel speaking about this, there will be others. An example would be star elixirs used for healing found in the work of Tolkien in *The Lord of the Rings.* Remember that this is to touch something old and something new in you—this capacity to recognize kinship.

The kinship is born initially of light. Then it also comes to human values and those things that you find important for your own transformation, for your own issues in the world. Beings in other star systems have dealt with some of the same problems you have. They have not always solved them the same way as you. Many times they have dealt with powerful energies such as nuclear which destroyed their home by inadvertent or accidental means. Others have experienced an involution of societal values where such values as greed or power have come in place of harmony and truth.

The Law of Opposite Expression seems to hold throughout the galaxy and most of the universe. So therefore most civilizations that have risen to some degree of consciousness and awareness have had to deal with their own negative aspects, transcended the shadow self, or understood all aspects in themselves of lightness and darkness. The very nature of consciousness is to bring awareness. Therefore there is always an upliftment by dealing with the aspects of negativity. Rarely has a civilization moved through various aspects of awareness and consciousness with what you would term ease. Indeed there are always periods of struggle or difficulty or taking several steps backward to take several forward. So these beings sometimes have something to share with you: an energy of source that says you can solve these problems by the love we see in you.

Most civilizations which have reached some degree of conscious awareness, spiritual growth, or technological development and understanding, are quite aware of Earth as a civilization. Beings on Earth broadcast much about themselves to the universe through their radio and television broadcasts, through their own powerful mental thought forms, and through their creation of wars and various violent difficulties on Earth. So it would be very hard for such civilizations not to be aware of the Earth. Yet those civilizations that wish to provide energy of an uplifting and helpful nature to humanity do so out of their very nature. And it is only those who have very powerful specific messages—the ones associated with the brighter stars, those civilizations we have discussed in detail—that will provide these energies in a very powerful directed way towards people.

Humans have not reached a place of consciously broadcasting what they have learned. They broadcast to each other for the influence of relationship, or in the case of broadcasting through radio, television, and so on for the selling of products or the making of money or for the purpose of communication or for the purpose of influencing of others for the garnering of power. It is very much in the nature of all beings to broadcast who they are as an important part of their own existence. So therefore these beings in other star systems will consciously or unconsciously broadcast who they are, either by deliberately directing their awareness or not. Yet most of those stars that have civilizations associated with them that are helpful to humans, that are deliberately seeking to assist people on Earth, are doing this broadcasting very deliberately and consciously and allowing the very best of what they have to be broadcast. But it is in their nature to broadcast anyway, so it is simply a matter of influencing this process.

When we speak to such beings, when we meet with them, or know them, or feel the light from their stars, many times what we recall is not only what they have done, what they have created, but a question they have for you. It is not always as you would think, like: "Why are you screwing up your planet?" But it is often: "Why not love more? Why not find some place in you that is deeper, stronger, and clearer, and which can allow this loving aspect of you now to be applied so that your problems become instead a joyful solving together?" This question is not verbal in nature. As you go deeper and deeper into the subtle levels of this, you will begin to feel this deeper question about such things as the natural resources of your planet, and of how these things can be appropriately shared. This may even inspire certain visions within you that can welcome this.

There is a powerful change—largely unconscious and unavailable to humans at the current time—that is moving throughout the galaxy. This is an influence that has been accelerated greatly since the awareness of the Christ presence on Earth. This is an awareness that has brought deeper understanding of the potentials for many capacities to come into beings. There are many pieces to this puzzle. Most of these have already been laid in place. The one remaining piece of maximum importance is that which humanity will add. It is not that the piece that is put in is that much larger or has greater influence in and of itself. But because it does then complete the whole, it does then activate a tremendous energy. Therefore humanity's contribution to this is of so much importance because in the completion of this whole, so much becomes activated for so many.

When an individual finds some specific attunement to a particular star, it is possible, utilizing the Law of Help, to ask that star to influence or assist that individual. One can attune to the star by meditating on the star or taking the elixir, but then asking for that help, even though it is not that which that civilization has specifically offered as we have suggested in the text, this energy may still be quite available for the person. It is really that simple. An individual's consciousness is quite powerful and can indeed bridge over millions of light years to make some association with the consciousness of a group or of an individual in another place. The ability to share consciousness across huge distances is one of the important properties of thought. But beyond thought, consciousness can be shared through the understanding of essence, for indeed essence transcends time, space, and most dimensional limitations; and bringing this into form yourself is quite possible.

CHAPTER 2

★★☆☆☆☆☆☆☆

Working with the Energies of the Stars

Star elixirs will help most individuals. But if you go out and look into the beautiful sky full of stars and you don't get anything from it, probably star elixirs are not going to be very helpful for you. Many of you recognize a certain kinship around this. How many of you can gaze at a sunset and not be moved by it? Then a similar thing applies. The underlying energy here is the shared consciousness which exists because all of you have understood and worked with the stars all your past lifetimes. Half of your life is the night life, and whether you look at the stars or not, they are influencing you. And many of you in many of your lifetimes have looked at them. So it is likely you are going to get something of value from working with these energies.

When you would gaze at a star, you are attuning to its innate vibration. These vibrations may have a lot to do with the civilization that has grown up with the star or the star itself, but the point is that such vibrations are accessible once you open to them. The idea of bringing the light of a star into pure water is to bring the association of that star and its vibrational characteristics into that which on Earth is most easily able to vibrate and hold the vibration of that star. Pranic forces in water are unique amongst all of the compounds found on Earth. Water's unique physical properties form the basis of life on Earth. Water is able to capture and hold much of the vibrational qualities and characteristics of other substances, other vibrations, and other energies that it is exposed to. This is the principle underlying homeopathy, flower essences, and gem elixirs.

What occurs in star elixirs is that the light from the star is allowed to vibrate in pure water. What is transmitted to the water is a holistic vibrational representation of the energy of the star and the civilization and other factors associated with the star. The water holds such a vibration, ready to be released into the water within your bodies. This characteristic of water transferring to water is what brings this vibrational signature into a person. This process is influenced by consciousness, and therefore this process will be enhanced when you are more aware of your ability to draw in this vibration. But because the water in the elixir affects water of the body, these effects will still go on even if the person is not aware of them. The idea of the transfer of vibration to the subtle bodies has been discussed extensively in the previously channeled material, in particular, *Gem Elixirs and Vibrational Healing, Vol. II.*

The point is that this transference of vibration has a lot to do with the microbiological properties as well as the physical properties of water and its uniqueness as the sustainer of life in so many different forms on Earth. Thus, the water when taking on this higher vibratory characteristic is able to transfer it to individuals. This transference may continue over a long period of time after one exposure to such water because the change may be gradually felt as it shifts and moves from one water molecule to the next throughout the human body. When such changes reach the brain, there will usually be some shift in consciousness. This will also apply to changes in consciousness which are influenced by the heart and the spine. As these changes come more and more into consciousness and awareness, some of the characteristics of the star will be transferred to the person.

We have the difficult job of sharing which of these characteristics will be transferred to people. We must assess the potentials of the star based on the civilization and the quality or personality of the star itself. We must then assess which of these vibrations will make it into your telescope on Earth. This will be influenced by environmental conditions, upper atmospheric conditions, the Earth's own aetheric energy, and the nature of the influence of thought forms on the aethers of the Earth itself. Then we must assess how these energies will be captured in water, what will stay and what will not, and which of these qualities is most likely to be transferred to the majority of individuals who then ingest such water.

Certain individuals as providing representation of larger civilization are called upon to assist in this process. Individuals who have a deeper understanding of their own history are utilized.

Yet it is also important here to bring through the general characteristics, which are known and well received by so much of humanity. To receive and pull that information is very simple. It is a matter simply of looking at how individuals are influenced by the stars, how they have always been influenced by this, how it is as if carried within the genetic coding of individuals, and how it is shared within the collective conscious of all of humanity. So in bridging across all of these areas, it is really a matter of deciding what not to say, than what to say, since so much is available. A civilization has an extensive history, dealing with so many different things. A star may have been in existence billions of years, providing vibrational influence for many civilizations, for many beings. So it is a matter of deciding what is not to be shared.

Now many will ask, who is involved in this project? These include a number of ascended masters, but also a number of beings whose specific task is for the gathering of scholarly information about such matters. There are also personal guides of the questioners, including Fred and Michael. In addition to this, there are a number of guides associated with many who will read this material in the future. These guides are also influencing this process. For those who have picked up this book for no particular good reason, as if then they were drawn to it and felt they must buy it, acknowledge the influence of these guides, and ask them to provide you with their experience of this information, and you may have a much deeper insight and understanding about it. It is as if your guide already knows about this and wants to bring you the information through the reading of the book as well as through their own influence.

And then beyond this are influences purely mathematical in nature for the deriving of information, where information is stored as in globular clusters, particular crystal matrices, various Atlantean records, and many other things available to those with ability to attune to such vibration. Most individuals on Earth have such abilities but keep them dormant or locked up because they are not yet ready to access such capacities. Yet we see it very likely that very soon more and more individuals will attune to such capacities in themselves.

The most important influence in this process are the energies of the Sun. Sometimes known as Helios, this entity is able to overshadow and directly assist by informing us which of the energies that might be useful for beings on other star systems will not apply to Earth people, and which energies appropriate for other stars will not apply in the Sun's environment.

Alcohol has the property of causing some of these vibrations to remain fixed by slowing down the process by which water reverts to the neutral state. This is why alcohol is generally added to such vibrational mixtures. Also alcohol will tend to lower the effects of external light, particularly from the Sun, that might interfere with some of these subtler stellar vibrations. Thus, diluting the water in alcohol tends to preserve it for a far longer period of time than if the water was kept in its natural state after it has been exposed to the stellar vibration.

When combining star elixirs with flower essences and gem elixirs, the elixir form is the most subtle when there is the maximum isolation to light and the maximum amount of pure alcohol. Therefore this light exclusion and alcohol presence will not harm the presence of other substances. So therefore it would be better to put the flower essence, gem elixir, or inert gas elixir into the star elixir bottle. A combination is best mixed in alcohol in a light-tight bottle, because the most subtle of these elixirs will be the most sensitive to the various contra-indicating and difficulty producing other substances.

Don't be confused when we say subtle to think that this means not effective, not powerful, not having an effect that you will notice. In fact it is the opposite. It is in these ways of vibrational subtlety that the maximum transfer will generally be seen to come into the person. The most subtle of flower essences, such as Lotus and Silversword, the most delicate of these energies of the gems, perhaps such as diamond, these are the most powerful as well. But you need a little more alcohol, a little more care in preserving them, a little more beautiful energy around them when you make them for the same reason—that these energies are very subtle. These energies move through and very powerfully connect multiple levels of existence. Thus a lessening of density occurs—that is what subtlety is.

These energies are also more sensitive to densifying influences such as strong magnetic fields, energies from substances with powerful smells such as coffee, and of course sunlight. The general influences to be avoided are the same as with flower essences, gem elixirs, and homeopathic remedies. The only additional ones to be avoided are those substances of petrochemical origin which are becoming more and more troublesome to vibrational remedies, and of course the influences of light and energies derived from the Sun.

In terms of dosages and utilizations of the elixirs, these are done according to individual's own attunement and capacity. But generally the idea is to repeatedly give some vibration to the person, giving them a time to absorb it and work with it. So giving a vibration a few times a day is helpful. When there are numbers of some higher significance associated with this, there will usually be additional benefit because of the deep symbolism that numbers hold for people. Thus numbers like three drops or seven drops, making combinations and putting them under pyramids or tetrahedrons for ten minutes or two hours come up over and over because of the numbers. Two hours representing one twelfth of a day, ten minutes representing 1/144 of a day. The day is an essential primary component as it relates to basic internal cycles, the nocturnal/diurnal cycle that all people feel.

It is hard to overdose on the elixirs when taken at the stock bottle or mother essence level unless there is particular sensitivity to a particular elixir. At which point a person should not take it at the mother essence or stock bottle level, but instead take it at a higher homeopathic potency, perhaps at 12X as a good neutral homeopathic potency for perhaps a few weeks, and then take it again at the stock bottle level.

As these are vibrational enhancers, you don't really have to prepare quite as much as you might with some of the more powerful vibrational tools such as flower essences for the purification and shift. With most of these stars, there is less chance of what might be called healing crisis. There can be a great shift, but it is not likely that it will manifest so much physically—it will be one of insight and change.

The best preparation for working with the energies of the stars is to find a place of quietness inside. Go out and look at the stars a little, learn about the characteristics of the stars, and welcome their energies. If you are out at night and you are feeling those stars, this feeling of quiet may be with you even if it is in a noisy environment. Find the quietness inside, even if that means a stilling of the mind, a meditative technique, a movement, a dance, or whatever it takes to help you be a little quieter. This will enhance tremendously the effects of the star elixirs as you take them.

Choose them wisely. Choose them in a way in which you have some willingness to change. And manifest that willingness, feel it within you as you work with the elixir. Somewhere inside you state: "I am willing." A phrase such as this which draws your attention to this willingness to open will be of great benefit. This is true of all vibrational tools, all vibrational remedies. But with the stars in particular, this can help deepen this experience to reach a place of questioning. It might even be years of working with it before the benefits seem to shift and you have gained what you need from it. But after you have received benefit, after you have used the star elixir, look for that question and find the way to answer it in yourself. It may relate very much to some application of love in your life.

Meditation upon the Stars

One would gaze upon the star and then one would internalize it by whatever means is appropriate. For the visually oriented this may mean to attempt to recreate the vision of the star inside oneself. For those who are audibly oriented, to attune to an inner sound that the star might be stimulating in them. For the physically oriented, to bring the star into oneself, to imagine it warming ones body, to put it inside you somewhere. To those who are attuned by other modalities, they use that which is appropriate. And then sitting with that for awhile, holding that within one's own self, one closes one's eyes and focuses on this internalized aspect of the star. This can take place very briefly, for a matter of a half a second, or as long as five or ten minutes, depending on what feels comfortable and appropriate. The eyes are then opened and one would again view the star and drink in then the star's inherent characteristics. These do not have to be known, one can simply open oneself and let these things flow in.

In some ways it isn't so much a technique, it is really a non-technique. It is as if saying here is an object of tremendous brightness, power, energy, radiance, and although it might appear somewhat faint, but still knowing that its light does reach you convinces you in some ways of its great power when you recognize how far away it is. And so it is as if trusting that energy, saying that this energy itself is powerful enough, useful enough, and that which can correspond enough with one's own consciousness to have benefit. One simply accepts this and then is able to more easily accept the benefits of that light itself and need not go further in figuring it out. It is simply a matter of opening to it and in this way drinking it in.

Exposure to the star itself by gazing upon it will usually affect the body on many levels. The idea is to transfer vibration to the holism of the body. This vibrational transfer takes place through consciousness by a direct attunement to the vibration of the star. This is why when an individual has difficulty in attuning to the vibration of the star, yet wants to work with some of the effects suggested, they are better off utilizing the star elixir. The difficulty may have to do with the temperature or environmental conditions under which they would have to go to see the star, or difficulty in locating the star. But it may also have to do with the energy of the star itself. Such a presentation at a conscious level may be difficult for the individual, as if they are being asked to move too quickly or to learn too much.

As the energy that is available from the star moves through the person, there will be some transfer into the water of the body. This is a way in which the body is able to store and work with the vibration of the star. After you have completed the meditation upon the star, it would be wise to spend a moment or two of thinking about the water in your body, directing consciousness to it so it would continue to hold the vibration of the star. This is true also when utilizing meditation upon a flower or a gem, the water in the body can be used as a storage mechanism. But this is not of great importance. Far more important is the way in which you deliberately bring the shift in vibration caused by the consciousness of the star into all portions of your life, into your understanding of yourself, as well as into your awareness of your relationships and your physical body as a symbol affected by this energy. Your understanding of yourself will be shifted by this new awareness. This takes place through either the elixir or meditation upon the star because of the similarity of the way in which this energy moves through you. A shift is created when the vibration of the star is added to or coupled to the vibration of your own being.

If an individual has attuned to the star through meditation and gone to a certain extent with that, and then they take the elixir, they will usually find a deepening of effect. The reverse is also true. When you combine these methods at the same time, you are utilizing two mechanisms to bring the consciousness into the vehicle of the person. So you are bringing some of this in through direct awareness, through alteration of the thought forms and consciousness in the brain and the higher mind, and you are also doing it through the physical body through water uptake mechanisms, and that is then transferred into higher levels of consciousness. It is as if you are working at it from both ends moving in towards the middle, and this is likely to be more effective for most individuals. This is a holistic process in which many aspects of the individual are affected at once by such a technique.

Some individuals may experience sensory overload when meditating on the stars in an open area. The solution to this is not that far different than what is currently utilized by those who subject themselves to loud music or powerful stimulating experiences that would seem overloading to most individuals: one becomes as if transparent, clear, holding nothing, and in this way energy from the various stars sweeps through you. It is as if then you attune to all of them at first. Then you see yourself becoming transparent, not invisible, but clear so that the light of these stars simply passes through you and then into the Earth. Then as you focus on a single star, you allow that to fill you up, you become as if then in your imagination filled with the light of that star, glowing with it. This way then is one in which such a light is stronger than that of the other stars, in your imagination, and thus the light from them either is seen to pass through you or as if then go around you, as if repelled by the light of that star that has filled you. The point is that you do not seek to shut out the awareness of the other stars, you simply allow this energy to move through you with no influence or attachment in your own visualization.

If one gazes on that star, there is a focussing of the eyes on that particular area. When the eye is focussed at infinity, it is naturally possible to attune to many things at once. When one begins to notice this occurring, it is usually good to close the eyes, and imagine that starlight, the one you have been gazing at, pouring into you, as if it is then illuminating you from the inside. For some individuals this will mean it appears as if imprinted on the inside of the eyelid; for others inside the mind; for others, inside the heart or the physical body. Each must find his or her own way. But other techniques such as this acknowledgement of the other energies, and allowing them to pass through, may be very helpful if you have an intimate knowledge and awareness of many of the stars, and it is very hard to shut them out.

A simple device can be constructed with a small hole to view only the star of choice, special environments can be constructed, or trees in a forest can be used appropriately. This has been done by those in the past who seek the influence of a single star.

Starlight Elixirs and Dreams

In general it will be observed that various vibrational tools of any kind that have significant effect on the higher bodies, the spiritual bodies, the mental body, the astral body, will translate into dream experiences, as you understand them. When you are asleep, you do not have a deep awareness of the difference between astral body experiences or dreams, and such a differentiation is unnecessary. It is also useful to recognize here that many of the civilizations involved, many of the higher forces, the beings that allow their energies through these stars to assist individuals, are blocked in their efforts to do so by the conscious mind. When the mind is able to sleep a bit, to stand out of the way and allow these things to come through in their own way, in their own form, then such can come through in magnitude. This is one reason that vibrational tools which attune one to energies that are of higher intelligences than are normally made available to people will come through that much more quickly and more powerfully in the dream state.

In addition, besides the conscious mind getting out of the way, there is often a willingness within an individual in the dream state to process various forms of information that are presented at an emotional, and to a lesser extent, aetheric and physical level. This can be very important when one utilizes a star that can attune one to a source one already has had contact with in a past life. This may be an awareness of a particular civilization by being in that place or being taught by such individuals, perhaps an experience of contact with such beings in this lifetime, perhaps an awareness of their symbolism and the whole idea of the assistance of other civilizations. All of these things contribute to the naturally creative unconscious, which will tend to work these things out in the dream state. Although this may not be available at the conscious level, the powerful emotional issues that are discharged in dealing with the attunement to higher knowledge and other matters can be dealt with so much more easily in the dream state. The body's own wisdom directs the course of how this energy and information can come in. As you attune to these things in the sleep state and find your dreams that much more vivid, there are being given to you many tools to work with in the waking life. To use dream recall, various dream interpretation techniques, ways of deliberately making what you have received in the dream more conscious, and then relating your own interpretation and feeling back to the star, you can have a deeper attunement and awareness of the civilization associated with that star, as well as deeper awareness of your own issues dealing with some of the things that star has brought up.

Star Elixirs and channeling

Individuals on planet Earth right now are attuning to channeling more and more. The reason for this is that there is so much energy pouring in from so many sources as if to say you are more than who you think you are, more than you have remembered. Individuals who are attuning to extraterrestrials of positive impact on people on Earth can do well to utilize star elixirs in a slightly different manner. Here a group may wish to work with a focalizer, a person who will do channeling. That focalizer has a particular attunement to a star chosen by the group. They choose a star or extraterrestrial civilization they are already familiar with or interested in, or choose one arbitrarily. All of the people in the group then utilize that star elixir or meditate on the star, and then the channeling begins. A specific request is made to attune to a being from that civilization. The vibrations of all of the people linked together will significantly improve in any channeling situation. But by attuning to an energy that is already pouring in, this can be quite powerful. At the same time for the person who is doing the channeling, they may find it much easier to do such work because they have the inherent vibrational support of the various contributing factors of all of the people in the group.

We mention this because there are people who will naturally think of this and wonder if it is appropriate. This will work best if there is a clear consensus amongst the individuals involved that the star system they wish to attune to has positive benefits, is something they are all interested in, and is helpful to the evolution of the people in the room at that time.

The ability to transform, to change, and to create their own vibrational shift as a result of the channeling process is so important at this time and can thus be engendered better in a group. This can be done with any of the star elixirs, perhaps better than with flower essences, gem elixirs, or homeopathics, because you are attuning to a very intelligent force. You are not simply attuning to a reverence and working with the Earth that might be found in the connection between the devic kingdom and a flower, but to a developed level of civilization from other stars.

A Brief Description of How Starlight Elixirs Are Made By Fred and Michael ★

Most of the elixirs are made in the foothills of the Sierra Nevada Mountains of California, near Calaveras Big Trees State Park. This site has very little light pollution, being far from any major city. As this house is solar powered, there is also no interference from power lines. We use a Schmidt-Cassegrain telescope with silver-coated mirrors. The light of the star is captured by suspending a quartz bottle filled with extremely pure water directly in front of the eyepiece. The telescope has a clock-drive that enables it to follow each particular star as it moves and keep it centered within the viewing field. An interesting pattern of starlight is revealed within the bottle of water, like a three-dimensional viewing screen. Inert gas devices are used to eliminate the possibility of negative thought form contamination. After two hours, this vibrationally altered water is placed within a light-proof container. Pure grain alcohol is added as a preservative for this stellar energy.

As for directions to use the star elixirs, take one to seven drops either directly or diluted in pure water. Avoid exposing an open bottle to sunlight. Three seconds is the maximum time that a star elixir can be exposed to direct sunlight. For indoor use, there is a longer period of exposure that is acceptable, one to five minutes is an approximate range. After this time period, indoor lighting might start to influence the elixir. The best solution to the problem of light contamination would be to use the elixir two hours after sunset or in an area with very little light, total darkness being the most effective. During the time of the new moon or after the moon has set, the elixir can be taken outside in conjunction with gazing at the star.

These star elixirs can also be used in massage or in bathing. The best source of illumination would be the indirect light of natural, undyed, unscented candles. Bathing in pure water with a few drops of the elixir can allow the energy of the star to permeate all of the subtle bodies. As a bathing ritual, there may be a memory of the light of stars as they were focussed into large bath chambers. This was done in Atlantis and early in Egypt during special times of initiation. Depending on the level of the initiate, specific stars were utilized. We are now able to recreate some of these ancient techniques by taking the starlight internally in addition to immersing ourselves in a cosmic bath.

The original liquid mixtures are made into a stock concentration by adding seven drops of the mother essence to a mixture of pure water and 40% grain alcohol. It is at this stock level that most people have been using these elixirs.

CHAPTER 3
★★★☆☆☆☆☆☆

Historical uses of Starlight Elixirs

The Lemurians utilized the stars in many ways: gazing upon them, journeying to them in astral form, utilizing them in ritual when there was a particular essence or focus needed in that which was carried on at night. These were usually moonless nights, but occasionally lunar influence was also a part of the ritual.

The Atlanteans sought out information. They looked at the spiritual essence and capabilities of the stars. They then discovered many technological ways which could be used to emphasize, strengthen, and bring these into greater form. Many of the techniques they utilized caused difficulty in the long term, and we have not commented on these or described them. They usually utilized resonating crystals to form a latticework at an aetheric level that transfers or translates the star's energy into a new form that can then be captured in various different ways utilizing oscillating crystal matrices or various technological devices. These were the principles that were also employed in producing energies that could later be applied for the movement of specific DNA patterns.

However the techniques that were far simpler, the mere capturing of these starlight energies into such as water, these techniques were utilized in the early technological development of the Atlantean civilization. Some Lemurians did not find this acceptable. They said: "You are missing the point, you are missing the ritual, the awareness, the direct connection with these stars." They did not understand that many of these Atlantean beings had lost their inner connection with their will and with the Earth and with their own understanding of themselves as Earth beings. As a result the Atlanteans needed a deeper and more powerful spiritual awareness, and the only way they could receive this was through these subtler forms. Thus merely meditating on the stars was not sufficient for some of these Atlanteans.

In their own way then both civilizations and societies were deficient. The Lemurians required forgiveness for the Atlanteans, and were unable to manifest it. The Atlanteans required will and awareness of their connection to their roots and to the Earth, and were unable to easily assimilate this. People today in working with flower essences, gem elixirs, homeopathy, various herbs, and the star elixirs will naturally be working with all of these principles. In this way they will be touching in themselves both will and spirit, and developing a deeper awareness of the many attributes of their own lives, their own personalties, and their spiritual awareness. There is no segregation, no inner division, when you work with all of these vibrational remedies. If a person was to work with star elixirs exclusively, there could easily be a tendency to excessive development of spiritual principles without will, without the actions which occur in the day. But if there is a balance, if there is even a little attention to daylight matters, we do not see very much difficulty.

The Lemurians developed a deeper sensibility and awareness of the characteristics of the stars. This often began with the inner meditative work. Then the Lemurian would reach out with their consciousness to the star. The connection to the civilization and to the stars themselves was emphasized and initiated by the Earth people. Then when this energy reached its climax, its most powerful point, the civilization or the star itself then returned the energy. It was as if their effort was well rewarded. This occurred first with the brightest stars. A great development of musical form was then transmitted by Vega, this deeper awareness and healing by Capella, and deeper concentration and focus of mental energies by Polaris—all of these different things by the different stars, each of them in their own ways. These gifts from the stars have changed somewhat over time as the Earth's own rotational axis has shifted, various characteristics of aetheric density have changed, and so on. But back in Lemurian times, the awareness of these stars gave the Lemurian culture a deep understanding that they were not alone.

The Atlanteans thirsted for this understanding, but were unable to always follow the path of knowledge which the Lemurians used. Thus the influence of the concentrated vibration of the star was of benefit in re-awakening in the Atlantean much of this inner consciousness. So there were many techniques developed far beyond that of the telescope, but the essential principles of the telescope were employed for the development of elixirs.

The greatest use of this was as a great celebration for an individual's transformation. This occurred midway through the first Atlantean epoch, thus this is allied with the early development of Atlantean civilization. A large reflecting mass which could be that of a crystalline object, a metallic semi-sphere, a parabolic off-axis mirror, or various other structures were utilized to reflect the light from one star into a bath and then the person was to go into that bath. It was a beautiful meditative experience, one in which the water was very powerfully purified and cleansed. The water was then utilized for the development of plants that had specific capabilities related in some way to this star. When those plants grew, this person might partake of them by burning them and smelling the burned residue, by eating them, or by utilizing them as a flower essence. There were many other techniques. These are similar in many ways to the underlying Lemurian principles, but there is here in working with these in the nighttime alone the tendency observed by some of the Atlanteans to disconnect from the deeper roots, to have very beautiful experiences that were not made very physical later. And so you see the beginnings of the difficulty.

And though this technique could be utilized at the current time, you would generally find it too expensive, or you would not be able to get sufficient light to cover such a large area as a bathtub. But some people can experience this for themselves by taking a few drops of the star elixir and putting this in the bath. But it is best if this technique is utilized in a darkened room. Utilize only candlelight, and if possible, this should be shielded so that only the candlelight reflected off the wall or ceiling is visible to the person. Then you get into the bath and meditate on the characteristics of the star after putting a few drops of the elixir into the water.

Meditation on the stars has gone on for all cultures. Each culture has developed their own favorite stars, their own ways of working with them, their own particular awareness of this. The seasonal attributes of the various stars is an important part. The Mayans in particular have a great deal of lore and understanding of much of this. The Mayan civilization has been influenced by Lemurian civilization from subtle levels as well, and the deep awareness of this is an important part of Mayan culture. The Egyptians had ways of working with the stars themselves, and they developed various techniques of drawing in the energies associated with the different stars as part of their rituals. However this is just a natural sort of thing. The development of all cultures relates very much to their own observance of the heavens and their observance that although they are earthbound, they are still somehow connected to the light that they see in the sky.

CHAPTER 4

★★★★☆☆☆☆☆

The Seeding of the Earth

It was as if in the beginning there was a light. This light burst forth—it was that which you call the Sun. But it was of such tremendous energy that time, space, and gravity did not exist. Instead there was a great questioning—what will be? As this question resonated with the Sun, energies poured in from many places and times. Transcending this were the energies from many other stars as if saying let this one be a little different. As the Earth was birthed from the Sun, there was also born a question about how love might be formed. God's energy is the energy of the combined forces of all of the billions of galaxies of billions and billions of stars. This is an energy that asks: "What will allow this to be more of what it is?" What was asked was could this be a planet that could support love? The answer to this was unknown at the time, but it looked like a good shot.

As the Earth was formed, what was seen was that a lot of water would be helpful for developing the emotions. Energies of all kinds were attracted to assist in seeding the Earth. This seeding was a cross-fertilization from many civilization and many developing technologies. Many energies of pure mental functioning alone were reflected to the Sun to create the genetic structures that gave birth to life. First there was a setting of a scene, and then the seeding itself.

Humanity may be seen as quite distinct in many ways from other life forms found on Earth. Such a distinction cannot be ascribed to Darwinian evolutionary processes alone. There are too many differences in DNA structures, intelligence, consciousness, and certain unusual capacities of the human body to simply be explained by random chance or mutation processes. For instance, the hairs on the human body are aligned in such fashion as to promote naturally occurring efficiency in moving through water, yet no aquatic phase has been identified. Nor would any primate other than man share this trait and capacity, as the fur of chimpanzees, apes, and other primates does not promote efficient movement through water. So therefore you are left with many questions about this if you look at this from a purely evolutionary point of view. Neither can the evolution of humanity be understood by the miracle described in Genesis of God placing on Earth certain beings fully formed and ready to do what they need to.

This is because of the tremendous prehistory, the powerful influence of multiple civilizations going way back in time, and the powerful conscious affinity so many people have to animals and plants that goes far beyond those things of recent civilizations' developments. People also have an affinity for powerful energies that extend way back into humanity's past. Therefore recognize that the real answer to this question of genetic influence, seeding, etc. lies in your very being, in the cells in your bodies, in the DNA structures found within you. These contain the real answer to this question as to the nature of humanity's history in a biological sense. This has not been unlocked yet by your scientists, but when it is, the final question of evolution will be put to rest. Many of the influences on humanity can be traced to powerful energies which are extraterrestrial in nature. These influences have certain patterns associated with vibratory signatures of other civilizations. Certain genetic aspects have been removed, changed, or modified far beyond that of current understanding—this could only happen through these other technologies.

Because this happened over an extended period of time, it is not as if there was one coherent policy developed that was then continued all throughout humanity's evolution. As various other civilizations wished to contribute to this, many changes were made. Initially there were direct influences from a concordance of a number of civilizations that were directed through the highest level of awareness in the center of the galaxy. This was a coordination with powerful energies of pure starlight nature, not anything resembling human or organic life forms.

But as humanity's own potential began to be recognized by other civilizations, various other contributions were made. A few were made quite outside of the approval, consent, and assistance of humanity's guides, humanity itself, and the other beings that had been previously involved in the seeding. Therefore it is important to recognize that this was not always done with humanity's highest interests at heart. Luckily, most of these aspects have contributed in generally beneficial ways to humanity, much to the chagrin of the civilizations involved, and the delight of those who wish the highest and best for humanity.

Indeed humanity is a synthesis of many influences, terrestrial and extraterrestrial. As a true melting pot of such energies, humanity cannot be so easily distinguished from other civilizations, yet has its own unique characteristics. Most people on Earth are a combination of the many beings that have existed in various forms on other planets. But you have adapted specifically for Earth. Your lungs have to adapt to the higher concentrations of various substances. Many things that are unique and special about Earth would be things that you have held into your own formulation. The stature of beings on Earth suits the gravity, so you are not as tall as some of those who have seeded you. People on Earth have a genetic memory that tells them things could be different, air doesn't have to be breathed quite this way, and that they could be a lot taller and live a lot longer. These are genetic implants that can allow transformation for people.

These civilizations have powerfully influenced the DNA structures, the cellular structures, the anatomical structures, the digestive system, the skin, the hair, the nails, as well as the very physical appearance, the size, the shape, and form of the human body. The ability of individuals to communicate through various subtler forms, not just through the vocal or written forms, but also through telepathy, psychometry, and by passing information through sacred rites and many other things—these things have all been influenced by so many different civilizations intertwined in so many different ways. The motivation behind this is different, of course, depending upon each of the civilizations involved.

In some cases this influence has been that of a seeking of an upliftment or a help to humanity. But in others it has been for the production of specific limitations. In others it has been so that the limitations are in alignment with humanity's own need to understand emotion, to work consciously with the understanding of death, and to work and understand in ways that eventually give rise to the overcoming of these limitations and the bringing of consciousness in the form of love, without the full consciousness of past lives where love was understood. Humanity's request to understand and work with love could not be accomplished without certain limitations. This way an individual would not have to carry the guilt from a past lifetime into the current lifetime. Yet the individual would also have a deep understanding of disease or death processes so that he or she would understand the power of emotion and work with it appropriately, this always leading to a development of greater love, compassion, and understanding. This is not an easy concept to understand, yet it relates very much to humanity's evolution and the purpose of humanity. This is why humanity's purpose is so difficult for so many people to accept and work with, yet the meaning and power in humanity's purpose begins to come forward once you begin to appreciate some of these concepts.

The influence of other civilizations on humanity has taken place in many different forms. Some of the more recent influences are to provide greater awareness of immortality and a sense within individuals of a contact with their ancient roots. This is through the Pleiadean influence which has influenced individuals through the legends in ancient Greece which have been transferred through Rome and the Catholic Church and many other forms into some current day rituals and understanding. Some of these ancient legends, the particular forms of your religious activity, and the various rituals that humans are involved in, have a large influence on your civilization. Such things as Candlemas, Easter, or Christmas have an influence for long periods of time. These rituals and awareness do not come only from terrestrial sources. But going much further back in history one observes the powerful influences of many other civilizations, including those of Sirius, Arcturus, Aldebaran, Procyon, and even to a milder extent, though certainly at an important mental level, the energies and concepts of Fomalhaut.

As you go back through history, you will find influences in various different ways. Some of these influences have come from genetic manipulation where certain specific strains of DNA were introduced through interbreeding with beings from other planets and stars. Some influences have been as subtle as an idea or a thought form placed clearly into humanity to see if it would accept or reject such a thing. Some influences have even been secondary as in the creation of certain new genetic strains of plants that would by their signature affect individuals, as is the case with corn and amaranth. Yet individuals are also affected by other means as well, those that affect them on subtle body levels and those that invite individuals own participation in their own genetic changes, as occurred often in the early periods of Atlantis. So then you find these influences in so many different ways.

This development of life on Earth must be seen in its true form. This is not just a matter of interference or ways in which these beings weren't always in concordance about how this was to take place. It is important to see that there is a core energy in humans that these beings really cannot touch. It is a core that is based in Earth's own existence and in the genetic structures of people. But most importantly, this core is an energy that is akin to light. This is the capacity within a human being to love and to allow love to be a stronger and more important part of your lives. This is the characteristic within you that is the reflection of God from which you began. Before taking form as a mountain, as a dinosaur, or as a human, you began as that starlight, as that great explosion of love that formed the Earth. As a part of you, the Earth can awaken this.

It is not decided how this love will come into form. There are many suggestions, many avenues to explore, many things to know. But there are also many things that only the love itself will tell you. This history is important. It is important that the mistakes not be repeated, and you understand your roots. But what this history points out to you is your capacity. This capacity can transcend the history and the difficulties. This will be of great importance in charting the future history of humanity with consciousness, so that you do not blunder into it, but walk into it with your three eyes wide open.

Now to deal with this issue is to begin to look at these things in a conscious, mental way. But as soon as you begin to do this, because the vessel for consciousness is your body and it is made of DNA and it is made of these patterns that are associated with these other vibrations, you begin to stir up all of these energies in yourself. Your own understanding of the genetic influences on humanity will come from your awareness of your own DNA, your own naturally inherited characteristics. As humanity understands more about these core characteristics and the many influences on human DNA, it will no longer be possible for these civilizations to influence humanity with humanity's rejection of such influence. When this understanding is combined with the accelerated energies on Earth now, it is highly likely that soon humanity will influence its own genetic development by seeking out certain influences and emphasizing these over others. This will affect individuals in a single generation. This will lead to the changes in humanity likely to be observed over the next few decades. Humanity will do better with the acceptance and creation of its own influence.

When you recognize that another race has genetic structures similar to humans because they look like humans, because in some ways they have functional structures similar to humans, then you may be certain that these are seeding races and have had a strong influence genetically upon humanity's structure by the best means, a giving of a part of themselves. This is different than genetic manipulation by scientific means, but an actual way of transferring what may be seen as loving and helpful factors into humanity. This may stir within individuals their capacity to accept just who they are. As you recognize in yourself many components from other star systems, there is also this underlying sense that comes through that these beings wish to be a part of this. It is as if to say there is hope, there is love, and that you are worth it. Indeed God's love is with you strong enough to create this attraction to the beneficial energies provided by all of these different beings in all of these different ways. This is much stronger than being simply observed. It is a way in which these beings wish to participate because humankind as a race has such tremendous potential for love, for change, for awareness, and for the education of these capacities back out into the universe.

The Seeding of Plants, Animals, and Minerals on Earth

This incredible variety of plant and animal forms on Earth is not just the product of the bountiful nature of the Earth herself. It is also necessary for a developing civilization to have much to draw upon. Some of the plants were taken from other worlds and genetically altered to be appropriate to Earth's environment, such as corn and amaranth. But by and large the beings working with such energies found that there was little to be gained. Many of the species that were deliberately altered in order to provide change for people did not survive nor did they provide the valuable and useful changes that were anticipated. It was seen therefore that the people themselves would do this better with telepathic influence. Thus there is a continuing influence, not just by extraterrestrials, but by humanity itself to seek variety, and to encourage its own development on may levels. This was especially understood in Lemuria with their creation of such variety of plants and devic orders and all sorts of things that could give rise to other evolutionary characteristics in humanity's future. In many cases the Lemurians would go off on their own, and when they encountering difficulties, they would ask for assistance from extraterrestrials.

However in the formation of certain powerful energies that would also affect genetics as in the entire rose family, to a lesser extent the orchids, and certainly with the way in which quartz was to be manipulated and utilized by many civilizations, there was a very conscious and deliberate influence by a number of extraterrestrial civilizations including those from Sirius, Alcyone, and in some cases Aldebaran. The point was to bring certain energies into form so that individuals could work with this, but also have a choice about it. Other civilizations brought such forms into Earth where humans had very little choice; but this was much rarer as the usual consequences of such were rather drastic and difficult, and in many cases simply led to the dying out of a plant species seeded on Earth.

With stones it is a little different. Here the idea of seeding on many levels has taken place over many millennia. In fact before there was concrete understanding or awareness of the potential for a race such as humans, millions and millions of years ago, interesting transference energies were utilized in the formation of a number of stones. This was not the direct implantation of a stone, but rather the awareness of an energy that would form such a stone deep within the Earth. The point of this was for the creation of a potential that might eventually give rise to civilizations, to things of beauty, to things of benefit. This was not a work with a direct aim. It was rather an appreciation of their beauty that allows them a primary link. It was an expression more in the way of flower arranging or bonsai tree pruning. These beings would share an energy with the volcanic forces and the forces of energetic action deep within the Earth for the formation of these substances. These underlying potential energies, which generally were beneficial and magnificent, gradually made their way into civilizations later. These were seeded by what you could imagine as telepathic, creative, manifesting abilities. But the ways in which humanity has used this potential and these stones, that was never foreseen.

In this way many of the older stones, those that take many millions of years to form, certainly continue to act as a bridge and a link between humans and beings from other civilizations. Certain stones, even certain forms of quartz as found in the Earth, are still utilized by other civilizations. These are taken from the

Earth and used to seed other civilizations with certain higher capacities that Earth people may have. This is not a genetic seeding, but a general influence.

Because Earth is the receptive meeting ground of so many energies in so many different ways from so many different places, including those influences from Earth's own development, the seeding of the Earth is a little more of a hodgepodge than a deliberate concentration. Where civilizations who work extensively with time travel are involved, these things are not by any means seeded with Earth in a linear manner.

PART TWO

CHARACTERISTICS OF THE STARS

CHAPTER 5
★★★★★☆☆☆☆

The Brightest Stars

Sirius (Alpha Canis Majoris)

[m –1.45] Binary, a blue-white star and a white dwarf, 8.6 light years. Their point of closest approach to each other happens every 49.5 years.

Utilization of Sirius can set up an internal vibrational resonance between the subtle bodies. This will bring them into a temporary state of harmony while the person is viewing the star or immediately after the elixir has touched the physical body of the person. Using visualization at the same time can cause this effect to be deeper and deeper with each time the meditation or use of the elixir takes place. It would be recommended that individuals work with this for seven days in a row to make this effect as deep and long lasting as possible. This could be done by repeatedly meditating on the star over a seven day period or working with the elixir or any combination seven days in succession.

Sirius can enhance communication between the subtle bodies. This is that which normally goes on under healthy conditions for most people and is generally cut off between certain of the subtle bodies when there is disease or difficulty. Communication will be enhanced between the physical and aetheric bodies, and to a lesser extent between the aetheric and emotional bodies. This will be of great benefit for anyone who is working with healing.

Sirius can be of some benefit when the healer is working with any level of sympathetic, empathetic, or symbiotic healing. These are techniques in which the individual is consciously or unconsciously taking on the disease or negative thought form of the client, and then it is the practitioner who works with the negative thought form or disease on some subtle level. Sirius elixir can be used so that the healer is able to rectify the problem in themselves quickly.

At a higher spiritual level of work with Sirius, the deeper meaning of the disease will emerge. Some difficulty may exist in understanding the reason for the physical body impairment, difficulty, or disease, because of some unlearned aspect in the person's life. This could be some level of denial, difficulty in working out one's lessons in the world, a misunderstood aspect of one's personality, or even some information from a past life not fully received. In working with this star, there can be a shift in which communication from the subtle bodies provides a different perspective for the individual. This can give him or her a better idea of that life's lesson, that missing component, or in the more powerful cases, the aspects denied in the person. This must be sought after, however.

The civilization associated with Sirius extends back a long time. People have a deep unconscious awareness of this civilization, which has great love and caring for humanity. The beings from Sirius have been involved in the seeding of some of the genetic constructs that have given rise to the DNA structures that influence heredity on Earth. The beings from Sirius have an awareness of the underlying vibration from which these genetic components come. This awareness has been a guiding light for their civilization. This energy is shared with humanity on many levels. Sirius may be one of the extraterrestrial civilizations that humanity will work with in the immediate future, maybe as soon as 2015 to 2025.

The underlying message of Sirius is that the transformation of the physical body is of great importance at this time. There may be a sense of a gap when people wish to understand the nature of the physical body, their own genetic makeup, and who they really are. This can be experienced as a wall of energy, an impenetrable obstacle, or something missing. Use of Sirius can bridge this gap so that additional information is made available for the person to have the flash of insight necessary to complete the healing process. This can directly affect all of the things you are doing in the physical world to make that healing more effective and all of the things done vibrationally to work with the physical body. This will also directly affect assimilation. As the components of your body come from the Earth, the ultimate secret to understanding the health of the physical body is to realize that you are a part of the Earth.

Sirius can be combined with other stars and other vibrational remedies to direct specific attributes of healing into the physical body. The healing must be asked for at a deep level. The person should be willing to receive this healing on the deepest level by bringing it most powerfully into consciousness at the cellular and subtle body level as well as through the chakras.

An excellent time to utilize this star elixir is just before falling asleep. During sleep the healing capacities of the body are increased and the ability to absorb healing energies is also increased. There may be a dream with insight, understanding, and deeper awareness of the life's lessons involved. The individual may remember this dream better after using Sirius elixir.

At the highest level of working with Sirius there can be additional energy for people to shift vibration. The vibration of the physical body can be changed to better match that of the spirit or the vibration of higher-dimensional levels. When in the presence of extraterrestrials, the influence of Sirius can help people to better be in charge and in a place of understanding of one's own consciousness, and better able to work with the energies of extraterrestrials. This is particularly true for extraterrestrials who would be helpful in your own evolution. These beings will often find it difficult to be with individuals who are not able to change their vibration easily. Meditation on Sirius or use of the elixir at regular intervals can assist with such vibrational shift.

VISUALIZATION ★

The visualization to use when working with Sirius would be to draw in the energy of this star with each breath and focus this energy into that part of the body that you wish to affect. Then on the outbreath recognize that energy pours from the affected part of the body throughout your physical body and then out of the skin, as if filling the subtle bodies. As you do this meditation over and over, you can imagine this connection from physical to aetheric to emotional to mental and astral bodies and see this energy transfer as each of the subtle bodies gets lit up one after the other in sequence. The exact sequence is unimportant, the exact way in which this is created is unimportant; it is simply the idea that there is this transference of energy taking place.

After doing this meditation for two or three minutes, you might imagine a second image of yourself going to a place of great knowledge like a library or a place of great inner peace where you could receive information such as a special spot in a forest or by a waterfall or by the ocean. Then in a state of calm, you imagine that second image of yourself bringing in this information by looking it up in books or absorbing it by a meditative process. Let the deeper understanding of that universal principle come into consciousness, in symbolic form if necessary.

You could go to sleep and ask that a dream come that can assist you in the deeper understanding of this. You could also enter into some therapeutic relationship where the therapist is able to help you understand more of these aspects of the symbols of the body and the life's lessons involved. The idea being that you more consciously ask for this information by your actions.

Arcturus (Alpha Boötis)

[m –0.06] Yellow giant, 36 light years.

The mechanism by which Arcturus enhances transformation of subtle energy is of benefit to understand and gives way eventually to other applications. The energy of Arcturus influences the connection of the aetheric body to the physical body. In any healing work there is an extension of the subtle bodies of the healer into the subtle realms of the person the healer is working with. The influence of Arcturus will purify this energy and make it of a singular resonance. The healing energy is usually more clearly observed, felt, known, and absorbed by the person being healed. This connection at a subtle level is an unconscious action between the healer and the client in orthodox or nontraditional medicine. Most people involved in the healing arts are not aware of the true nature of this connection. Being able to emphasize or strengthen the subtle bodies is the key to all healing.

The aetheric body takes the last step in the transformation from subtle energy into physical energy. Therefore the healing energies that are available from drug substances, healing modalities of intervention, or subtle or psychic healing phenomena are all powerfully influenced by the aetheric body. There will usually be several points during the healing process where a resonant condition is very powerfully shared by both parties. It is during such time that the influence of Arcturus will lengthen the established connection, deepen its intensity, and allow its energy to connect to other parts of the body or to more subtle levels and other subtle bodies. This is of great benefit in the healing process.

Arcturus can provide a healer with the inner sensibility to understand the true nature of healing. The healer may be unconsciously connecting to the person they are healing. The healer may also be connecting to someone in their own past with similar patterns to the one they are healing. Energy may be going unconsciously in many directions. Arcturus can bring this into a place of greater conscious awareness and deeper resonance. This can help the healer to know their true capabilities and essences more clearly so they can work with the energies and the potential they already have. What is assisted here is a transference of information, a shift of a point of view, and an awareness of energy that takes place in a resonant condition between the healer and the client. When this resonance can be established more powerfully, such a transfer will take place more easily. In this way the healer can help their client to help themselves.

In conventional medicine there are powerful intervention techniques utilizing drugs, surgery, radiation, and various different experimental techniques. Arcturus can be useful when combined with such intervention because the person must still deal with the clearer understanding of the disease or disfunction or even some of the side effects of the intervention technique.

Arcturus elixir when taken by both people involved in this process will cause more questions to be asked of the healer and more energies to be exchanged between them, even if it is conventional medicine that is being utilized. The doctor's real role is far beyond intervention, but also that of education, prevention, and assisting the other individual to understand. This may not always be the doctor's conscious role; but at the soul level, most doctors and health practitioners of all kinds have been motivated to understand and work with others. In most cases this is their reason for being drawn into the healing arts.

For those not involved in the healing arts, there will be some assistance in learning any life lesson dealing with the transference of energy between the aetheric and the physical body. For most individuals, this will be around health conditions. Self-healing may be enhanced, but there must be a resonant condition to join to or this effect will quickly fade away. This resonant link could be established with a friend, an advisor, a counselor, a guide or a teacher, or perhaps even one of the great healers from the past embodied at a subtle level. Arcturus is best used when there are two parties involved who are able to share amongst them insights, understanding, energy, and this principle of resonance.

You could conceive of the beings inhabiting the planetary system of Arcturus as great healers. This would be accurate in the highest spiritual sense only. They are excellent transferrers of energy from one resonant condition to another and have learned a great deal about this. This is the essence of the healing principle. In their life systems the learning of lessons through disease has been discarded a long, long time ago.

Vega (Alpha Lyrae)

[m 0.04] Blue-white, 26 light years.

The Vegan system has within it several planets in which civilizations living there have understoood interconnectivity and musical expression for a long time. They have projected some of this energy to Earth. Vega can present to most people an awareness of the essence of interconnectivity from a common source. This is the basis from which much music comes forth. The awareness of the vibrational characteristics of one's own soul come forth from this common bond that people share. The energy of Vega relates not only to music but to vibration, soul interconnection, and bonding at deeper levels.

Vega can attune people to these underlying principles. There can be awareness of the inspiring source of music. Some individuals with a great desire to work with music but a great deal of blockage in ability may benefit well from this as it shifts the context by which they work with music. Vega can be of some benefit if an individual who is considered tone-deaf wishes to improve his or her ability to appreciate and know music. The correct application of musical phenomena will also be enhanced. Group interaction will be assisted when where there is a common goal to bring through a specific essence or an awareness of musical source. Thus Vega can inspire groups of classical musicians to bring through the essence of the composer whose piece they are playing. Vega is easier to use for individual work and must be applied with the highest spiritual principles in mind in group work.

The soul note is an essential vibration associated with one's soul family and the roots of that soul family in the greater whole of humanity as one. There was a time in Atlantis when, for attunement to one's soul note, a number of people would meditate on Vega and then take a sort of astral body ritual travelling experience to the Vegan realms. The use of Vega in meditation or in elixir form with techniques that would give greater attunement to know one's soul note better will help one to determine this note. Vega can strengthen the ability to more easily play with this note as well as with the harmonically related variations of it.

Vega can create a deeper attunement to soul note, soul purpose, soul vibration, and connection with one's soul for some individuals. This may take place by an attunement to universal language, a sort of interdimensional communication. The language of music can connect third-dimension concepts, fourth-dimension interconnection, fifth-dimension time displacement, and sixth-dimension ability to create. As they work with Vega over long periods of time, many individuals may find a deeper sensitivity to multidimensional facets of their own existence and an easier way to communicate with other people.

Universal language is different from the language which you use every day to communicate expressive information. Universal language is based on expressive principles, principles of universal connection, and an awareness that transcends cross-cultural boundaries as well as intergalactic, interstellar, and interdimensional boundaries. Individuals who wish to attune to their connectedness to universal mind can do so through many avenues. One of these is musical expression. Many individuals have a sense of oneness or connectedness to others when sharing musical appreciation or musical creativity with other human beings. Vega assists this and also helps individuals see a little more of its source. Individuals who use Vega for the creation of a oneness will naturally be drawn to music when dealing with such interconnectedness. When you attune to the universal source, this can result in interconnectivity, awareness of other beings, and shared consciousness. This has less to do with the music than it is a way of communicating and knowing and accepting that all of this is shared together.

People are interconnected at the soul level that is the congruent, amorphous, and intertwined entity called the lifestream of humanity. The nature of this collective soul is not constrained by the usual boundaries of time and space. There was time long ago when the energy that was to be humanity first came to Earth. This was a spark of light and a piece of God-stuff that said "I am", and very little else. This energy was able to interact with the energies provided by other races, other thought forms, and the energies of the Earth herself to help it come into form. Eventually such forms began to differentiate into the individualities that now are perceived as human beings. Each of these individualities still has this deeper connection to a whole pool of light, awareness, and understanding that goes far beyond any individual form. Thus it is not just a matter of becoming one, it is a matter of knowing you have been one and will be again.

MEDITATION ON INTERCONNECTEDNESS

Close your eyes and imagine yourself in a time of great beauty a long time ago on Earth. There are many beautiful sounds of nature surrounding you, such as the sounds of birds, insects, and animals. These sounds seem to coordinate and become their own musical expression. And as you breath and feel this, you then tune to the physical nature of your body, the air, and the physical Earth around you. And notice that as you do this you are experiencing multiple realities, you are experiencing many beings at once attuning to the Earth, to these sounds, to you, and to each other. As this attunement grows more powerful with each moment, you are as if breathing as one: breathing the lungs, the air, the physical bodies of many thousands at once. Then this begins to shift into the way in which you are breathing as if with the Earth herself.

This coordinated effort of breathing and consciousness with eyes closed now gives way to an openning of the eyes, and as this occurs a great light pours out from the eyes of many. This light forms itself into a magnificent pool of light that surrounds the Earth in a liquid, loving sort of way. It is this light which contains the consciousness and awareness of so many at once. It is this light which is the essence of the soul energy that eventually comes into individualized form but now is to be viewed and understood as this beautiful light and nothing more. See that from this light comes the experience of individualization of various bodies, of various souls, of various patterns. But it is within this beautiful pool of light so inextricably connecting to the Earth herself, that so much potential, energy, and love can come forth. Then see that this light has characteristics that transcend limitation and that this light exists now. Even though at this time you may not be aware of the ancient Lemurian roots, the ancient times when humanity was one soul, still see that that light exists.

We recognize that this is paradoxical, but it is only paradoxical because of your limited view of time. It is as if the time of one is in existence in coordination and simultaneity with the time of many. This is an important concept to hold for a moment briefly, briefly breathing it, feeling that others are doing the same, and then letting it go. Return your consciousness to individuality where you are and what you are doing and let these ideas sink in a little.

Capella (Alpha Aurigae)

[m 0.08] Yellow, four stars, 46 light years.

This star system can help people bring spiritual ideas into a form that can be practical and applied well in the world. This is an energy of resonance and connection. When translated into human terms, these energies are best shared by working with love, compassion, and understanding. Capella can be helpful in strengthening family connections, family ties, and awareness in one's own biological family of certain pastlife connections that can improve family relationship.

The seventh chakra energies relate to religious understanding, one's own personal awareness of God, or any other attribute of spirituality as the person understands it. These spritual energies may not always be clear and conscious and understandable. Many times individuals need some focus to understand and work with these energies. They need to put the energy into form or do something with it. Even if it is only as simple as explaining to a child your concept of God, this principle of bringing some form to an energy which is essentially formless is important for people.

The energy of your soul wishes you to know yourself but does not make this knowledge available from the spiritual essence itself. You learn about this spiritual essence by bringing it into a form that you elect. It is your experimentation with this spiritual essence and your working with it in some way that does bring some knowledge of who you are. It is important that this not just be knowledge that can be communicated to another, but a knowledge that is internalized. When the internalization of this knowledge is complete, some aspect of your physical being will be affected at some vibrational level. This may involve your relationships, but more likely it involves the brain itself. As the brain shifts a bit, the third eye center may be able to transmit to the soul your deep awareness at an experiential level of this spiritual force. This completes the circle. The soul grows as a result. More importantly, a powerful link is established between the soul and that part of it that has broken itself off to form the physical body.

A strengthening of this connection to the soul can take place with repeated use of Capella. Capella is a powerful link-maker and gradually over one's lifetime can intensify this interchange between the soul and the physical form. This may make it less likely that a being in subsequent lifetimes would easily allow a piece of the soul to be separated and lost by being drawn to a state of darkness or difficulty.

The physical form is influenced by the higher self, the conscious self, the superconscious self, the unconscious self, the physical self, the astral body self, and so on. These models make it clear that separation has taken place and that the entire essence of your soul has not been allowed to be easily transmitted into your physical aspects. The influence of Capella can bring additional understanding of the many different ways you can bring this essence of your soul into form.

The energy that comes from the essence of your soul is unique and is you, and is at the same time bridged beautifully and powerfully to a oneness that extends through God to your entire universe. It is up to you to make this experience of the bringing into form of spiritual energy something that you understand in your own personal way. This may be intuitive, it may be physical, it may be emotional, or it may simply be an inner knowledge or an inner sense of satisfaction. It does not matter which form this takes. In searching for the correct path for the development of intuitive principles, much assistance is required. You thirst for it when you are on the spiritual path. Capella will help people become more aware of these opportunities to be assisted.

The star systems of Capella have a number of shared entities of different types who have understood much of these ways of interacting in the universe. Some have entered into periods of dormancy where they do very little for thousands of years. A single clearly focused idea emerges when they awaken from the period of dormancy. This is instantly shared in a great celebration by all the beings on these star systems. This powerful energy that is shared between them becomes a resonant factor that can exist for hundreds of years. Several layers of these resonant factors are available at a subtle level throughout the universe to those who wish to understand them. And so for humanity, it is a way of condensing this principle so that a small fraction of it is made available for people to bring some of their deeper awareness into form on some level.

One of these beings who had been in hibernation for a long time has very recently reproduced and is now clearly broadcasting throughout the universe this understanding of the interrelationship between all beings, and specifically between beings of similar vibration, history, family ties, and soul connection. For these beings from Capella, reproduction is at a vibrational level. Beings who are similar in vibration come to a place of resonance, clarity, perfection, love, and understanding and then take the highest and best within themselves and in one split second are able to merge that into a powerful energy that is nearly identical to the highest and best of themselves. A soul spark is created that can form a being, a planet, a galaxy, or something as simple as a beginning of a new idea or a transformation. This beautiful idea and concept was broadcast initially in August of 1949.

There are many direct parallels in this for humans. This idea has gradually permeated through much of society. The ability of the family to share burdens and to work these things out on many levels is gradually coming into deeper awareness. This applies to the soul family as well as the physical family. The strengthening of the connection to your soul will naturally create a resonant condition to your soul group. Your family will be affected where there is karmic connection. Many people that you feel connected to in your family are related to your soul. This powerful vibrational aspect of yourself is reflected in the people in your family. At a higher level, the awareness of spiritual principle as brought into form can be influenced by your family too. Sometimes they can reach you in a deeper way than other beings would be able to because how they communicate with you is not merely words or ideas, but is deeply rooted in feelings, in associations, and in pastlife experiences. This emphasis on family connections will be enhanced by working with Capella.

Procyon (Alpha Canis Minoris)

[m 0.35] White subgiant, 11.2 light years. Has a white dwarf companion

Procyon provides a greater acuity of mental functioning that can enhance concentration. This may result in an ability to strengthen the physical body. There is some stimulation of the intuitive understanding of reflex points in the physical body. Individuals involved in reflexology would do well to utilize the starlight elixir. Procyon can also enhance the ability to absorb energy directly from plants, the Earth, and the Sun. In a healing process, the person receiving the healing energy will find the reception of such energy enhanced.

Procyon can enhance the direct transference of light into consciousness. Procyon will beneficially influence all capacities of thought. These will include release of thought addiction, the proper utilization of thought as a mode of expression, and the awareness of the proper utilization of logical processes. There can be increased awareness of telepathic connection to other beings, especially those one is close to or those in one's family. Procyon can assist the gathering of information based on the observation and attunement to many different aspects of light. This will benefit individuals who meditate, those who work with sunlight energy directly, or those who attune to any stars or luminous objects. Individuals who work with the mental processes to excess will benefit by bringing in new information, new energy, and new transformation from light into thought.

Most individuals do not fully recognize the real capacity of thought and its true purpose. It is all right if you think Procyon is going to help you by making your mind stronger, but that is really missing the point. Since thought comes directly from light into a being, the conscious ability to work with thought is an important part of your own development on Earth and of all people's awareness of their true natural capacities. With Procyon individuals can experience shifts in context, awareness of new forms of thought, and a new understanding of themselves. They may see results, feel different, and be able to communicate in ways they had not seen as possible before. These are the proper utilizations of thought. The higher purpose of this star is one of shifting the context through which information is perceived, utilized, and expressed.

Your own vibration is slightly shifted with the use of Procyon. This makes it much easier for you to absorb and work with subtler energies on many levels. The most powerful energy that is seeking to make contact with most humans is that of your Sun. The Sun has powerful vibrational attributes of many kinds. These are filtered through and are transferred by most substances exposed to the Sun such as plants, animals, other people, and your environment. This beautiful energy is not always well absorbed by all people. This energy is more powerfully taken in when Procyon makes it easier to shift vibration to momentarily become one with another.

There is a clear connection between Procyon and the Sun. They have a relationship through a bonding energy that transcends time and space. This is not a direct physical connection through an energy emitted as light from your Sun. This connection is at a subtle vibrational level in which the Sun says: "I love you, I care for you, I share with you your light and your life." It is this energy that these great magnificent stellar beings have in common, and it is this which is made available by Procyon to a person.

Procyon elixir could be combined with Sunlight elixir. This may assist the person who is working on making a deeper connection to the other kingdoms such as the devic realm or the realm of nature spirits. This is more than just seeing these beings, but actually feeling and knowing more about their life lessons and how these relate to that person.

Altair (Alpha Aquilae)

[m –0.77] Blue-white, 16 light years. Contains magnesium, iron, and titanium.

Altair can assist people in understanding resistance, potential, and flow. When there is a difficult obstacle, usually it is simply symbolic that one has the potential to overcome that resistance, to shift perspective in dealing with the resistance, to understand it in oneself in some way, or to mirror it outside in the world. Altair's influence is quite powerful to show the individual the truth of this principle. Many times this will only be felt at the most basic level as more strength and more courage to confront that resistance. This is the technique that you know best.

However at a subtler level, there will also be an understanding as to why the resistance is there. Higher understanding may be necessary in order to have ongoing encouragement, strength, and will in order to get these lessons or work with these energies. This does not always lead to the dissolving of the resistance. What may occur is enough strength to understand the manifestation of the resistance, to see the source of the resistance, and that the overcoming of this obstacle truly helps you grow.

Saturn can bring a great teaching that takes place in overcoming one's obstacles and in having the courage to move forward. Altair can bring a far higher vibrational level of understanding of this into one's awareness. The combination of Altair and Saturn elixirs is useful when working with matters that are not only physical but have some spiritual component of resistance. This may relate to deeper understanding of your own patterns or a difficult family situation that has been repeated over and over. You may then find that there is not only greater encouragement, but deeper awareness of the higher principles involved.

At the highest spiritual level, Altair can provide you with an ability to transform a difficult situation by making a step that is entirely outside your usual context. This must come from your contemplation of the whole of the situation and your awareness of all aspects of your own being as it interacts with this. It is usually very difficult to make such a leap to the highest perspective in the most difficult situations where the most encouragement and strength is needed. Sometimes this will be aided greatly by one's guides. Those guides who have the greatest ability to bring their own experiential knowledge of courage into the individual will make that energy far more available under the influence of Altair. At this high spiritual level, there can be a matching of energy between individuals and their guides.

The civilizations associated with Altair in the past have developed an ability to transfer energy of a subtle nature. These beings have recognized the powerful creativity available to them and are often about the business of creating universes, galaxies, and so on. The vibrational remnants of this awareness act as a beacon to tell others that as they work through the patterns they have created for themselves and bring energy and information into their lives to make the steps that are needed, that on the other side of this is more joy, more awareness, more strength, and more creativity. This can comes through many pathways, and these beings in their great wisdom understood that the pathways should not be defined. Individuals as well as the various civilizations who might be touched by this beacon should find this way of greater strength and awareness in their own way. This energy is utilized by your civilization to assist people to shift out of the necessity for using resistance in order to understand themselves.

Betelgeuse (Alpha Orionis)

[m 0.8] Yellow-orange supergiant, 650 light years. Irregular variable, magnitude varies from 0.4-1.3 over a 6 year period. The star expands and contracts 20%. 90% energy is infrared.

This star provides substantial increase in communication with energies of a physical nature, particularly with the Earth energies. The root chakra is stimulated and the digestive system is enhanced. Betelgeuse can significantly enhance the ability to perceive the difference between survival connected energies and true spiritual awareness. As a result, fears are lessened and insight into the source of the fears is strengthened. An awareness of the purpose of such fears in one's own life path is enhanced. Betelgeuse elixir is a good companion to the Mars elixir.

This is based on the principle that you might call spiritual recycling. This is a way in which energies are transmitted in many different forms in the universe and eventually come full circle. These energies in coming full circle bring with them the learning, the vibrational characteristics, the various changing attributes of the beings involved, and the influences of higher forces. The exact nature of how this transference of energy takes place will depend on the nature of each civilization. In the human form there is a powerful recycling between the highest spiritual awareness which has in the past been linked with the bond between the seventh and root chakras. This now relates to the energies of the twelfth chakra and the root chakra. This transference of energy is a great cosmic miracle because such an energy must transfer to many dimensions before it returns to the physical form.

An individual will usually move through several phases in distinguishing and working with all facets of this. The first phase involves root chakra energy. This is an awareness of physical survival and the ability to transfer this energy into the basic physical body systems: reproduction, digestion, some forms of nervous system interaction, and the structural systems based in the spine. Most people become aware later in life that many of the things which they thought must be there are not necessary for survival. They become aware of the soul's survival, the survival of the higher essence of the being: that the being will go on anyway. There were many times in the past when life was lost but the being went on.

As this awareness comes more clearly into focus, the true nature of survival emerges as a choice to become physical. There are several points in life when the individual must make this choice again. This can relate to a disease or some disharmony in the body. There are also endocrine shifts at the time known as mid-life crisis where individuals again rekindle such an energy and decide whether to be here or not. Do they choose life or do they turn away from it?

In an understanding of this for the person, this star can certainly influence because cosmic recycling is what this star does so well. It is able to recycle various forms of energy, and in the process, infrared light is usually emitted in fairly large quantities. In comparison to visible light, ultraviolet light, cosmic energy, and x-rays, infrared light is less energetic and causes less change. It is more dense and less subtle than these other energies. As this powerful being known as Betelgeuse is able to create transference of energy of many different forms, there is usually that which is no longer needed because it no longer takes intelligence with it. This residue is that infrared energy. The beings on this planet are able to cooperate with the star to influence this process so that the infrared energy that is left over can be of an inspiring character, though in a subtle, gentle way with non-specific attributes. This powerful infrared light can go all over the galaxy causing a certain degree of change. This is the true recycling in which even the energies that are left over from the process have value and are utilized on other levels.

The inspiration of this for people can be a way in which you become more in touch with your own true survival instincts, the true nature of why you are here, and the way you use these energies in your own personal ways. Eventually you may be able to make your understanding of this more available to others so that they know that their own survival is not based on that which they thought it was initially or that which they perhaps were taught as children.

There is an inherent tenacity for life inbred into the genetic structure of most people. This dates from a time long past when genetic material was extracted from the primates and energies were added to them and changed, and then made into human form. One important component taken with it was this survival nature. The genetics involved have a period of change built into them. This is an explosion of energy that the person can utilize in many ways, and usually occurs for most people at least once in their lives. As they move through this change, survival as a choice to come into form is made observable or utilizable by the person. However when they have the additional energies and assistance from this star, it is possible that this energy will be seen in its true capacity. At the highest level, this energy connects the choice to be God, the choice to be aware on all levels, and the choice to know yourself no matter what the cost. This can be of great benefit because it shows the individual the true purpose of rebirth, karma, universal movement, and this connection between the highest chakra and the root chakra.

Aldebaran (Alpha Tauri)

[m 0.85] Yellow giant, 70 light years.

There is a loving energy associated with this star that extends back in time. There was a contact between the being that was born as Christ on your planet and the beings from this star system. This was a period of training in one of Christ's past lives long ago. These beings from Aldebaran have a deep compassionate awareness of the true nature of death and the difficulty of loss as humanity works with it. The beings associated with this star system have worked with death, loss, and destruction and have come away from it understanding that these are entirely unnecessary. The utilization of powerful techniques of mind interaction, cosmic awareness, and technology allowed them to bridge through such a difficult period and come to a place in which the real nature of grief, sadness, and loss was understood. Their transformation enabled them to understand the underlying principles of this without further emotional development. This understanding of grief and loss has not yet been made available to people on Earth and as a result these beings are projecting a great deal of compassion and kindness towards people on Earth.

By the very nature of the broadcast energy from this star and its connection to other life forms and other stars, there has been occasionally set up a network of many other stars all around Earth. These beings understand how loss and the understanding of it is unnecessary. Yet they broadcast an energy to Earth to tell you that your creation of this as a learning principle is bold, is to be admired, is to be understood, and eventually when the lessions are understood from it, then discarded.

With use of Aldebaran there are certainly many ways in which the entire grieving process is accelerated and assisted. As a result of coming into contact with this compassionate energy, individuals can find their own inner love and their own inner strength. There is a sense of consolation and an awareness of grief transformed into the true nature of the lesson involved. If you have lost something, there can be some awareness of why you do not need it and of how this energy could be moved. If it is a person you grieve for, you perhaps then have the awareness of the finality and certainty of this and the understanding that death is a transformational process in which you change as well as the other person. This deeper awareness eventually gives way to a sense of peace and calm. There is also a sense of hope and positive energy in a recognition that there is a oneness between those who might have passed over and those who are alive, between those things that you might wish for and those you have, and between that which is desired and that which is no longer needed. There then comes an awareness that there is a powerful energy available that simply says: "You are, you exist, and that is enough, and that is praised and loved." This is the underlying message of this star.

Many individuals have benefitted already by the use of Emerald gem elixir in working with the grief process. This tends to bring certain conscious aspects into better focus for many people, and the entire consolation process is a little easier to work with. This could be combined well with this star and could be utilized in many forms. Combining Emerald and Aldebaran elixirs will provide additional energy for people involved in the grieving process.

Antares (Alpha Scorpii)

[m 1.0] Yellow-orange supergiant, 400 light years.

Antares can bring to consciousness an inner awareness of pastlife connections to deep states of malaise. This can include suicide, misunderstanding in relationships, or dark energies that have been dealt with in the past. As this information becomes more available, this can enhance the ability to understand the shadow self, know it, and release certain components of it. There can also be deeper insight into how others struggle with their shadow selves, and this may enhance group meditation. Some dispersion of negative thought forms also takes place.

Those who live near this star and those who have travelled from very far away to work with it have done so for the specific purpose of compression of various energetic factors into lower dimensional forms. This initially took place on much higher dimensional levels and brought the energies into the fourth dimension. Your civilization is now moving towards an understanding of the fourth dimension. This is an ability to understand information that you usually access in the dream state or in unconscious, superconscious, or meditative states. Antares can make this energy more available to all beings on all levels who wish to access it.

Many other civilizations have recognized that working with the Law of Opposite Expression at the third-dimensional level for the production of the negative in order for the positive to understand itself, is a path that only leads to the creation of a great deal of karma. This karma can tend to intertwine upon itself for endless numbers of lifetimes or endless numbers of interrelationships with very little being accomplished. This is an attitude that has no emotional underpinnings, for the willingness to love is the ultimate solution to this karma. The star is transmitting an energy that is able to influence this process to always bring it to the place where love and some way of spiritual evolution and acceptance of the Christ principle is a part of this picture. This star can have a negative influence on those civilizations or beings that wish to exclude love from their way of understanding and working in their universe. As a result, these beings have good cause to turn away from it and not utilize such an energy. This star may be utilized by such civilizations as a transference point or as a repository of knowledge, but the star's energy is not directly used.

In your civilization on Earth, you have an ability to utilize love for the awareness of the deeper hidden parts of your being that oppose your spiritual progress. These aspects are healed or changed by love. The transformation of the shadow self energy by forgiveness creates a magnetic light that draws opportunities for karmic balancing into form to correct the cause of the difficulty. The understanding of this from a cosmic perspective has been powerfully influenced by this star.

This star is useful if you are working on deeper psychological issues and wish to change certain aspects of yourself that you do not see as beneficial for your own progress and evolution. Each time you use this star you will kick into action a sequence of events. These can last as long as five years, though with most people the primary influence will fade after about two weeks. During such time period you may notice an acceleration of karma. Events from your past, beings that you have known, or beings that remind you of ancient things will seem to come into your sphere of influence. This indicates that you now have more power in working with them. It is as if you can then choose. You can create an influence of a beneficial nature by a releasing of karma, a forgiveness, a change that manifests greater love, or a way in which you learn and teach the shadow self of its true place. Or you can create more karma for yourself by using this influence from the past to control others, to cause difficulty, or to bring more energy into a place of ignorance or misunderstanding. Antares influences the place just before choice and does so in a very beautiful way. If you attune to this in any way, asking with love in your heart for the higher path to be shown, so it will be. The opportunities for this may come forth in ways that were perhaps unexpected.

Spica (Alpha Virginis)

[m 0.96] Blue-white giant-subgiant, 250 light years. Eclipsing binary with 4 day period.

Spica can promote the transference of consciousness from the superconscious into the waking conscious state. No new information is imparted as with some of the other stars, but that which is already available is made much clearer and brought into consciousness more easily. This can enhance lucid dreaming states and some psychic abilities including psychometry, levitation by the use of pure mind energy, and remote viewing. Spica may be able to strengthen the physical body in the cervical vertebrae region of the spine. The neck often symbolizes separation between the physical, represented by the trunk of the body, and the mental, as represented by the skull. These vertebra are often highly stressed, for in the evolution of humanity they have served many different purposes for earlier mammalian life forms. This area is also symbolic of expression, and so there is a reminder that expression in loving and healing forms can be useful in bridging this gap and releasing some of these separation ideas.

Spica is useful for those who wish to be within a singular vibration associated with some higher vibrational aspect of themselves or who wish to become one for a time with the higher self. An individual who wishes to channel their higher self might be positively influenced by Spica and be able to hold such a state a little longer.

These energies are based on models of separation in which you recognize that there is a being that is separate from you that is called the superconscious, or a being separate from you called the higher self or the soul or the soul group. It is as if you become more of a integrated being by drawing through information and welcoming more consciousness from these separated beings. The real influence that Spica creates is an easier interchange of energy between the separated selves. In point of fact there is no separation. Vibration is a change from one state to another. The higher aspects of your being have the highest vibrations, the most rapid aspects of change. This rate of change at its most rapid is that which you have most difficulty working with. By separating artificially from these higher aspects, you have allowed yourselves to concentrate on earthly attributes.

Yet reflected to you in so many ways are all of the ways in which this earthly existence is reflecting and showing you these aspects of higher consciousness. The magnificence of nature shows you the interrelationship on so many levels of so many things in such power and energy. And so it is as if the illusion of the separation becomes clearer and clearer. Spica can help you to lovingly accept that you chose this path of separation to know better about earthly existence and about the nature of form. This can lead to an acceptance of these higher vibrational attributes as not being separate from yourself but only those things which you have chosen not to access as often as you might the more common levels of waking consciousness.

What actually happens with Spica's influence is that a more fluid state emerges and the model of separation becomes less and less useful. As these aspects of your own highest vibration are more easily brought into form, you could say that the highest self is now being made available. What may be noted in individuals who work with Spica regularly is a gradual increase in the auric field and a gradual increase in their ability to work with higher spiritual forces and energies. This is natural as this ability to release some of these aspects of separation takes place.

But eventually the entire model of separation breaks down, for after all, you are one being. It is the essential transmission of great teachers such as the Buddha that this oneness extends far beyond individuality and uniqueness of form into that of oneness with the universe and with the highest aspects of all beings. Spica can gradually bring this principle of oneness into consciousness for people.

Fomalhaut (Alpha Piscis Austrini)

[m 1.16]Blue-white, 23 light years.

This star has an excellent ability to release addictive states by bringing to consciousness the purpose of addictions. These can include addictions to relationship, thinking, sex, or various substances. The awareness of pastlife connections that create the necessity for such addictions also comes to one's consciousness with repeated use of this star. Fomalhaut can strengthen the ability to change patterns of behavior that have addictive components. On a psychological level, the use of this elixir is timely and important for most people on Earth now. There is an enhancement of inner quiet as the addiction to the thinking state is reduced. You do not yet really comprehend addiction to thought as a difficulty. To really understand this is to show you that you can take addictive principle to such a far-reaching level that it really changes how you perceive yourself and your own survival and denial issues.

You might think that addictive principles are unique to earthly life. Most civilizations have moved through ways of working with addictions. This is understood very deeply as an important method for creating awareness and forms of consciousness in beings. The principle of addiction is one of being so tied to specific forms of what one accepts as the only possible reality, that this is thought to be the only way to exist. The necessity for the addictive object is linked to a false sense of survival. Each time the addictive principle is understood at its next higher level, what emerges for the beings involved is a sense of their own beingness and their own uniqueness. By the Law of Opposite Expression, addiction shows them that which they are not. They are not the addiction. They had thought they were, but now they know they are not.

This underlying principle is shared by the star itself in working with various civilizations. The most important of these civilizations were those beings addicted to the energy of Fomalhaut itself. From this there came a symbiotic relationship that eventually yielded great understanding, compassion, and awareness. Sunlight energy on your Earth is utilized for the development of chlorophyll based forms that eventually provide the energy for all other life on Earth. Imagine instead that you decide you will redirect human destiny and physical evolution to absorb energy directly from your Sun. As you draw these energies directly from the Sun, you find there is a great sense of pleasure, a sense of consciousness, and an awareness of life. You might think that this would be a very spiritual evolutionary journey. As you reach the place where you depend totally upon the Sun for these energies and these forms of awareness, you would find that you had made a grave error. This mistake led you to only a higher form of addiction in which you were addicted directly to the sunlight energy. Now compared to current addictions, including the addiction to thinking, this is certainly a preferable state for humans.

The beings on the fourth planet around Fomalhaut took this to its ultimate degree with the use of technology and various ways of actually being with the star to receive such consciousness. Far beyond levels of consciousness as you understand it, these beings were directly absorbing and working with the energy from their sun. The beings of Fomalhaut were not in physical form as you understand it when they were involved in this process. The star itself was able to communicate with these beings and say to them: "Look what you are doing. You in your awareness of my energy are turning away from the highest energy that God has presented to you directly." They did not understand this but worked with the principle as best they could for quite a time. The star eventually sought assistance and help by bringing to bear various powerful influences from other stars to distract these beings and show them that there were other ideas. Gradually what came into form was this sense that they were stuck, that they could not evolve further.

Working with the energy of their sun they realized almost in an instant together that they had turned away from a powerful energy source. You would consider this a loving source of energy. To them it was the inner essence that created the universe. With their tremendous realization of this, most of these beings died. A few were left to regroup the civilization and come to a place of correct utilization of their sun's energy and correct absorption of the higher energy for the development of their own spiritual evolution. From this they returned to source and came to know God's energy in their own way. Their civilization was eventually transformed. In their transformation, the essential and best characteristics of the larger part of the civilization were extended into the next dimension that they entered into. In this process several other galaxies were created in places far away from your universe. Enough energy remained to merge their experience back with the star itself. Fomalhaut as a result has been influenced so that this essential core principle: "I love you enough to see you transform and release all addictions." is that which remains vibrating as an important characteristic of the star at this time.

This tale is a journey through levels of energy and awareness to a place where your very survival is at stake. The larger portion of this civilization did not have to die. Yet they found it was their only choice given the limited circumstances they had set up for themselves. Addiction is that which, in your understanding, depends intimately on denial. You must choose to not see the true source of your energies or what is really nourishing you. If you make such denials, if you choose not to see the larger picture, the addiction can remain. Sometimes it is enough only to see the truth and stop the denial. But the opposite is also true. If you understand the addiction more completely, sometimes the denials will melt away.

The important thing to recognize is that the falsehood at a deep level for so many is that their survival is somehow based upon certain concepts or ideas that are essentially limiting. In understanding those limitations, in recognizing that survival is not as you think it is, there are many ways to approach addictions. With the use of this star, the entire process is speeded up. This can create a willingness to look at these truths, to allow them forth, and to release denials. This is not just because these beings have deposited their information and their experiences into the star which are then vibrated as if by a beacon to all beings in all places. It is also because there is a certain characteristic of love that the star created for these beings as if this is a way of saying: "I recognize how I am involved in this process and I love you so much, I bring this energy of care, of compassion, of change into you so much that you are changed as a result—and I do so with great power." This sense of great power is the characteristic that the star also brings to people so that they can change. It may not be very clear as to how this will happen, what they should do, what they should be looking at, or what could no longer be denied. But there can be a sense of this hope and this power moving through them, as if to say, "You do have a choice."

Pollux (Beta Geminorum)

[m 1.15] Yellow giant, 35 light years. The closest giant star.

Pollux works with the intuitive, non-dominant side of the brain. However, the brain model is a bit inadequate to explain higher processes. What is observed with the electroencephalogram is the stimulation of various nerves in that side of the brain and therefore it is assumed that in the formation of electrical impulses, thought occurs. It is not that way at all. Thought is manifested on multiple-dimensional levels and then transmitted through receiving mechanisms to the physical form, and then manifests as electrical activity. Because of this, the intuitive energies that connect to subtler realms have components that are lost in the translation process. These lost components are still available, since thought in its true essence and form does not have the same constraints on time that three-dimensional processes, including electrical activity in the brain, must adhere to. As a result, these thoughts that have not been fully received are able to remain accessible to the individual. There is no time limit on this. These thoughts don't just fade away over time, but can become available as the person attunes to them.

Should a person utilize Pollux occasionally but regularly, perhaps even as little as once a month for extended periods of time, he or she may be able to receive thoughts of a more varied nature, thoughts relating to past activities, and energies to complete thoughts left incomplete. This takes place at the level of true awareness without temporal constraints. As a result, creativity is enhanced, the ability to work with various new ideas can be strengthened, and the ability to take in information and bring it into a new form may be more available. People may simply feel more in tune with their past, their future, and their relationships as if it is the feeling and the sense of it that is strengthened more than the concrete logical thought processes.

When we refer to thought, it is very difficult to define these terms in ways in which individuals can separate this from what you would call mind chatter or even thought addiction. We are referring to the energies that precede the actual process of electrical activity. These are often energies of magnificent and beautiful inspiration. These are generally lost to most individuals. Pollux can enhance the process of absorbing a little more of this, making it a little more practical, and accepting that this is all right for yourself.

Deneb (Alpha Cygni)

[m 1.25] Blue-white supergiant, 1,600 light years. One of the most luminous stars.

Deneb has the ability to create in people deeper inspired states, an awareness of the teachings of the masters, and an enhancement of the channeling process to connect to non-physical beings of light, assistance, and love. There is a deeper stimulation of the higher aspects associated with the lungs and circulatory system. The deeper understanding behind pranayama yoga and the martial arts is made available to people. When this star is utilized in group meditation where the group meets regularly, there will be an enhancement of focus when a single idea is meditated upon. Some assistance with the process of creating matter from the aethers will be noted with use of this elixir.

Deneb is a multidimensional being. Its primary dimensional aspects and realities are beyond that of your third dimension. The relatively constant transference of various energies and beings causes the formation of energies at a third-dimensional level which you perceive as a star. The extreme gravitational forces created by powerful movements of energy from other galaxies through this as nexus point cause energies and transferences that clearly step far outside of time-based systems as you understand them. Deneb is able to influence time and space in a relatively innocuous way so that it appears as a constant light, a particular form that is the influence upon your three-dimensional world.

Deneb has been utilized as a powerful transference point for many civilizations now long past and forgotten, as well as many of those now in existence. These powerful energies connect Deneb to many galaxies. Because the star has taken part so much in the transference of beings from one physical location to another and the transference of energy in many ways, it has been intimately involved in the process of information transfer. Deneb significantly influences the transfer of formless energy into a form of energy that brings information into the being.

Only those beings who have some connection to their own highest evolution along lines returning to God are even aware of the higher properties of the star. Only those influences from higher vibrational levels seeking their way into lower vibrational levels will have some influence over this transference of vibration. The influence from various masters and the energies of beings of light is a natural part of this process. Deneb makes its energy available to individuals who wish to utilize it for their own highest good, and it cannot be misused or utilized in ways that could harm. This self-governing property is in alignment with this way in which these energies are able to be transferred into information that is valuable and useful.

It is always the case when a process of this nature takes place that there is secondary vibration which moves from the receiving entity back to the star and then to the beginning point. The masters are so interested in your evolution that they become a natural part of this process as if drawing out more of your true nature and capability and what you can work with in the world. Deneb influences your meditations, your spiritual evolution, your soul's evolution, and your soul group's evolution in so many ways by creating the transference of energetic principles. It does so on guiding principles that are very powerful, but because of their subtlety, move in ways that are very helpful.

The star has completed a number of evolutionary cycles in which it became aware in multiple dimensional ways of its connections to other star beings in this galaxy and in others. Deneb is able to assimilate and work with the underlying principles for which the transfer of information takes place. This transfer of information takes place harmoniously and beautifully, but is governed by a force which is not judgmental, opinionated, or working from sets of concepts or precepts with which you are familiar. This is the nature of the evolution of this being. It has achieved this high state without the necessity for comparison or for judgment on any level. It is strictly in tune with the powerful source that allows the energy to transfer. It is a source that says: "I give to you knowledge. From this knowledge it is hoped that you will extract wisdom. From this wisdom it is hoped that you will extract love and that special way of your own uniqueness." This is a very poor translation. A better approximation would be the ancient Chinese concept of wu wei. This property that Deneb transfers is then allowed to permeate the being and create a new force of some sort. This is not known at the beginning of the process exactly how it will be released; and this force returns along the same lines back to its creator.

In this process there is a strange and wonderful thing. More than any other star, Deneb responds to you. Your thought form is received instantaneously by Deneb. In this way the uniqueness of your being is added to Deneb. The star is in its own way nourished by this and acts as a library or repository for some of this. It eventually integrates it and shares it with other beings. Thus it is a nexus point not just for interstellar travel, interdimensional shift, but also for the information itself in the way in which it contributes to other beings and their awareness. The two-way action of the elixir is minimal. The two-way action of meditation with the star is preferred. If you find yourself inspired or if there is some assistance in the physical condition and you wish to share this back with Deneb, then find the star in the nighttime sky, and send your loving thoughts in that direction. That is all you have to do, but it is valuable here to actually gaze upon the star.

In helping with the lungs, Deneb can influence the process of how you receive energy and choose how you will utilize it. As the lungs symbolize energy, such an energy can be misused easily or used in ways that might not be understandable. Use of Deneb in elixir form will be valuable for individuals struggling with lung difficulty particularly where a life lesson is involved as in severe or chronic lung problems including emphysema, asthma, and lung cancer. In these cases individuals may have new insights. But more than this, they may find some peace inside. The uniqueness that is born from the energies and information they have received in their life may be created in form as something valuable and useful for others.

Martial arts disciplines have several capacities to transfer information and understanding. There is the physical way in which you are learning new ways of working with the body. But there is also the meditative way in which you are able to change your perspective, move to a place of quiet, and let the body simply do what it does and receive. This is what Deneb influences. This is actually the core of the martial arts work. Though it is only the state you strive for, it is still that which is brought into form by the physical. As soon as the form is received, it is transferred immediately back to the physical. This then gives you immediate feedback: you see the body performing better, you see the results that you desire. As a result of this you recognize the intrinsic value of the higher consciousness associated with the martial arts movements. Deneb's influence here is to bring this inner core into greater strength in most people.

This is but a small portion of the information available about this being. The civilizations that have worked with this being do not do so anymore in any concrete form. There is no one civilization associated with Deneb, as this is an important meeting point for multiple-dimensional energies, physical transference, and other energies. However approximately every 11,000 years of so there is sort of a celebration, an energy of connection in which a singular thought form is presented to the star to allow a more powerful transference from multiple civilizations simultaneously through the star. To translate very roughly, this is quite gratifying, satisfying, and helpful to the star's own evolution. Such a celebration is scheduled for May 11, 2007. On such date the adding of your own loving thoughts to Deneb would be valuable. In the cosmic scheme of things, this is quite close in time, though it might seem quite far away to you.

Regulus (Alpha Leonis)

[m 1.35] Blue-white, 85 light years. Has two dwarf star companions.

Regulus can unblock deeply buried subconscious patterns. At first there is a simply a sense of perseverance, greater emotional stability, and a willingness to look. But then within a few days of repeated work with this star, what begins to emerge is a sense of how one fits into the patterns. Still, observation of the patterns may not come forth for a while. When one has the sense that these are important, a sense of patience and a deeper appreciation of these patterns can take place. As your awareness continues to deepen, the natural understanding of these patterns comes forth. There may be an ability to express them, to learn of how they compare to others' patterns, or to learn from them based on what others might suggest you look at and learn about. But at that point in time the individual is usually able to appreciate this, accept it, and know it in themselves.

There is a great difficulty when you are involved in working with the recognition of a long-standing pattern when someone else reveals the pattern to you. This observation may be entirely correct, perfectly logical, and that which makes sense on all levels, and yet you simply cannot accept it. Sometimes this is because the pattern is accurate, but the things that have allowed you to take that pattern in the first place stand in the way. These can be swept away by psychological techniques such as emotional therapy work, various ways of bodywork, deep movement, and other things. But sometimes when one is confronted with the patterns too soon, there are too many emotions to deal with and one simply wishes to turn away. It is a natural way for the consciousness of the person to work in such fashion. If the pattern involved has anything to do with drugs or various addictive patterns via addictive relationships and so on, the individual involved may turn to those again as if to shut off the deeper awareness and understanding. If the person can discover the pattern themselves or can at least be better emotionally prepared to receive the information from someone else who might help, then a great deal more benefit can take place.

The star itself tends to influence this for many reasons. One reason is that the beings who have worked with this energy for a long time have seen the experiments with the development of love, the development of deeper consciousness, and the development of powerful mental abilities with many other civilizations in the galaxy. These beings, you might say, have seen it come and seen it go. They have a deep appreciation of this and a deeper sense of patience and awareness. But more importantly, they recognize that there are patterns that take place. But within these patterns there are usually unpredictable micro-patterns that are important for the development of the personalities, the people, the entities, the intelligences, and ultimately the very planets themselves. As a result of this, these beings have seen that where some impetus toward deeper self-awareness of these patterns is made available to the civilizations involved, they tend to last longer, affect transformation more readily, or more importantly, manifest the very things they came to work with more easily. This has a relatively recent implication in that the individuals involved have only been working with this in such a conscious fashion for about the last 21,000 years. Because this is a relatively recent development, the beings involved are not very certain and wish to compensate with some degree of what you would call compassion for humanity and Earth at this time. Though they will not interfere with any other civilization, they do pour energy of all sorts into their sun, into the broadcast systems that they have developed to enable others to work with patterns.

The success of an experiment usually yields results beyond the expected ones. This is where the scientific method is inaccurate, as it does not take into account that when the hypothesis is proved, a great deal usually changes. There is an attitude shift, a deeper awareness, and many consequent applications. Should humanity come to a deeper awareness of itself, manifest forgiveness and a way in which change can be accomplished without war, without great struggle, but instead with greater love; it will be possible to transfer this, to transform it, and to share it with other civilizations, including these beings of Regulus. And as a result they will be all the better for it. It is this which they actually choose to remain in form to work with. Rather than taking the path of some of their brothers in the higher civilizations, such as becoming centers of galaxies, creating various other systems, or manifesting significant dimensional change, instead they have chosen to expand their own awareness and understanding of all facets of existence. The facet of love is the one that humanity can share with them the best, at least from the long-term perspective of the next 21,000 years.

CHAPTER 6
★★★★★★☆☆☆

Second Magnitude Stars

Adhara (Epsilon Canis Majoris)

[m 1.48] Blue-white giant, 650 light years. Contains silicon, magnesium, and oxygen.

This star can enhance the absorption of minerals and food in the physical body. The spiritual property that is brought in that eventually gives rise to this enhanced absorption is the ability to become one with the physical substances that are taken in. This can be visualized as an aetheric light moving between you and the food or the substances taken into the body. Over time, the use of this star will shift digestive disturbance, various mucus coatings of the intestines, and other things in the body that prevent good absorption. This will allow easier absorption because the ability of the physical body to ease such blocks is made clearer. This is because Adhara is broadcasting the raised vibrations of the substances contained within it. These are far beyond any electromagnetic or measurable spectral vibrations. The enhanced absorption of these various minerals, oxygen, as well as some vitamins, can assist in the release of toxic substances. This ability to shift one's vibration and be aware of the process can allow people to become one with plants and animals, rocks and minerals of all sorts, and to a slightly lesser extent with vibrations of human and non-human beings from other civilizations.

The civilization that existed on the sixth, seventh, and later the first planet around Adhara had worked for a long time on learning how to absorb electromagnetic energy from their sun directly without the intervening processes of photosynthesis. When they learned to tolerate such powerful energies, a number of these beings relocated to the first planet around Adhara to be very close to their sun to draw in energy directly. These beings eventually merged with their sun and have provided Adhara with this characteristic of the ability to work with absorption. These beings, as part of the consciousness of Adhara, are now seeking to absorb and work with the energies of other civilizations.

At a higher spiritual level, there can be a deeper absorption of spiritual concepts that may be hard to understand when first presented or which may bring up certain blocks within the person. The consciousness associated with these blocks will increase. Thus the ability to perceive denial and cause this to shift in a conscious and easy manner will generally be felt. There is also shared amongst Adhara and the beings that have worked with this star a sense of humor, which can be quite valuable in any process dependent upon absorption. In working with this star elixir or meditating on this star, one can sometimes find a sense of humor about the issues and blocks in one's life coming to the forefront.

This star elixir can be added to ozone or hydrogen peroxide therapy. Any oxygen therapy will generally have more impact and have greater benefit in the presence of this star elixir.

Castor (Alpha Geminorum)

[m 1.58–2.6] Three binary stars. 46 light years

There is a tendency for Castor to influence the logical processes and the various aspects usually associated with the dominant left hemisphere of the brain and the corresponding opposite side of physical body. This awareness is one that leads to the enhancement of various biological functions within the brain structure itself. This works first to influence at a cellular or metabolic level the uptake of small amounts of minerals necessary for these processes. Calcium, magnesium, chromium, and selenium are all essential for such brain function. Manganese becomes very important at the higher levels of brain function. Some influence of its uptake into the brain will be enhanced by using the star as a vibrational tool.

What takes place is that these metals are used by the brain tissues to create a hierarchical organization. This organization is the natural function of the dominant side of the brain in that this is necessary for interaction in a hierarchical-based society such as yours. In such hierarchies there is always a transfer at subtle levels. Long periods of preparation over many past lifetimes and the current lifetime all influence this process to more easily create this organization into hierarchies of the holographic phenomena known as brain function. As a result of the influence of this star there can be for many people the ability to form such hierarchies easily and work with them as needed. This allows in the brain balance the correct positioning of the hierarchy: to be used when needed, to be released when unneeded.

Logical function will naturally be enhanced if that is what you are drawn to. Castor will also enhance the ability to share information in a hierarchical form so other people can work with it appropriately. Castor can enhance interconnectivity within the brain. Certain logical functions will be speeded up. But do not think that all mathematical or logical functions are held in this context. The mental functions which are very rapid actually take place in the intuitive brain. Thus such functions as the instantaneous ability to multiply two four-digit numbers together and instantly receive the answer is a combining of factors which only begin and end in the left brain—all the rest takes place in the intuitive side.

It is important to realize that in working with this as an elixir there is no forced function here. It will not make you more logical. It will simply allow you deeper awareness of these conscious processes and give you more choice about how you will utilize them.

Shaula (Lambda Scorpii)

[m 1.62] **Blue-white subgiant, 350 light years.**

Repressed emotions can be brought into consciousness and understood with the use of this star. These emotions can be released and the energy brought into coordination with other facets in one's life. This can enhance recall of emotional blocks felt in childhood and to a lesser extent from past lives. The reasons behind the emotions are better understood and forgiven. In some people this work with the emotions may have a cyclic nature which matches the five hour period of this star.

Group interaction with the star was an important keynote for this civilization. Their understanding of the emotions was very different than what has been created on Earth. The ability to coordinate emotional awareness with free will as it relates to many levels of consciousness is an important hallmark of the star. How people will use this is influenced primarily by the shared nature of emotional bodies amongst people. The ability of people to work with emotions in many different ways has created a shared emotional body amongst humanity.

The group soul of all of humanity is broadcasting feelings and emotions which are disturbing to the Earth. This is an important contributing factor to some of the geophysical changes that occur, such as in volcanos and earthquakes, which are an important facet of the Earth's cleansing. The Sun is also affected here. In its communication with other stars, the Sun is able to as if ask for help and share this information with the Earth. This has created a gradual bond between the Sun and the Earth over the centuries at an emotional level in dealing with this issue. This has allowed Shaula to project energies of some assistance in the direction of your Sun.

In many ways the maturation of the shared emotional body of humanity is important for humanity's evolution. The karmic purpose of the relationship between Shaula and the Sun is the way in which these energies are able to encourage maturity, deeper awareness, consciousness, and choice in dealing with the emotions. This is not to encourage emotional repression or to change the way in which people relate to their emotions, but to make them more aware of all aspects of emotional awareness, emotional involvement, emotional understanding, and the appropriate sharing of these emotions in the world. The use of this star by meditation or taking the elixir will improve an individual's own ability to deal with emotions by consciously providing emotional energy and information to the mental, aetheric, astral, and physical bodies.

The beings from Shaula have a completely different way of dealing with what you would understand as emotions. But there is enough similarity here that this is the star with energy of the most benefit for humanity's own continued evolution. The civilization has a capacity to transform energy at different subtle body levels but has found that most energies from Earth beings are too primitive and uninteresting except for the shared emotional body of humanity. This has influenced some of their development of emotions and they are returning the favor by helping the communication between these two stars to assist people in working with feelings.

Bellatrix (Gamma Orionis)

[m 1.64] Blue-white, 300 light years. Ejecting part of its atmosphere into an expanding cloud.

The use of this star can expand the ability to observe the aura and to understand its significance in yourself and in others. The first step is to see through and know well one's own aura. This is an ability to understand your own aura, to recognize its coloration, formation, and also the ability to clear it and to strengthen it. This refers to energies generally perceived as visual, to a lesser extent felt, to a much lesser extent heard. These energies are generally observed to exist between the skin surface and an area three to four feet away from physical body. There is also an enhanced ability to perceive and work with the aura of other people.

There is also an ability to work with negative thought forms that have plagued one for long periods of time, and eventually reveal some enhanced information and understanding about the purposes of such negative thought forms and what they represent. These are primarily thought forms relating to other people, and might be perceived by some as "psychic attack" thought forms; but they are not such, they are simply energies that the individual has drawn to his or herself as a result of interaction with this other person.

The beings from Bellatrix have dealt with the awareness of visionary activity for many thousands of years. This is an activity that still brings them interest and excitement. Genetically they have found ways to re-engineer themselves to have much wider perception of electromagnetic, gravitational, strong and weak forces spectra, as well as the ability to perceive subtler dimensional energies that might be characterized as fourth and fifth dimensional. When Earth beings are looking into these areas there is an unconscious broadcasting that transcends the limitations of time and space to ask these beings for help. When you are studying auras or looking into the matter of subtler seeing or opening the third eye, there is a certain sadness that you usually experience that is the source from which some of this asking for help comes. The Law of Help would state then that as you would ask for help, so it must be given. Imagine the frustration that your guides must feel when they seek to help you with seeing auras and opening the third eye. It is not only that they cannot do anything on a physical level, but they also are able to see these sorts of things easily themselves, and so they also assist in this asking for help process.

Humanity unlearned these capacities of subtle seeing at the time of early Greece. At this time emissaries from this star were sent to assist people when they wished to continue such learning. This has been an important contributor to the various mystery schools and other techniques that have preserved the ways in which auric vision has continued on Earth. The star elixir is helpful here to remind people of past lives where they had some of these capacities.

Meditating on Bellatrix can help a being connect with this civilization in a direct fashion. While you are meditating on this star you can close your eyes and imagine a connection from your third eye to the star and in this way allow Bellatrix to give an energy to you. This is utilizing the Law of Help in a clear way. This can awaken the third eye a bit, and if you are successful you will begin to form an image of that star in your own sensibilities. This does not necessarily have to be only vision work; it can come through other modalities such as feeling, or perhaps sound.

Now as this sort of connection to Bellatrix is increased there is a natural tendency for people to shift their consciousness. Though these beings from Bellatrix have learned much of the capacity to see, how to use what they see for the betterment of others has not been easy. Thus it is not simply a matter of diagnosis that seeing the aura of another person can provide, or working with the perception of the incoming ray to enhance counseling or to help other people in deciding their jobs or direction. As people become aware of these subtle energies they are naturally more in tune with each other and able to communicate by color, by sensing, and by feeling, and not simply by words, actions, or sounds. This way of communicating is sought and understood by these beings from Bellatrix. They may attune to this in people and recognize how people's emotions, love, and other beautiful aspects of healing will contribute to the civilization of Bellatrix.

The aura of the Sun extends to just about 3 million miles outside the widest orbit of Pluto. Outside this area the primary aura of the Sun is minimal in character. The auras of most stars extend to their outermost planets. There has been a deliberate attempt to intensify the aura of Bellatrix to extend many millions of light years into space. This is its natural tendency to some extent and the beings who lived with her simply found the way to increase this. Thus at times this aura can encompass Earth and be a part of Earth, and this can be helpful for people to connect to Bellatrix.

El Nath (Beta Tauri)

[m 1.65] **Blue-white giant, 200 light years. Outlying member of the Pleiades.**

The energy of El Nath can assist individuals with the ability to perceive on multiple dimensions. This can include highly inspired channeling states, but is especially important for deeper understanding of the essence of mathematics, physics, and science. Ideas of form and geometry that relate to multidimensionality can be brought to some level of inner understanding. There is an enhanced ability to intuitively perceive cosmic principles and ideas. Those who struggle with even simple mathematics or arithmetic are likely to benefit by utilizing this star. Use of the *I Ching* is enhanced as well.

The individuals on El Nath have achieved a high level of interdimensional functioning and have been involved in seeding processes, loving processes, and processes of expansion that have provided a powerful inspiration to many other civilizations. The genetic seeding which has presaged some of the genetic seeding on Earth is an aspect that runs very deep for all beings on Earth. Some of the genetic structures that beings from El Nath seeded into many other civilizations, including those in the Pleiades, Zeta Reticulli, and Sirius, have been utilized in the genetic influence of Earth beings to create a continual genetic thread. Some basic discoveries and essential improvements in genetic structures, as they are influenced by subtle energies (especially the connection to the aetheric body), were pioneering works created by the beings connected with El Nath. These beings have left these abilities to influence genetic structures as important ways of revealing inner information to people.

Many of those involved in Pleiadean civilization came to understand this quite well and in their own seeding of humankind there were some deliberate attempts to put a few genes into people relating primarily to the mind, the mental body, the understanding of civilization as a whole, as well as some filters with regards to past lives. These were genes that were almost identical to those originally developed by El Nath. This extends through genetics going back many millions of years on Earth. People who are drawn to spiritual capacities and deeper awareness of themselves, or who have an attraction to understanding about extraterrestrials on any level will certainly benefit by working with El Nath. Simply because a part of them is connected to El Nath, working with El Nath can remind many people who they are, even if they do not have attunement to these stars or understanding of subtle energies.

This civilization from El Nath came to a balanced way of working with science and is still broadcasting a very important message about the use, versus misuse, of technology and science. Mathematics and the awareness of science in all of its facets can be extremely important for people to understand their universe, not in a rational scientific way, but an emotional, appreciative, praiseful way based on awareness. Einstein is a leading example of the awareness of the awe observed in working with and understanding nature.

What language could be utilized to communicate between civilizations to share genes and information about genetic structures and development of physical forms over many centuries between many civilizations, over very long distances and even between multiple galaxies? This question was of primary importance to beings associated with El Nath for long periods of time. The answers came in a deep appreciation and understanding of the universe and of the cosmic laws which are primarily mathematically based. These laws are not based on conceptions or ideas of people but on the stars and on the actions of the cosmos itself. The appreciation of this universal language is a natural tendency that is increased in people when they work with El Nath. This is certainly beautifully brought through in the *I Ching*. This is a divining technique that is not based on Earthly technology but indeed comes through many levels of awareness, including those from El Nath. People who may not be attracted at all to such things as science or mathematics may still find a great deal of pleasure and awareness in working with the *I Ching*. Thus they are attuning to universal principles and reminding themselves of these as a powerful universal language. This is the real idea of mathematics at its highest level. As any trained mathematician can tell you, it is a way of understanding and communicating with the universe.

Alnilam (Epsilon Orionis)

[m 1.70] **Blue-white supergiant, 1,600 light years.**

Thus star can enhance the ability to work with responsibility. The shoulder region and musculature in the neck is strengthened and assisted. The ability to perceive shortcuts that bring the purpose closer in one's tasks in the world is enhanced, and the correct use of such shortcuts without harm or difficulty is provided. In addition, the ability to more correctly balance the ends and the means, and be able to put these into proper perspective, is somewhat assisted. This business of personal responsibility is of great importance for people of Earth right now.

Alnilam's denizens divided into two races. The two races had a number of conflicts and eventually found their way through it by shared responsibility. They were able to cross-seed and develop a third race that encompassed all the capacities of the other two. This new race had a natural ability to travel through space without space ships in ways that are quite ethical, responsible, and conscious. In this way they are occasionally beings who act as guides and helpers for people on Earth or helpers and guides for the personal guides of people on Earth. They are also involved in sharing information that people can work with to act more appropriately.

Their way of understanding and working with the universe is very different from humanity's. They cannot comprehend the underlying message that humanity is creating with regards to self-responsibility. How can beings fight each other, destroy their planet, and create for themselves an environment which will not only kill them but also the other beautiful life forms they are with? Why do they not seek knowledge and awareness of their environment, of the people around them, and of their purpose in being here? Certainly these beings from Alnilam understand that people have certain aspects of their genetic composition missing which makes it hard to know these things. Certainly they understand the development of many separate civilizations that come to war and fight against each other just as they once did. But there is this underlying feeling—it is not an emotion, but if anthropomorphized it would turn out to be like a feeling of disgust with the human race. As they are responsible beings seeking ethical awareness as a technique and way of providing compassion, understanding, and evolving in their universe, they naturally must deal with this problem. This then draws their attention to Earth because that being that projects to you the maximum amount of difficulty can act as your teacher to show you about yourself. Earth beings are thus acting as a mirror for these beings. As people grow to a place of greater self-responsibility, the attention of these beings will naturally be drawn elsewhere.

Energies are temporarily stored in the shoulder region to be released by movement through the arms. There is a natural alignment and tendency for such energies to deal with responsibility. Because they are so ethically motivated, these beings from Alnilam will not ever interfere. But they will provide knowledge and information to your guides and helpers. When nuclear weapons are utilized on

Earth, these beings from Alnilam will assist in the transmutation of this energy so that no great damage occurs to the galaxy.

At a very high spiritual level, these beings are available to act directly as teachers. This may take place in the dream state when you dream of a teacher who says to you: "This is the right way, this is the wrong way." In many cases you have thought of this as your conscience, and this is often the case. But sometimes it is an energy whose source is from this other world that is provided to you in dreams in the veil of a conscience so that you can choose it or not.

Alioth (Epsilon Ursae Majoris)

[m 1.78] Blue-white pulsating magnetic spectrum star with strong lines of europium and chromium.

The star can strengthen the ability to create enhanced loving states and to communicate love appropriately. The use of this elixir is recommended for counselors working with individuals with mental difficulties including schizophrenia, manic depression, and other very disturbing psychological states. There will be no direct benefit to the patient; it is to assist the counselor in the counseling process.

There is an enhanced ability to correctly metabolize and work with sugar substances and understand unconscious associations with sweetness in order to correctly balance loving conditions and understand the principles regarding weight loss. Some individuals with bulimia or anorexia nervosa will also be assisted by the star.

The ability to bring love into people's hearts is very difficult because of barriers to this that are created by negative forces on Earth, by Martian forces, energies that are created by people's own naturally occurring negative thought forms, disease structures, pastlife denials, and many other things. These give rise to thought forms that say you cannot love more than one at a time and if you do there is a great struggle, and that the love must always be personal, nurturing, and self-fulfilling, not something that is expansive, universal, or something that assists your planet. Communicating this love between people is hard because there aren't sufficient techniques and availability in the language itself. These beings from Alioth just want to assist or help where possible but have found that this energy blocks anything that they would do and makes it very hard for them to assist humanity in its own lessons. Their true capacity is to assist any civilization in developing their own lessons. As it is so important for humanity to learn about love, it is this energy which these beings have focused on Earth.

Jesus the Christ, Mohammed, and Confucius, spent a little time on this planetary system. It is a rather unusual system consisting of three moons and a central planet that come into close contact with each other in such a way that the love energies and other energies utilized by these beings change the gravitational fields to maintain the three moons in a stable orbit. Even though this should not have occurred naturally, it was a way of working with gravity and understanding the aethers that were natural to these beings. Some short periods of time on these worlds have taken place for people from Earth at various times in the dream state, in states of deep consciousness, and for these enlightened beings we have mentioned, by direct physical intervention. However the interchange of energy in these places that people have worked with have not been transferred to Earth with any degree of success.

All that is left is a way in which this energy can be beamed to Earth. The idea was to create a bridge by causing an oscillation in the atomic spectra of the chromium contained within the star. Chromium has an important ability to overshadow in people their understanding and working with love on many levels. Part of this is because of the sweetness aspect associated with love, and that is well placed for most people. The appropriate utilization of glucose, the proper production of insulin, and the balance of blood sugar with regards to hyperglycemia or hypoglycemia are influenced strongly by chromium. The idea was that this star would project a vibration added to the characteristic signature of chromium that would then come into Earth. These beings have specifically focused energies of a loving nature, of a compassionate nature, and of an awareness nature into their star and focused it on the chromium vibrations so that these could be transferred to Earth.

This is frustrating for such beings because all over the Earth at this time depletion of the soils is taking place. Some of the first minerals to go include chromium. Chromium supplementation is often recommended at least in small quantities for most people as chromium is becoming less and less available from the usual sources. This is usually from large quantities of vegetable matter such as grass that is eaten by cows and eventually turned into butter, milk, and other products. These products, now devoid of chromium, were the last source of such material for most people. There can be some additional benefit here if you expose chromium in aqueous solution to the starlight. There can be some benefit in taking the starlight elixir and putting a drop into a bottle of aqueous chromium. The ability to work with the vibration of any substance is significantly enhanced when it is in a water-based form, as water is an important transformer and transferor of many energies.

Mirfak (Alpha Persei)

[m 1.80] White supergiant, 500 light years.

Some enhancement of mental functioning through cleansing of the mind will be noted. The ability to incorporate the natural cleansing functioning of the primary ray that the individual works with will be seen and the ray energy will be accelerated. There is a strengthened ability for the person to release negative thoughts or various patterns of behavior that have been difficult. Also the cleansing of certain physical substances, particularly toxic metals, is strengthened. This would be wise to do in coordination with the visualization of a waterfall, as if the speed and strength of the waterfall sweeping through the body from top to bottom would be significantly enhanced by the star.

The energy of this civilization and star are interconnected. There was a problem about 570,000 years ago where beings who had lived in peace with their star began to observe increasing solar flare activity. This became a great problem as the flares became stronger and larger. They recognized an ability to take such energies and deflect them or shield themselves, and realized that for the karmic purpose of their own planet and for the awareness of their own civilization, such was not the best path. Instead it was seen as valuable to understand the higher aspect: that a destruction then gives way to a creation. They recognized that the solar flares themselves could be utilized for sweeping away psychological debris and subtle level energies that were not necessary in their civilization.

These beings from Mirfak have been influences for Native American civilizations, both North and South American, certain individuals in Scandinavia, and for Eskimo cultures both in the Soviet Union and the higher areas of North America such as Alaska and the Canadian Rockies. Emissaries from Mirfak came here to teach methods of cleansing. These are very important techniques and have been acknowledged and worked with by these native cultures for a long time. The sweat lodge or sauna is one of the very powerful techniques that were given. When in a sweat lodge or sauna one will often naturally imagine such as a cooling waterfall, not just because of the heat involved but because of its cleansing capacity.

As people attune to the energies of this cleansing, they may come to know themselves a little better. It is a way in which you accept the naturally occurring energies and utilize them to your own highest ability. This is a capacity and property that these beings have developed for themselves but not one that has been easily shared on Earth. This whole process was seen to have a magnificent personification in the waterfall. An ability to communicate with Indian guide spirits may be enhanced for people who stand near or in a waterfall. They may also find that this can attune them to this star and its civilization. The use of the star elixir for deeper communication with Native American spirits can be quite beneficial for many people.

The beings from Mirfak were able to utilize these apparently destructive solar flares as a positive, clearing device. This is a way in which people can take the very energies that would appear to be negative and difficult for them such as energies that relate to poisoning, excessive toxic materials, or various physical body processes that are clogged or having difficulty completing themselves, and not only clear those energies but also recognize the message they bring. A new energy is welcomed by clearing out what is not needed. This is the underlying message of these beings. There has been a direct incarnation from this star system in the being known as Shiva in the Hindu religion. This being has through legend acted as a beautiful symbol for this cleansing and this destruction to give way then to creation and magnificent energies that are necessary for people's own evolution.

Kaus Australis (Epsilon Sagittarii)

[m 1.81] **Blue-white subgiant, 150 light years.**

The ability to speak appropriately and to modulate voice tones to generate a desired response is strengthened. This star can also enhance the ability to listen to others accurately and understand what they are saying without imposing your own ideas. Clairaudience is strengthened. Most people will be able to share information honestly in a more balanced way even though it may be disruptive to the other person.

The star itself is pulsing in such a manner as to project energies at very subtle levels that correspond to near-exact octave translations of various frequencies of aetheric energy. Those who attune to musical and spoken forms will naturally translate these into various notes. This is a repetitive pattern that is not particularly musical but is quite inspirational for people working with sound. This is projecting an ability into people to understand the power of voice. This is an energy that can have powerful effects on many beings by presenting choices, showing them their own strengths, and more importantly, illustrating for them that the star is there by aetherically projecting a presence that states "I am". The naturally occurring vibrations of this star are projecting a powerful reminder of the great power of the Law of Speech. This law states that speech itself has a tremendous capacity to penetrate and to cause change. Civilizations that have sought this star's energy have learned a great deal from it. It has no planets but has frequent intervibrational contact with other beings who come there to learn of some of these energies.

This star has been used in the past to create sounds for healing and for moving objects. There have been many other activities associated with this star. The ways in which words are used to harm were also supplemented by this star, and this did not have beneficial outcomes. The various beings closely allied with Earth's own evolution have coordinated their energies with the star to filter the energies of this star now coming to Earth so that they will be perfectly appropriate for people. The energies now being pulsed and projected aetherically from this star are only those showing people the highest and best uses of speech, the best ways to sing to know their voices, and most importantly the truths that naturally come forth when voices are used appropriately.

Dubhe (Alpha Ursae Majoris)

[m 1.8–1.9] Yellow giant with three other stars, 105 light years

These stars can strengthen the ability to project energy from the heart that can be healing, warming, and regenerating. This energy can be directed with greater consciousness into the person themselves, another person, the world at large, animals, gems, or plants. A particularly good application here is the pouring of such an energy into a clear quartz crystal to allow this energy to strengthen further and vibrate on its own. The combination of free will and love can be better communicated to others. These stars can also create certain deeper states of forgiveness of the elderly in your life, be it your parents, grandparents, or ancestors.

These stars can assist in the creation of an energy that can exist independently of loving conditions created by people. This is a powerful method of providing love energy in which the independent existence of this allows people free will by giving them a choice to work with it appropriately or not. This has been developed by a concurrence of several civilizations that have lived on several planets that have gone around these stars. Over time they have worked out ways of dealing with free will. This has not been worked out completely and they are very interested in how people will come to know this.

During the early Lemurian period these beings from Dubhe recognized that working with raising the vibration of gold would be an important method of allowing this communication of love more deeply for people. This was attempted and some of the remainders of this are still available. Gold as a physical material has some natural benefits in being near a person and Gold elixir certainly has benefit in opening the heart. But it was also observed that people were able to misuse gold because it was physical and fairly rare on Earth and so aspects of greed and other things could get started with it. This created a problem and so the Lemurians in recognizing humanity's future began to correspond with other beings about this. This process was not completed until the middle period of the Egyptian civilization and was shared only in certain limited localities at first. The civilizations on Earth from approximately 200 to 500 AD experienced important changes in their relationship to gold. Incan civilization and various primitive South American civilizations understood the value of gold but would never associate it with greed. At the same time there were certain civilizations in Western Europe which were willing to kill over gold.

It was recognized that it was necessary to create a new energy that people could seek out in their own way and be reminded of love. This was a way of utilizing the gold on Earth as a jumping-off point for these energies. The energy of gold has not been significantly changed but rather a new energy has been added.

Individuals who attune to loving energy but also seek it as an independent creation outside themselves can indeed imagine it as a healing force that can be poured into another person, a crystal, or a bowl of water. This energy can be utilized in many ways.

These beings will continue to make this energy available to people, but they will not interfere. They will continue to provide free will choices so that people can turn away from this at any time they wish. However this gives a clue as to other uses of the elixir that are a little different from other elixirs. It can be provided to people as a gift without their complete knowledge and no real harm will come. They will not be forced to make a choice, there will simply be a natural free-will opportunity for them to receive a little more love in their lives as a result of exposure to the elixir.

Alnitak (Zeta Orionis)

[m 1.8–2.1] Blue-white binary, Alnitak A is a supergiant, Alnitak B is a blue-white giant with a large ultraviolet output. 1,500 light years.

These stars can release the potential for higher energies involved with psychic functioning. These energies can be applied in many different ways but will generally lead to a significant vibrational shift in the individual. This will strengthen these abilities as well as provide more energy in using these abilities. These psychic abilities can include remote viewing, translocation, matter duplication, levitation, prescience, and viewing of internal organs of oneself or others. Meditating on Alnitak or working with the elixir can stimulate psychic functioning on many levels. This will generally be a subtle and deep empowering that will not directly create any enhancement of psychic functioning. This will happen gradually later.

Beings associated with the planets in the Alnitak system have developed methods of transportation based on subtle vibrational forces including what you would term psychic energy, fourth to fifth dimensional energies, and forces you might call supernatural. When they came to Earth in the very early seeding stages in the quiet period between the dinosaurs and the development of humankind, there were influences on the plants and the animals. Increased telepathy was noted just by their presence. This was incorporated into genetic structures in people and was an influence that has given rise to several of the genotypes that can enhance the development of psychic functioning in people based on their inheritance. These beings have overseen this and project an energy that naturally stimulates and vibrates with the human genetic structures to bring some of this into form for people. The effects of the thickening of the aethers on Earth have made these various talents very fleeting and hard to work with. These beings have pulled back from direct influence and are now concentrated their efforts in the star.

It was an easy matter for Alnitak to broadcast these energies of developed psychic functioning once the star was convinced that people's deeper conscious functioning would assist their brother the Sun. These energies are shared with people when they are aware of their connection to the Sun. Some people have blockages to psychic functioning. They know they have some capacities; the people in their family have some of this, but they simply cannot attune to it. The combination of Alnitak and Sunlight elixirs may be a powerful tool for unblocking such things in people.

Wezen (Delta Canis Majoris)

[m 1.84] **White supergiant, 2,000 light years.**

The use of Wezen can enhance the ability to perceive the truth in others especially where it relates to conditions of repressed love or certain aspects of potential connected in some way to a loving condition. Enhanced as well is the ability to perceive such difficulties in one's own self as well as in others and to know the truth of another's potential. The ability to assist others in manifesting their highest potential is strengthened. Coordination will be strengthened in physical activity, including group sports. There is some enhanced ability as well to move the physical body in purely creative states such as dancing or beginning learning of various martial arts disciplines.

Wezen has some ability here to allow transformation in people of long-buried energies. These are important aspects that were shared in the times in people's past lives when they were aware of great and important truths. This occurred as a powerful knowledge explosion at the beginning of the Atlantean civilization, as a powerful awareness of the nature of the Earth in the time of completion of the great pyramids at Giza, and in the time of highest recognition of the oracles in Greece and their ability to transform information and energy as understood and created by the symbol of the guide being Pallas Athena. All of these energies have been powerfully influenced by this star. This is because as people from Earth were able to work with various forms of their own understanding of civilization, a vibration took place which was easily sensed by this civilization and star. This resonated with the star to produce a minor flaring effect to make this star brighter, clearer, and able to project energy back to people on Earth. This star may become a bit brighter in the time of greater transition around 2012 or around 2026. Do not worry about the difficulties of the speed of light here as these things are timed appropriately for humanity's own development.

Now because of this there is an underlying tie to levels of unconsciousness within people where any past life existed where they had awareness of these greater truths and expansion in civilizations. It is very much an Earth-centered energy and an Earth truth that is emitted by this star. It is a reminder of what it is to be alive on Earth, to know people here, and to understand the nature of your civilization. This star provides a deep reminder to people of what they need and who they are.

In these times when buried truths come forth that are so important for humanity, a certain emotional spark is created as a powerful signpost. This is held in the astral body, which has a powerful ability to hold information from past lives. This is then released to the person in the presence of the star, reminding him or her of some of these ancient times. These were times that were portals to the future from that time forward and so one begins to glimpse large and important truths about oneself when exposed to such information.

The understanding of these truths at a verbal, conscious, or expressible level is certainly not of great importance. The astral body does not communicate by such means but through nonverbal or artistic ways. There can be a quieting of the mind and a deeper awareness of these internal states through movement of the body. These ways of movement and dance often had their beginnings in such points of great inspiration and great awareness, and a return to the roots of such energy are usually found in such movement and dance. Truth is generally held in the cells in the structures of the body and so movement of such structures can often encourage the dislodging and revealing of such truths.

Guide beings from this star have been assisting this process of revealing long-buried information about the stars and their messages.

Alkaid (Eta Ursae Majoris)

[m 1.86] Blue-white, 150 light years.

This star can assist in the integration of spiritual ideas with internal concepts of power, expression, and emotion. This can bring into consciousness long-buried emotions, a sense of power, and a deeper expressive ability. Insight into these areas will promote a deeper state of integration in the individual. The balancing that takes place as a result of this will produce deeper physical healing and a sensation of warmth in the physical body. Individuals who are moving away from eating meat who have difficulty with maintaining warmth in the physical body will do well to utilize this star.

The star has been causing an increase in temperature for the three populated planets around it for many centuries. At first this energy was used to increase their physical energy. As they ventured into space and were able to translate these things into subtle level vibrations, they found that a dimensional shift at the sixth dimension allowed them to travel through space as if propelled by the warming energy of their planet and star.

These three planets have a kinship with the Earth at a vibrational level because of certain underlying physical structures that are very similar. These are planets of great beauty with a tremendous variety in plant and animal species. These planets influenced the creation of the Earth herself. They were able to help the Sun to make decisions about working with the formation of the Earth. Because of this vibrational kinship, the natural ability of the Earth herself to work with energies from this place is enhanced. A natural tendency for a transfer of vibration will come into people as a result.

The Earth herself is a power planet. It makes its changes through great destructive principles and powerful creation principles: through volcanic action, the pushing up of mountains, and the changing of powerful weather patterns. This is a great understanding of power that the Earth herself is going through. Where power reveals a truth, a deep internal change, and an awareness of what it means to be alive, the Earth has made some progress. In working with this star in any form you will be more aware of this in yourself. It is not so much the Earth's own way of doing this that you become aware of, but your way. This is because many of the capacities at a vibrational level that were created in the Earth were then created as an overlay of capacities in most of the plants and animals and certainly in humans who live on Earth.

Sargas (Theta Scorpii)

[m 1.86] Blue-white supergiant, 500 light years. Contains ionized metals: titanium, iron, magnesium, and calcium.

Some of these minerals are symbolic of various components of will. The use of this star can bring deeper clarity to the aspect of will. Sometimes this will relate directly to a willingness to live, a willingness to survive, and a willingness to confront deep issues in one's life regarding survival or suicide. These issues are generally deeply buried in the unconscious. Most people have a past life that has as a primary core issue the question of whether to go on with the series of incarnations or whether to end it. By your own presence in the world you have made this choice already. To bring this choice into greater consciousness and clarity is the property of this star. At an even deeper level, working with this star can strengthen the will to survive and counteract suicidal impulses to some extent. When working with an individual dealing with these issues, there is benefit in doing hands-on healing work, massage work, or other touching work and the practitioner utilizing this elixir or meditation upon the star as well.

This star has the capacity to energize the connection between the Earth and the Sun. This will connect people to their own root chakra and to their own ability to bring energy from the Earth into the physical body. These energies already exist because they are based on substances found in the physical body. The many minerals that are found in the Earth's crust form a direct vibrational connection between the physical body and the Earth herself. Sargas has a capacity to energize some of the underlying connections which have not been fully acknowledged or understood. The higher power or strength associated with these energies are better known to people. Some of these energies can remind individuals of past lives in which there was difficulty accepting their role on the Earth. Part of this is generated through the minerals themselves and part of it is because there is a general awakening of many cellular structures in the body as a result of the influence of this star.

There is a long-standing vibrational connection that extends from the nature of the way the soul has selected cellular structures to manifest certain aspects of the soul. These cellular structures are stimulated by this star which will energize the natural connection to the Earth that has been established because those substances are drawn from the Earth. This blending of the soul and Earth aspects within a person will stimulate energies from the past. Though some of this will often relate to genetic ancestry, it is mostly aimed at the aspect that the soul has willed into the person. This is the development of inner will. It is a will that is generally in perfect alignment with what you are doing in your life but is usually tied to some unconscious aspect that is within you that you don't really understand. These unconscious aspects can be keyed into your consciousness by any cellular changes because these memories are a combination of the material and the spiritual. These cellular memories can be stimulated by the ability of minerals to affect the body.

A long period of awareness of the many substances found within this star was an important aspect of the work of the civilization and the star herself in different and coordinating ways over long periods of time. This became an awareness of the nature of mineral substances. Titanium and many other minerals were utilized by this civilization for buildings, space ships, various instruments, and other structures. As a result of their awareness of the vibrations of these materials, this civilization began to understand that it was partly by the nature of the materials themselves that they were learning, not just by the function of these devices. This deeper awareness eventually gave rise to a new form of communication utilizing the vibration of molecular structures to communicate ideas, feelings, knowledge, and other matters that do not anthropomorphize very well. This communication became a way of transcending the limitations of time and space, and allowed this civilization communication with many stars.

When communication was set up with the Sun, this energy exchange was quite powerful. These beings recognized some of the deficiencies in the human race, animals, plants, and other things growing on Earth. They recognized that these ways of unconsciousness or misunderstood expression could be stimulated through awareness of vibration with the mineral kingdom. These are certain long-dormant capacities to communicate utilizing the vibrations of these minerals. In Lemurian times deeper communion and direct awareness of this powerful race of beings took place. Some of the techniques learned by the Lemurians for working with gems, minerals, and metallic structures of all kinds were influenced, and in some cases taught directly, by these beings. As people welcome certain aspects of the unconscious, some of these capacities will come into greater prominence with the influence of this star.

Alhena (Gamma Geminorum)

[m 1.93] Blue-white binary, one of which is a subgiant, 100 light years.

This star appears to offer individuals the ability to rapidly change modes of thought and to shift context. This will give them the ability to see things in a whole new way and to utilize the information from a new perspective or to change their minds in a way that is appropriate for their own development. This may mean seeing several sides of an issue in a genuinely touching way that really brings consciousness to the situation, which makes it helpful in the decision-making process. Use of this star elixir will stimulate the chakras in the feet.

This star system is a binary that has the ability to allow shifting vibrations as the two stars move around each other. Evolutionary processes on this planet are greatly speeded up. Changes in plant and animal structures take place quite rapidly, even in just a few hours. For the civilizations there, this was a very interesting sort of thing, as if the colors, their perceptions, and the plants and biological species changed all the time. The beings in one of these systems of planets around Alhena began to grow in a new way by recognizing that there was a certain deep gravitational effect that was shifting for them as the stars moved. The awareness of this led to a new form of sublight space travel. These planets were as if shared in terms of trade, awareness, context, and other things. The ability to shift context in relating to one's neighbors was very powerful.

The cross-seeding from one planet to another severely stressed the ability to maintain ecological structures and to work out social systems. The solution to this was found in their stars. In working with their gravity, these beings received communications from their stars. Alhena's energies became deeply involved in the civilizing process of these beings by encouraging and assisting them to see things in new ways. What was unknown to them for the first few thousand years that they did such work was that each time space travel was undertaken their star system also received some of their communication. Once this deeper communication and higher awareness through vibrational transfer took place, the star began asking questions and saw that its energy could be useful to other developing civilizations of the galaxy.

This led to its broadcasting of these energies as these ideas of shifting perspective and seeing things differently. As much of this is based on the gravity of the star, this energy reaches Earth about a hundred years or so behind the current development of this civilization. This is of no great importance since these beings have evolved far beyond humans. This message has a certain level of underlying strength, a certain perseverance and ability to push and continue when the going gets tough. This is done is by shifting perspective, seeing new ideas, and bringing in another way of doing something so that you can make progress. The perseverance of this energy affects the Sun which then transmits this to the Earth to stimulate the feet.

As these beings have shifted in their own modes of space travel they have pretty much discarded physical means of transportation. Their ability to shift vibration, context, and awareness has allowed them to work easily on the subtler planes. People who are very spiritually inclined or who already have some deeper awareness of their mind's ability to allow contextual shift will find that they can make contact with such beings in the sleep state. They are generally presented as humanoid in nature with soft features and perhaps resemble at times in your visions the Nordic race of people on Earth.

Algieba (Gamma Leonis)

[m 1.9–2.2] **Two yellow giants, 110 light years.**

The use of these stars can balance aspects of love relating to full acceptance of male and female qualities in an individual. Individuals who are struggling with sexual identity and how they are relating to others as male or female will do well with this elixir or meditation on this star. At a deeper level there is some release of blockages at physical level that can be hormonal in nature and thus endocrine balance can be assisted in most people, which will assist in regeneration. Meditation on the star or taking its elixir will also provide a deeper aspect of love in a relationship where role reversal is an important part of the relationship. In the case of the woman who works while the man stays at home, the role reversal is based upon certain conscious messages drawn from society. Understanding the true place of these messages is enhanced by use of these stars.

These two stars are able to switch roles even though they are of different sizes and capacities. There are no planets around Algieba. These stars have developed an ability to transfer energy, information, vibration, and they had noticed that when the transfer took place there was a natural drawing in of lessons, awareness, and consciousness. The first time this transfer took place the stars were dramatically changed. This was approximately 4.3 billion years ago. As these transfers took place more often, physical changes were lessened and only the subtler-level changes were allowed. At one point in the development of these stars, approximately 1.6 billion years ago, these stars became equal in all ways and shared their essence and characteristics. As the stars came to understand the importance of personality, they developed individualized characteristics to make the stars different from one another. Because these stars are able to transfer consciousness, they have found that by having differences they can learn a great deal. In becoming aware of these differences and accepting them and knowing them and eventually sharing them with others, there have been some rather dramatic changes. The stars are able to easily transcend the capacities and limitations of time and space by the tremendous gravity that is available between the two stars.

This is a star to be experienced and known in your heart, to be felt with your body and your mind, but especially to be known in your innermost being. Algieba can make instantaneous transformation available to people. This is especially available to women who are attuned to transformation through the understanding of throwing off the old patriarchal systems and coming to new living systems. This energy is also available for men who are seeking an internal balance by understanding the coordination of the female aspect of themselves with the male aspect. An understanding of their uniqueness and their ability to have many beautiful combined capacities will generally be brought into most people's consciousness. This will release blockages, cause shifts in the awareness of love, and bring balancing at the level of male and female. Humanity has made a fairly arbitrary choice with division of the race into male and female polarities; and so other polarity divisions will also be affected by Algieba over the next few thousand years.

Around Algieba are clouds of energy from a race of beings from Andromeda that are learning from this star system at this time. It is possible that in about two or three hundred years some of these Andromeda beings will recognize through the binary Algieba an awareness of other stars that have civilizations with them that they could learn from, and it is likely that Earth will be chosen. This will likely enhance contact with this race which is the bearer of communications from Andromeda and other galaxies.

Menkalinan (Beta Aurigae)

[m 1.9–2.7] **Two blue-white subgiants, 90 light years. Eclipsing binary: magnitude drops each 4 days. Also a smaller third star.**

This four day cycle is symbolic and connected to powerful energies associated with most people's ability to apply information derived from powerful dreaming states or energies associated with astral travel. This is a resonant capacity reminding people of the natural ability of the body to be involved in these processes of the astral body coming into the physical body. This work with the astral body generally takes 72 hours to permeate into consciousness. Approximately a day later the individual in applying this information and experience will reap the rewards. The use of meditation upon this star or elixir is recommended at any time during such period, but most importantly immediately after the astral experience. This can bring out the highest consciousness of the lucid dream or of the astral travel experience. These energies can then be applied with greater force and understanding in the world, and the true benefits of the experience will generally be brought into consciousness for the person. He or she will have more energy when dealing with the issues brought up by such experiences.

There is also some benefit in using this star where an individual is perceiving a block that seems to have some cycle associated with it. The cycle does not have to be three, four, or five days or anything close to that of this binary but rather can be a cycle that the person has simply noted occuring in his or her life. It could be a certain cycle of health or disease. It could be a relationship cycle where one notices at certain times of the month one is close to ones mate and at other times not. For all such things there will be a general benefit in utilizing this star or its elixir so that a shift in the energy is available and the person can have deeper awareness of this. It can be especially helpful if the person involved utilizes it to bring in a clearer dream state or to assist with lucid dreaming. It can be well combined with Krypton elixir for a general enhancement of the dreaming state.

Mirzam (Beta Canis Majoris)

[m 1.96] Blue-white giant, 700 light years. Slightly variable in two different superimposed six hour periods.

Some deeper acceptance of what would be termed magical phenomena will be felt by most people in utilizing this star. This can mean acceptance of everyday actions in the world as miraculous or it can mean acceptance of various paranormal, supernormal, superconscious, or unusual phenomena. Though this can apply to psychic gifts, it is generally where energies about the natural phenomena in the world that are not normally a part of one's existence become more acceptable. This can include witnessing of the devic orders and working with the ability to sense the aura in other people. It will allow individuals deeper acceptance of miraculous phenomena outside themselves such as channeling or healing work that appears to circumvent the principles normally observed in everyday life. This is a good elixir for Westerners to take in preparation for psychic surgery or other forms of healing that might be seen as miraculous or paranormal. It would not be of any value to someone from the Philippines who had understood such principles from birth. In such cases it is a cultural phenomena that one wishes to understand more deeply. The deepest use of Mirzam is for understanding and accepting the miracles in oneself.

Miraculous or magical phenomena are simply those things that you have not understood yet but are also those things that do not generate fear. There is usually a sense of awe or wonder. This separates it from other things that you might not understand that do bring fear. This can become a way of exploration that is inherently without context. It is the very nature of the contextless situation that brings the magical quality into mind for most people.

Many of the phenomena that have been unacceptable in a given civilization are now becoming more available as individuals are naturally attuning to each other and learning about other cultures and civilizations on Earth. Over the next hundred years these will become assimilated and actually utilized. Therefore it is not out of the realm of possibility to imagine a formalization of the schools of teaching of psychic healing as done in the Philippines shared worldwide, where people themselves are able to do such because they have been taught how from an early age.

If you look into the history of humankind, a simple acceptance of magic and miracles has been very important for people's development as far back as can be seen. At this time these energies of the miraculous are coming from awareness of all cultures on Earth and the increasing awareness of such as the deep sea creatures and the creatures found only in unusual ecological niches throughout the world. This is an awareness of what is possible on Earth. These beautiful or unusual phenomena can deeply affect a person as if to say: "This is the world I live in, I had no idea!" This deep feeling of awe and wonder is very important for people to be aware of so they can be stimulated into new contexts all the time.

As people become more aware of the other cultures and the natural kingdoms on Earth, there will be a greater need for the miraculous on new levels. The next level will be awareness of the other planets, the stars nearest the Sun, and extraterrestrial civilizations. There will be a much greater difficulty with people in allowing these new contexts. Though they need it, they do not know how to relate to it because they have very little training at a conscious level. Over the next few hundred years this will pass as people begin to accept such awareness of other civilizations and encourage deeply shifted contexts in themselves. All during this time the influence of Mirzam will be more and more useful as people need to attune to contexts way outside of what they already know. The further afield it is or the more miraculous it would appear to be, the more an awareness at a vibrational level is necessary to understand it. The assistance given by Mirzam elixir or various meditative techniques such as meditation on the stars will be extremely helpful for creating this vibrational awareness.

Alphard (Alpha Hydrae)

[m 1.98] **Yellow giant, 100 light years.**

Alphard can enhance the ability to bring emotions to consciousness and to work with them with others, particularly in dealing with the emotion of anger. The true source of anger may be felt more deeply and be easily released as a result. Individuals in therapy where anger is an important issue will benefit in utilizing this elixir for more understanding of the purposes of the anger. This elixir or meditation upon the star is often able to transform anger into enthusiasm more easily for people. There is some benefit in combining Alphard with Mars elixir.

The civilization associated with Alphard moves through periods of deep attunement, awareness, and love for the people of Earth. This will usually alternate from time to time with disgust, revulsion, and fear as if it is impossible to understand why these people of Earth would do the things they do to destroy their environment, each other, and so on. What these beings have attempted to do over the last 2,000 years in looking at people on Earth was to take the highest and best of their ideas, put them in the star for continuous broadcast, and then withdraw from communication, awareness, and understanding of what is happening on Earth. This is a general tendency that has lasted with these beings for a long time as they have worked with other civilizations at various times.

Only a few individuals from this civilization have been allowed to make direct attunement with the people of Earth. These individuals became aware of the powerful influence of Mars over the many centuries and the continuing influence of the Martian thought form. There has been a deliberate attempt on the part of these beings to gradually shift the energy of Alphard so that it is able to in some ways neutralize or assist with people understanding this Martian energy. This star is also broadcasting an underlying aspect of an enthusiastic, all-powerful universal love. This is naturally inspired by the beautiful yellow color of the star. These beings have recognized that to transcend or go around intellectual or even emotional qualities would be a useful way of bringing the energy of this star to bear on Earth. These loving, encouraging, and enthusiastic aspects are non-verbal energies that come to people of Earth to provide a general source of inspiration and encouragement to shift and understand the nature of the anger.

At the current time much anger, fear, pain, and other negative emotions have biologically based aspects. These energies have a purpose. These energies can show you where love has been inappropriately applied with other people or in relating to oneself. This can lead to an understanding of repulsion and attraction and the ability of natural phenomena in the world to interrelate.

Transformed negative emotions can encourage other aspects of emotional awareness based on many variations of universal love, compassion, awe, praise, faith, and the awareness of deep levels of pleasure and understanding. The negative emotions themselves can show a path of transformation. Most people would tend to be trapped in the negative emotions for long periods before they can see how the transformation can be willed. This is not by repressing the emotion but by understanding what it means and why it is there. All of these things are naturally affected by the warmth, love, and compassion of this beautiful golden color of Alphard, as well as its spirituality and its resonance with the Christ energy. This can bring clearer mental functioning to people by stimulating the yellow ray.

All of these things can work now for people with the transformation of anger into enthusiasm. Earth is a planet of action, moving, doing, and creating. The principal energy that the anger is creating at a biological level is usually the energy to move faster, be stronger, or perhaps yell or make a loud sound. These are biologically based actions coming from the primates that are part of the genetic structures of people. People have the capacity to understand this and allow such energy to transform into enthusiasm. This star can influence many other processes of transformation such as the transformation of fear into a deep love, compassion, and oneness, and the transformation of pain into the awareness of healing and change.

Polaris (Alpha Ursae Minor)

[m 1.99] **White supergiant, 350 light years.**

Polaris is more than other star anchored in the symbolic understanding of humanity at this time. It is the pole star, thus utilized so much for navigation. It therefore represents at a deep level the unconscious ability of individuals to align with a common source to bring through energy that can be applied in the world. This can create a subtle alignment with the nature of the God energy that supports and sustains humanity as one. In understanding this deeply within people, what eventually emerges is the exact unity that they seek. Thus in meditating on this star or utilizing its elixir, there can be a deeper awareness of unity amongst people. As a result of this, what may come forth is actual application of the energies found in the sense of unity. This will assist individuals because this will naturally flow only along spiritually evolved lines.

The use of Polaris at this time is simply to align people and to bring them into a state of some common awareness. This shared energy will be utilized for whatever project or energies an individual wishes to put them to. While they are utilizing such an energy, some characteristics of the collective consciousness will also come through. These will be most directly tied to one's own questioning of what actually brings people together. Most individuals will recognize that this force bringing people together is not based on selfishness or individual actions, but instead on the unifying God-energy that has brought people into existence. Thus there will be a continual gradual realignment with higher spiritual principles when this elixir is utilized. This star is best used in group situation where there is action to be done but there is a possibility of being sidetracked into areas that are not entirely beneficial to the whole or into areas not spiritually oriented or aligned with higher universal principles. When the elixir is utilized, there is far less tendency for this sidetracking to take place.

Hamal (Alpha Arietis)

[m 2.00] **Yellow giant, 75 light years.**

Clearer states of concentration, the ability to hold a single thought for longer periods of time, and the ability to communicate that thought telepathically, these are all strengthened by the use of this star. An ability to understand the true nature of the thought process eventually results with repeated use of this star. Concentration is not thought alone, but an awareness that comes into being that relates to emotions and body feelings as well as subtle biological processes. This star is of some benefit to understand many of these processes.

Beings from a higher dimensional body in the space adjacent to Hamal have a capacity to overshadow how people understand symbols. They have contributed to the development of astrology by their ability to create powerful symbols of many other civilizations in people's consciousness. It was seen that such powerful symbols could be brought into a new form with the development of humanity.

Any symbol can be understood by utilizing history, channeled information, psychic sources, intuitive inner direction, deeper awareness of themselves, and all the other things that have been used throughout history to understand symbols. If an individual also used that symbol to allow them to concentrate by keeping their full attention on the matter with all aspects of their being, very wonderful things would result. Concentration can result in the ability to materialize an object, to bring into form a particular event or circumstance, or to bring certain emotions into form for other people, or to communicate ideas. On an inner level this can result in a deeper understanding, kinship, oneness, awareness, and deeper intelligence. These beings associated with Hamal gave to people the whole idea of symbols with free will, but they also left this extra key. In the deep ability to concentrate would be found aspects of free will, deeper love, and an ability to change their world for the better.

This ability was seeded into Earth at a multidimensional level a long time ago. It is a capacity shared amongst many mammals though rarely used by any of them, and is something inherent to the human condition. For a reminder of this and a path back in time to touch little pieces of this, the star Hamal acts as a wonderful symbol.

Alpheratz (Alpha Andromedae)

[m 2.03] **Blue-white binary, 130 light years. One of these stars is a magnetic spectrum variable containing manganese, gallium, and many other metals.**

This binary star can provide a deeper state of awareness of cellular structures in the physical body. Individuals utilizing meditative techniques or inert gas techniques for regeneration will find that such kinship with the cells is enhanced. Regeneration of nerves is accelerated. The ability of the physical body to enhance the process of conscious understanding is increased. Utilization of this star is recommended after a long chronic illness.

The changing magnetic fields associated with Alpheratz affect the small quantities of inert gasses found in her atmosphere. The nature of these energies is fourth dimensional and thus transcends the limitations and boundaries of time and space. People can have some regenerative energy and some deeper awareness of their own bodies by imagining themselves journeying into the star. Many of the most valuable elements found in the human body are mirrored in this star. Such a journey into Alpheratz can stimulate these substances being released appropriately into the human body. The correct use of these minerals is the very basis from which the body is able to reconstruct.

Small amounts of xenon trapped in what could be termed magnetic bottles on the star's surface and deep within her core are able to cause a transmission of energy throughout the galaxy. This can affect xenon on Earth to create some additional benefit besides the usual capacities of xenon for regeneration of missing body parts or for shielding of the Sun's negative energies. There can be in addition to this an awareness of Christ consciousness, higher awareness in the crown chakra, and a regeneration of the pineal gland. The way this is done is that a mixture of Alpheratz elixir with Xenon elixir is taken internally in the presence of a xenon beam. The xenon beam can be projected from an inert gas device, threshold pressure 300 PSI, even a few hundred gauss should be sufficient of magnetic stimulation. The xenon can be mixed with other inert gasses as long as there is some presence of xenon at this pressure. In the presence of all of these three influences, there will generally be experienced by the individual easier regeneration of the pineal gland. This is a gland that is not utilized at the current time very much in people. It is something you generally turn off as you grow older. However its capacities are merely dormant and can be awakened again in people. One reason this technique is so useful is because the volcanic activity in the Earth is increasing at the current time. It is as if the Earth's own awareness of blowing her top is connected at a symbolic level to the pineal gland. This sort of energy is now being made more available to people.

Over the centuries Alpheratz has become a place for the regeneration of societies, relationships, and beings that wish to understand and know each other better. Many beings who have learned techniques of regeneration have created a library of such techniques in the star and some of the planets that surround her. These are energies that you would not understand very well. In civilizations that do not require death in order to learn, it is a little easier to do things that don't need to be regenerated, started again, or destroyed and recreated. These are techniques of regeneration and awareness that eventually will be understood on Earth.

Diphda (Beta Ceti)

[m 2.04] Yellow giant, 60 light years, neutral metals.

The ability to perceive aetheric interconnections between individuals is strengthened. The unconscious ties made between individuals are brought into consciousness. The second chakra energies that may be depleted by such unconscious ties are relieved, and healing in this area is generally enhanced. The ability to touch others and both give and receive the subtler energies as well as the gross physical energies is enhanced. This star can enhance massage techniques where there is movement, such as Swedish massage or Shiatsu.

What occurs here is a way in which these subtler energies that are so important to people but not very well known are made much clearer and much more understandable for people. The aetheric energies might be termed modeling energies. Generally these are energies that are not conscious. The net result of many vibrational tools is to bring these aetheric energies into greater clarity and focus. When you are successful in deeper awareness, healing, concentrative ability, understanding of yourself, and even what you might call enlightenment, many times you will note that the aetheric body is intimately involved in this process and may even be partly responsible for it.

Diphda has some very beneficial capacities in working with all sorts of energies. The beings associated with this civilization on the nearest planet to the Diphda sun have learned rapid techniques of space travel utilizing electromagnetic energies as carriers to move faster than light packets. This ability to work with what are essentially fourth-dimensional characteristics has given them a great deal of understanding of this mode of being. When they look at Earth they see so much unconsciousness with regards to the fourth dimension and so little understanding of the way in which people are continually manipulating the aethers by their own love or hate. The beings who have studied this problem for centuries have over the last 300 years or so focused on this one area very deliberately. Free will choice is so important for humanity's own development that to interfere by giving too much understanding about the nature of the aetheric body would not be wise.

This star can bring a non-verbal energy into people to encourage the aetheric body to understand itself and for people to have deeper awareness of it. This is created by a strengthening of the aetheric body and a bringing of its energy into deeper form for people. Humanity's own expansion into the area of relationship is a way in which aetheric bodies are shared between people. The energies that are least understood in relationship relate to the second chakra. These energies can shifted and transformed into more positive color patterns relating to the color pink. Any things that encourage the development of the aetheric body will be assisted by use of this star.

Saiph (Kappa Orionis)

[m 2.05] Blue-white supergiant, 2,000 light years.

For most people use of this star will result in a deeper ability to be patient. This can strengthen one's ability to wait and see the overall picture, as well as bring a deeper awareness of correct timing and the way in which time can be appropriately utilized. There can be awareness as to the right place and right time to express oneself and to make powerful moves in the world, be they in one's business or in political, social, or economic areas. This ability to perceive the grander plan, though largely at an unconscious level, is enhanced and so the ability to be in the right place at the right time is somewhat strengthened. Deeper knowledge of this plan and how things are unfolding is enhanced in using this star.

There are many aspects of the development of time associated with the beings from this star. Most of them existed in a huge gravitational field somewhat similar to what you would recognize on Jupiter. But other conditions provided for their planet certain optimal opportunities for life. The huge gravitational field and minimum availability of dense materials made it difficult to produce the technological developments other civilizations have had access to such as space ships or other forms of starship drives. As a result their own technological exploration as coordinated with spiritual development focused on time. In their third-dimensional representation and awareness of this, they were able to make great leaps in consciousness, spirituality, and other functions to understand all forms of time. These beings have learned that the relatively arbitrary assignment of time to the locality of the solar system that Earth is in is that which is easily changed by consciousness. The beings from this star area have powerful capacities to shift and work with time in ways that are difficult for you to comprehend.

From this they were able to achieve space travel and able to visit other civilizations. They were able to neutralize some of the excessive gravity of their own planet and engage in interstellar commerce and working with other beings.

Their awareness of Earth was that individuals who had no conception of the true nature of time flows were trapped. You are within a linear time field by your own reckoning, you appear to move through time in an obvious and linear fashion—yesterday, today, tomorrow. Such a flow of time to you appears natural. To such beings it is the bars on a cage. It is a trapping of energy, life-forms, and awareness. The tiger who has been born to captivity is not fully aware of how she is trapped in the bars of her own cage. You might pity her, but she does not understand this nor is she aware of the difficulty. There is only a sense, perhaps vague, from other lifetimes, from the shared soul, or from the experiences of those around her of the possibilities should the bars be taken away. People also have a vague longing or awareness of the fluidity of time. As the awareness of people increases into the fifth-dimensional level of awareness, there comes this understanding of time, time flows, and its full impact on beings.

Until then all that likely can be imparted from these loving beings towards people on Earth is patience and a sense of the true span and scope of time. This can be an awareness of time's limitations, how to work with it appropriately, and the curiosity to explore and work with it in ways that are appropriate to each individual. This is all they can really do at this time as if then you in working with the trapped tiger know that you can do very little, that there are no environments left for the tiger to live in that you have access to or can do anything about. After you have moved through the place of pity what you do is that you love the animal, you do the best to feed it, to learn from it, and to grow with it.

These beings are not confined by the usual barriers of time and space as you perceive them and can direct their energy specifically as is appropriate to any developing civilization that would need it, and they have been doing so for people on Earth with greater intensity since about 1918. At such time the most important developments in quantum physics took hold. Though many of these were foreshadowed by earlier developments, from that time forward most of the important developments began to take greater form and there were inspirations here to many of the scientists and others who came to understand and work with time in a theoretical form. This has not been available to the general public and there may be benefit in taking the starlight elixir of this place when you study quantum physics, especially for understanding the time aspects.

Mirach (Beta Andromedae)

[m 2.06] **Yellow-orange giant, 75 light years.**

The ability to hear, to utilize the voice, and to release difficulties associated with the sounds one hears or speaks is strengthened. A deeper connection to physicalness and an opening of the root chakra results. The ability to hear the sounds of nature and the Earth will likely be enhanced as well. Psychic abilities, including the ability to perceive the rhythms of sound in the world around you will be somewhat strengthened. Some internal balancing of the connections between the thyroid and the pituitary will likely result from use of this elixir. There will be a strengthening of the hairs on the upper body and especially those in the ear which act as a physical antenna to translate aetheric energy to physical. Some states of hearing loss can be reversed.

This star vibrates and creates natural resonances with beings that are near it. These are in the aether of space, which does not transfer acoustic vibrations very well. Individuals who attune to the star will receive light wavelengths that will easily stimulate the underlying energies that relate harmonically to sound and other vibrations. In Lemuria the awareness of this star was often a part of healing rituals where music or sound was involved. Some of the early developments of transference of vibration into what eventually became healing techniques by the civilization around Sirius drew from this star. So there are energies of some healing nature here too, but mostly it is the awareness of these interpenetrating resonances and vibrations.

At various times in the star's life it has established resonances with other stars to communicate with them. The star benefitted greatly from this, experiencing a fifth, sixth, seventh, and eighth dimensional equivalent of joy. As is often the case when one experiences deep joy, this was something the star wished to share. This was encouraged by other aware beings, stars, sentient universes, and God. Such encouragement led eventually to the star working with specific energies of other beings to bring this into form for many civilizations. The individuals from Sirius with some influence from the highest thinkers of El

Nath were able to cause some shift in the vibratory properties of the star to create certain wave packets that are more available to those who would use them. These are especially available to Earth people in forms of acoustic vibration. There is a healing awareness of sound that people sometimes create within themselves when they work with sound for modes of healing, and this is influenced gently by the star. With specific focus on the star or use of the elixir there will usually be seen an acceleration of these natural properties by bringing what are usually unconscious forms of energy into some degree of conscious awareness in the person.

There are also some filters here. In the past humanity has abused some of these natural techniques. The atmospheric density on Earth makes an excellent transducer of sound. The high water content of the Earth's atmosphere also increases these capacities for aetheric energies to be transferred via the human voice and other vibratory forms into energies of sound and other forms to create motion, healing, materialization, or the movement of large objects. Some of this has been abused in the past and humanity has created certain filters for this which prevent the full explanation of this star's properties at this time. These filters are well in place and will not be disturbed by utilization of the star in meditation or elixir form and so we could certainly strongly recommend it for those wishing to explore these healing capacities in themselves.

Rasalhague (Alpha Ophiuchi)

[m 2.07] **Blue-white giant, 60 light years.**

Rasalhague can improve the transfer of aetheric energies into the physical body. These energies can strengthen the physical body when various forms of movement, martial arts, or dance are combined with visualization. Individuals involved in the development of the physical body who might have been attracted to substances such as steroids that artificially induce changes in the physical body would do well to utilize this elixir or meditation on this star.

Beings associated with this star learned interplanetary travel techniques from observation of gravity waves. Gravity waves are actually the expansion and contraction of the aether in the space near gravity bodies such as stars and planets. They did not learn this to explore other planets, although that was initially done and resources were discovered. But as they were able to use these techniques also for materialization principles, communicative principles, and other things, it was not necessary to travel to the other planets of their system. It became a dance or martial art form somewhat similar in principle to surfing. They are as if surfing the aetheric waves, and this was a great deal of fun. This was done for a long period of time and became a major sport attraction and way of relating to other people and other star systems. Eventually this became something that evolved into a dance form that was quite beautiful to other beings who could see what was going on at the higher dimensional levels. This was an energy that these beings left behind as they evolved into other realms of artistic and creative endeavor and is that which continues with the star and is broadcast to the universe.

People can use this energy to appreciate the perfection of the intertwining of the aetheric, physical, mental, and emotional bodies. The aetheric body is used to model and shape energies before they come into physical form. This star can benefit all individuals involved in creative visualization, this is the healing of the body by manipulation of the aetheric body. This will benefit those who wish to understand action learned at the physical level as it corresponds to aetheric energy pouring back into them and to the other levels. Anyone involved in movement will certainly benefit. He or she may be able to understand that this movement has a purpose, which cannot be adequately defined with verbal or intellectual concepts alone. This is one of the big problems in movement art or movement science. Those who seek to understand, explain, or describe the movement process only reduce its ability to inform, educate, and bring a sense of change to people. When they try to explain it they only belittle it. With this star there is a sense of expansion that can lead to a new type of expression that uses the movement as if to say the principles of "I love you" or "I accept this universe" or "I am willing to help" or "I know" or even "I am." These are important principles to be expressed through the language of movement itself in order to understand about such movement. This is a general encouragement because that is what these beings did. By the joy they felt moving through space and time, they were able to transfer these energies of joy to God.

Kochab (Beta Ursae Minoris)

[m 2.07] **Yellow giant, 110 light years. Kochab was one of the pole stars from 1500 BC – 500 AD**

This star can assist people in grounding information from their past lives. This is a way in which one becomes more comfortable with one's past lives, as if these lives are running concurrently or parallel to one's present life and can affect the person in positive ways. The ability to accept this easily, feel good about the information, and take it in by actually owning it and really knowing it, this is far beyond a verbal or intellectual process. This can generate a deeper sense of power within the individual.

In the future Kochab may be able to enhance people's ability to know about their destiny. This is an energy that is generally not available at the current time. Destiny could be thought of as a sonnet where the form is given but the words are chosen by free will by the person. Destiny is unique to each individual soul and their own development. Transcending time is usually required to understand this. Just as this deeper grounding and awareness of the underlying energies associating you with Earth can open you to past lives, so they can also open you to future lives. Those who wish to understand their development into the next life and the one after can benefit by utilizing Kochab.

These abilities are related to the symbolic associations this star has with earlier times. As the pole star it was a reference point for guidance and navigation and working with the Earth. Kochab had a powerful influence at the end of the Egyptian civilization and the beginning of Christianity. There was a certain deeper awareness of the Sun for Kochab, and these two stars were able to share information. In ancient times this star was a symbol for allowing one's connection to God to be felt. At the current time this is symbolized by the energies of Polaris.

Nunki (Sigma Sagittarii)

[m 2.08] **Blue-white, 250 light years.**

Nunki is in close alignment with the center of the galaxy. This star is one of those directly seeded by the center of the galaxy. A powerful direct connection exists between that star and the nexus of information, wisdom, and awareness that is the center of this galaxy. There is a transfer of energy from the center of the galaxy, and the civilization associated with this star has done well in assimilating and working with this energy.

As a result, mental transference of ideas and concepts in whole form is enhanced by use of this star. The deeper understanding of complex economic, political and social issues can be found in this star. This can relate to various components of diplomacy and the ability to interrelate in times of national crisis. The ability to transfer different aspects of cultures between countries will be enhanced. A deeper ability to motivate others in bringing some of these concepts into form will be noted. Some artists who are struggling with large concepts and visions that involve more than a single media will also be strengthened by use of this elixir or meditation upon the star.

The center of the galaxy is an origination point for energies of creative force. After these energies have manifested in the physical, what is left are guiding lights, gentle influences, more ideas, more potential, but not things that are forced into consciousness. Choice to work with these things can be encouraged by many different means and techniques. Information and awareness from the center of the galaxy can be accessed by intermingling these potentials to stimulate a new contextual view, a new idea, or a remembrance of an old idea now brought into form in a new way. These things have been transferred to a number of stars. Some of these are located near the center of the galaxy. Some of them are in a line with Earth to the center of the galaxy so that these information capacities and potentials are more easily transferred to beings on Earth, and of course to others who would assist and work with Earth beings. The center of the galaxy is concerned not only with Earth but with many of the other beings, civilizations, and experiments that go on within the galaxy. This star is one of those transfer points of this energy, awareness, and potential.

Exactly how this will come into form is not fully determined. It is a doorway to access many higher creative functions. A good way to access this is to stimulate in individuals all of the complexities of the world and all they have learned. Knowledge, wisdom, art, and the things that are the highest and the best of humanity are then integrated and combined in the person. Cross-cultural stimulation is the current form for this. When you learn about another civilization or another way of being on planet Earth, this can be stimulating from many different points of view. This can be from a pastlife point of view because of previous contact with this civilization or a birth in it yourself. But in other ways it is a different point of view because of the language, the appearance of the people, the customs, and the other things that stimulate on an unconscious level, such as in music, dance, and art. There is now an influence to increase these capacities of higher potential for humanity by the influence of these cross-cultural aspects.

There is also a stimulation of deeper awareness of the whole galaxy and of the many other beings, thought forms, and potentials that may come into form. You do not quite understand yet the magnificence of the center of the galaxy and of its capacity to interact with various civilizations. This is a way of working in modes of parallel computing to determine and work out all kinds of powerful and complex ideas. These ideas are then projected back to the civilization to ask consciously or unconsciously certain questions about those ideas. This can lead them to deeper awareness of themselves, and from this the answers are generated. It is as if internal processes are accelerated and assisted by this star.

Mizar (Zeta Ursae Majoris)

[m 2.09] **Blue-white, 90 light years, 5 stars. Mizar A is a binary; Mizar B is a three star system.**

Use of this star system can enhance states of multiple awareness, ability to channel, and the ability to organize various components of one's personality. There is an ability here to better understand the physical, emotional, and spiritual phases of one's life. A better way to integrate these is usually observed with individuals who work with Mizar. Channeling states can become more balanced, deeper states can result, and more information is likely to be transferred as a result.

In many ways, and more than with other stars, these beautiful beings known as Mizar have a natural ability to communicate to people about this message. In a sense, anything we say only reduces such awareness because after all these beautiful beings have their own capacities, and as people learn about these capacities and know them, they can certainly attune to them themselves. Obviously here you can create all sorts of energies. The powerful interconnections between these stars act as a magnificent symbol for many other beings. Most extraterrestrial beings who wish to channel to Earth beings will do some period of training or learning in the vicinity of Mizar. There will usually be a period in which they deliberately channel to each other, shifting energies and experiences. They will not just communicate with telepathic ideas by planting a seed thought or idea, but will work at much deeper levels by creating a natural transfer of consciousness: an awareness on multiple levels with thoughts, actions, deeds, memories, and senses. Some degree of practice of such is usually necessary before beings who are not of this Earth can channel to Earth beings. And so at the current time it is a very popular place amongst beings who wish to channel to Earth people. Pleiadeans make up the majority of beings right now near the Mizar system. When beings locate their fourth dimensional bodies in the stars or between them, some of these capacities are naturally heightened.

Human beings who wish to increase their capacities for channeling might imagine themselves playfully zooming around between these stars. This can be very helpful in coordinating some of these energies. There are certain points where the gravitational pull between these stars is equal. When people imagine themselves in such a place, they can be in a place of equalibrium with tremendous potential in any direction that is taken. Channeling is a state of delicacy, relaxation, and awareness; but the energy that can come through can be very powerful and can cause a great deal of change in the person who channels and the persons around them.

The history of Mizar is not all available. Some of this interrelates deeply to the channeling that people have done in the past. In some cases this is the aspect most shielded from people's consciousness in their awareness of their past lives. Sometimes the profound effect that such channeling had on their lives is something that is to be known by them only gently in this life so that they will not fall into previous patterns of difficulty or wish to recreate that which occurred in the past. The powerful gravitational fields between these stars creates a source energy that can be utilized by beings all over the galaxy. Such a source energy can be easily transformed into fourth, fifth, and sixth dimensional energies, and therefore is a natural source for any sort of channeling work.

Denebola (Beta Leonis)

[m 2.14] **Blue-white, 42 light years. Contains singly ionized silicon, iron, etc.**

The unusual heat within this star and its ability to create powerful magnetic fields has resulted in the unusual ionized states of these various elements. Silica has direct bearing upon will and leadership functioning. These minerals and the presence of this star in the constellation Leo all lead to this awareness of the deep meaning of leadership. There can be an ability to more consciously create the unconscious links between any leader and a group. The basis of charisma is that one becomes the voice for many, in a way in which the many are unable to express that voice. This is a way of creating deeper awareness between the individual and the group. This can be beneficial for individuals in leadership positions who are struggling with leadership and wish to understand the very nature of how they lead. This star can also be beneficial anytime a group focuses on an individual, even when it is group healing or receiving energy of the group, as this group energy then becomes one-pointed and focused within the individual. A deeper sense of will and stability may be felt. This star can benefit individuals who are experiencing difficulty with states of manic depression and schizophrenia, where these leadership qualities are an important component of the aberrated behavior.

Often in the development of such leadership qualities within an individual, there is a difficulty accessing some of the deep levels of humanness. A person who utilizes charisma needs to have deeper access to kindness, deeper levels of compassion, and mercy. When successful, such levels of leadership bring an individual to a position of power and these deeper human qualities such as kindness are usually the key to that power being properly utilized for their own development.

In many cases this rise to leadership or awareness of charismatic principles in past lifetimes affects the consciousness of individuals now. This is because they do not wish to harm, they do not wish to abuse power. Utilizing this elixir imparts more than just awareness of the power principle and charisma. It is also that which imparts a sense of kindness, by bringing that sense of humility, mercy, and compassion to deepen leadership capacities and assist individuals deeply with the whole issue of what it means to be a leader. People who may be involved in positions that take them to leadership that they stand away from or have difficulty accepting will benefit by the use of this star. This is a gentle influence that builds in strength which alerts individuals to the opportunities to develop charisma, leadership capacities, assisting others, but deepens these into the human qualities.

The civilization associated with this star has worked out several important bridges through multiple levels of subtle body interaction, and it is this which is transferred to humans. Though this is of some benefit in the subtle bodies, it is more a coordination of innate capacities that is transferred.

Mintaka (Delta Orionis)

[m 2.19] **Blue-white giant, 800 light years, binary.**

Mintaka can provide for most people a balancing of energies seen to be aggressive or animalistic in nature. This can enhance physical functioning, but can also be applied where overemphasis of physical functioning is wished to be replaced with deeper attunement to spiritual ideals, spiritual goals, and spiritual development.

The civilization on Mintaka had a great deal of struggle through various periods of factions, wars, and other things. These eventually led to genetic wars in which biological technology was utilized to perfect powerful aggressive tendencies within the beings so that they would be better fighters and better able to control their world. This eventually led to a period of some great emotional difficulty because the very same biological constructs that gave them the aggression and hypersensitivity to what the enemy might do next opened their emotional bodies and brought them to states of higher sensitivity to all feelings. This gave them long periods of sadness, suicides, and other difficulties, and even experience of the diseased states similar to some of the diseases on Earth.

As a result of all of this there was a certain energy that came into this civilization which caused the beings to put down the weapons of war and to join forces. The planet was fully ready for this inspiration from a being who simply visited and who poured out an energy of love. This is the same being who you know from Earth history as the Christ. This is an entity and an energy that can certainly extend through multiple time periods. This occurred a long, long time ago. These beings were ready for this gentle influence, and they then focused their efforts on the creation of happiness. They channeling these aggressive tendencies into that which could provide peace, strength, awareness, and a sense of happiness. This sense of peace and happiness could be genetically engineered to some extent when the aggressive tendencies were understood and worked with appropriately. That was the direction of this civilization for a fairly long period after the visit from the Christ.

This deeper awareness also led them to develop many animals that did not have high levels of consciousness but did work with these principles of happiness in themselves. This awareness of their world was not for the development of spirituality and form, but for the development of certain specific principles such as freedom, aggression, passivity, and learning about feeling in the world. Knowledge and understanding from this civilization was utilized in the development of the animal forms on Earth even as early as the first fishes, amphibians, and reptiles on Earth. The creation of aggressive animal forms on Earth peaked with the development of the polar bear some 70,000 years ago.

From that time forward the full understanding and enlightenment of this race has taken place. On this star system, from the planets that they have colonized, and the beings they have touched, has come an understanding and appreciation of how aggressive energies could lead to awareness, peace, and understanding. They saw that in the Earth system was a great difficulty. The Martian energies which have been associated with Earth thought forms but transferred and created in higher resonant intensities by residual Martian thought forms, the planet Mars itself, and the symbol of Mars have led to certain hostilities, hatreds, angers, and aggressive tendencies with Earth beings. One of the best ways these beings could show beings on Earth other capacities of happiness would be through the animal life forms, through people's unconscious, and through ways in which they were reminded of possibilities so that they could make choices about happiness for themselves.

They also gave Earth people an example of ferocity, power, and energy that would not serve a purpose that people would see as valuable and useful, but rather would create fear. This was imbued into the polar bear. To study this creature will teach you a great deal about aggressive tendencies as it seems distinct and different in this way of aggression from all other bears. These energies are not necessary for its survival, though they certainly assist on some levels. In some ways this is a creature that also seeks happiness in the awareness of the Sun and of energy that comes into it. Sometimes in their own inner physical meditations individuals will note the presence of an animal as they look into their own bodies. This is often seen as an animal totem, or a being that associates with one of your chakras, or an energy that manifests as an animal symbolically. Choose this star and star elixir should that animal totem be the polar bear.

The deep awareness of this civilization is an overshadowing influence that can lead to a deeper understanding of these principles in people. Understanding of the purpose of aggressive tendencies and how they can lead to a new sense of an awareness of peace and understanding is still a possibility with Earth. Look at the historical example of Japan , which transformed from a powerful aggressive force in the nineteenth century into the twentieth century. This was shifted by war into deep passivity and now to a place of economic domination without the need for armies or aggression, and with the principles of the sharing of harmony, which is still available in the world. This shows you how aggressive tendencies can be shifted and changed into ways of deeper awareness of other principles, and in the case of Japan, into principles of harmony and awareness amongst people.

Algol (Beta Persei)

[m 2.1–2.3] **Blue-white, 105 light years.**

Algol's ability to prepare individuals for understanding their destiny, their life purpose, and the ability to manifest this purpose more easily in the world, this is at once spiritual and practical. For most people what will usually result is an ability to understand their profession and accept it more easily.

Algol can attune individuals to harmonies deep within their being. These are partly genetic in nature, partly past-life in nature, but more importantly are in attunement to the shared soul of the lifestream of humanity. When this occurs there is a natural re-emergence of awareness of life purpose, direction, and choices that individuals have made for their own development. Sometimes these choices can be difficult for a person to accept.

Beings from this star system have visited Earth many times in the past and have sought to assist. They are pouring their energy to people now if they wish to attune to it. Algol's energy is sometimes unconsciously available to politicians when they are shown ways to make the best and highest choices. These energies are with you all the time, but when you wish to attune to them directly, meditation on the star will simply attune you to these beings who simply wish to assist humanity in a loving way.

This sense of purpose can connect one to universal principles. Awareness of all universal laws is stimulated. Awareness of how you have chosen to create resistant patterns to certain universal laws may come forth. These may not come in a fully conscious fashion, but is stimulated gently to help you look at some of these issues.

Many of these energetic principles are intertwined with the question of how humanity will choose to develop. If choices are dictated, the person will not know that free will is an inherent part of their being. The development of free will is really a shared purpose of humanity. Spiritually aware beings with a willingness to help will put out in their prayers, or in their invocations, or even in their work with channels, a request to know their destiny, to be assigned a destiny, or to be shown the best way to serve in the world. This presents a difficulty because it is in the development of their free will that the real choices can be made that affect humanity deeply and lead to the creative force being brought into form for humanity as a whole.

These beings from Algol have studied this problem and have worked with humanity's guides and various other extraterrestrials for a long time to present more choices, more options, and more possibilities to people. They also wish to show people the truth of their free will choices in the past, their willingness to work with higher concepts in the present, and their ability to attune to humanity's shared purpose and ultimate development in the universe in the future. The attunement to these higher principles is what is provided by the star, the elixir, and working with these beings. Then there will usually be within people a period of a little bit of emptiness as if this great desire for purpose, for being assigned a particular task, and for fulfilling this spiritual goal disappears. In its place is an emptiness, lasting perhaps a few days, but for most people a matter of just a few minutes. That is the time in which what you are being asked to do is understand what is—not what shall be or what has been.

This attunement to the present can often reveal what is to be created and what has been created as that which you choose by your own free will. This is the real secret to purpose: that you understand deeply within yourself, you recognize the possibilities, and after all of these considerations you let all of that go and in the quiet place of just knowing, you choose. When such a choice is made, usually powerful things will be created. What really tells you about yourself is the choice itself. The energies of these beings and of this star can be quite helpful to people in extending that period of quiet a little bit more to bring that deeper understanding of the true choices made. What is important here is to make that choice, and to see that it really does come from deep within you. Though this choice may be influenced by many other forces, these external influences can be put aside so that the true understanding within you is that which is honored.

Almach (Gamma Andromedae)

[m 2.2–2.3) **Yellow group of four stars, 250 light years.**

Almach can assist the transfer of energy from the mental body into the heart. This is an ability to bring concepts into a loving and beneficial form for others. The energies of love can be expressed and communicated more easily. There can be with such enhancement some integration of spiritual concepts for better expression of this energy. Some individuals experiencing difficulty in the knees and right knee in particular may find that in addition to other physical healing techniques to be utilized in the body in the work with the knee, the deeper concepts become more available in utilizing this elixir or meditating on this star.

Almach will bring most people an enhanced ability to shift vibration, a better ability to bring through clairvoyant ideas from multiple levels, and enhanced psychic functioning in transference of multiple ideas into a single integrated form. This is somewhat similar to Potato flower essence, though at a more perceivable level for most people. The combination of Potato and Almach can be powerful for individuals who also wish to attune to a single vibrational level and channel from a specific single being or energy pattern as long as such energy pattern is of spiritual impact and of benefit for most people. There is a self-governing principle associated with the energy from this star which will naturally assist people with clairvoyant and channeling abilities to transfer information from higher levels. This can lead to better utilization of this energy and information for the benefit of all. It will also tend to create certain levels of self-protection when utilizing these abilities.

In most individuals who use this star what is generally noticed is a more conscious awareness of the natural state of being. For many individuals this is going to be deeper awareness of what is going on for them in the fourth dimension in their awareness of how they are interrelating to others. For many people there can be a general acceleration that can be very helpful when they are feeling overwhelmed, when there is too much happening on Earth for them, or when they feel as if they cannot keep up with the increasing acceleration of life on Earth. This is the real benefit that comes out when working with this group of stars. Awareness of the subtler levels and the ability to transform or to shift vibration will be different from one person to the next due to the individuality of psychic functioning. The ability to understand what is happening better and to keep up with it will be enhanced by this star.

Almach can assist those people who feel a little cut off from others because they have deeper spiritual awareness but are unable to focus this, use it, depend on it, or see it easily in others. Anyone who takes this elixir or who would meditate on this star will find themselves naturally seeking the understanding of spiritual ideas, expression, contemplation, and caring in their lives. They will naturally tend to create situations to test this a bit to understand how God manifests. Look at spiritual expression throughout the ages. Where it comes into humanity, this testing appears to be such an integral part throughout the Bible and all of the great religious works. Deep in people's consciousness is this idea of suffering in order to bring results. This is because of an essential separation. To a large extent this separation is eased almost as if this oneness that can be imagined for all beings can take place within one personally, and this is encouraged greatly by Almach. The universal or the global sense of unity that one becomes aware of is also an internal sense of unity within oneself that is created by the joining of all facets of one's being.

Schedar (Alpha Cassiopei)

[m 2.22] **Yellow giant, 150 years.**

Enhancement of the spiritual principle of praise can be felt within most individuals. This can draw angelic beings and powerful beings of the devic order to one while meditating on the star or meditating after taking the elixir. A deeper awareness of the interrelationship at a spiritual level between the nature kingdoms, the plants and animals that surround you, and the Earth herself, can be felt more deeply by most people. This feeling of praise can radiate from an individual in a powerful magnetic way. To understand it and to work with it more easily is enhanced by this star.

There is some benefit here in understanding and working with this star for nearly all people. Some of this energy can be helpful to people who are seeking to understand their own relationship to the angelic kingdoms and the other beings who share humanity's willingness to evolve. The basic nature of spiritual evolution for people on Earth is intimately involved with the awareness of praise. Such an energy can often lead a person to deeper awareness of possibilities of manifestation of their potential. This is because it is an energy that directs them into those aspects that they know they are connected to and are one with, but which they also hold in the context of being outside of themselves. A merging with these aspects can manifest a sense of enlightenment, deeper awareness, and higher consciousness.

In addition to all of this there is the beautiful energy that naturally allows connection with these other kingdoms that is an essential capacity in the human heart. This is partly from genetics, because you all come from the same Earth matter and the manipulation of these elements by the simple DNA patterns as found in plants and animals and the more complex DNA structures found in the human body.

The mitochondria within the human being are another aspect of this. These are independently functioning cells that exist all throughout the human body and are developed from an incorporation in the past of those substances that were utilized for the correct utilization of gasses including carbon dioxide and oxygen. The creation of this balance in all cells is an important history for the shared beings on Earth. In this interrelationship it is as if the mitochondria were able to provide what the larger cell structures needed and a symbiotic relationship naturally took place. This has been going on for billions of years and there has been then a general thought form that could be anthropomorphized to the point that you could imagine that the cell structures praise the mitochondria and the mitochondria praise the cell structures. It has gone on long enough that the cell structures and mitochondria are intimately bound as one. As a result of this there is deep within the cells of every person an awareness of praise that goes beyond merely emotion or intellect. It is that which is inherently a part of your very being. The awareness of the interdependence of all beings on Earth and the awareness of these other kingdoms around you is a natural sort of thing to be accessed by any understanding of praise.

The beings from Schedar have seen and felt the tremendous benefit of praise, and have worked with it in many different ways. In their merging with God, when they discovered that the praise aspect could be brought out again and thus created in an even more powerful way, they chose to separate from God and in this way concentrate on working with praise. In this way Schedar is like a minor chakra of God manifesting many of God's aspects but specifically attuned to those of praise. These beings gain the maximum pleasure, awareness, and feeling of who they are from this energy of praise. After exhausting all the other choices, they began to recognize that here was an opening that was a lot of fun. The influence of beings from Vega was partly felt here with their ability to understand sound as a most magnificent way of creating praise. But it was the sound of the stars that they discovered, how they as if sing to each other the praises of God. It is the very nature of the bending of the aethers that all stars are involved in that creates this magnificent energy that reflects eventually back to God in a form that is most easily explained or translated in the human language as praise. Thus it is a natural development of the energies of the stars themselves.

They have seen that when people have choice about praise, they can go a lot further. In studying this and working with this in many ways, they have observed that humankind has tremendous potential in working with the energy of praise. The ability to merge with other civilizations in the future who have also understood this is the hope beings from Schedar have for the people of Earth. Because of this hope they are accelerating that capacity which is naturally available in all people. They do this by causing a pulsation within their star that connects it to the Sun. This pulsation is constantly transmitted to Earth in waves that occur at regular intervals of about a second apart. Thus you may find that when you attune to praise, it can increase within you and move to higher and higher levels. When you become aware of it and feel it, the energies of other beings who are also involved in praise are naturally drawn to you.

You can imagine that waves of sunlight influenced by Schedar are pouring through you. By imagining these beautiful waves of energy pouring through you, you will generally find that this aspect of praise is intensified and clarified. Schedar could be meditated upon the day before or you could imagining Schedar's energy coming into you and the Sun's energy at the same time. This would be in imagination since you are not going to be able to be bathed in Sunlight while meditating on Schedar since such meditation would generally require that it be nighttime. If this is done at night you will find that there is also an amplification of praise for the night forces, the forces of nature, for the stillness and quiet and peacefulness of the night, and the awareness of the other stars and planets. Schedar elixir could be taken and utilized with a meditative connection to the Sun while visualizing these waves of energy moving through you. If Sun elixir is taken at the same time it is likely that for most people the Sun elixir will predominate in character. But as people may have taken Sun elixir for a few months and gotten used to it, adding Schedar then is recommended. The subtler variations of the awareness of the Sun and its mixture with Schedar may then be differentiated from the Sun by itself. Under the influence of both of these it will be easier for people who are involved in the awareness of praise and understanding the other kingdoms around them to develop such more consciously.

Alphecca (Alpha Coronae Borealis)

[m 2.23] **Blue-white binary, 75 light years.**

The ability to juggle several ideas at once and make clear decisions will be enhanced. There will usually be an increase in a type of psychic functioning which can assist with extracting the truth from a situation or from conflicting points of view. Various aspects of understanding of truth will be made more available to most people when utilizing this star.

The beings associated with this star have a deep love of history. They made contact with Earth beings in the time of ancient Greece. The god associated with Mercury, sometimes called Hermes, was actually a manifested being from this civilization. Some direct influence beginning in the ancient Grecian period is associated with this star. These beings have assisted in this deeper awareness of integrating principles at various times and have sought to stimulate ideas and communicative principles for long periods with Earth. This is still in a period of dormancy but may open up in the next five years.

The brain in a human being is a repository of information that is then provided to the higher self at a sort of aetheric mental level. This higher dimensional construct then pours back into the brain in the form of information that rides on light. These are parallel processes that create multiple thought structures. They then come into conscious awareness linearly, one after the next. When deeper awareness of these processes takes place, the inherent parallel nature of these processes emerges to a person's consciousness. Those things that can encourage the awareness of the natural communicative processes between the higher self and the brain and within the brain itself and within the higher self all are of great importance in developing powerful thought processes. These thought processes are often not expressed, not even that which you are consciously aware of. Many of these are what you would call intuition. Intuition itself is inherently a parallel process working with multiple ideas at once. This ability to hold all these things in a state of somewhat increased consciousness is an important communicative ability within beings that is different than expressing and thinking. In societies that have developed telepathy and worked with it for long periods of time, such ability to create multiple ideas and share these appropriately amongst each other, this is common.

The juggling of many ideas and awarenesses, the willingness to create new civilizations and new approaches to life, and the coordination of all of these as burst forth in ancient Greece, was that which touched and inspired the civilization from this star. There was a natural coordination and affiliation which has continued to the present day. This is to encourage individuals to be aware of their own natural abilities to bring in many thought forms at once and to work with these at the level of superconscious thought. This is awareness at the intuitive level, direct knowing, and awareness of multiple levels of information, wisdom, praise, perception of artistic principles—all at once.

Sadr (Gamma Cygni)

[m 2.23] **White supergiant, 800 light years.**

This star can bring greater energy for understanding the nature of the physical body and the sense of gracefulness and easier movement. The ability to extract energy from the Earth through one's feet and utilize it physically is enhanced. Utilize this elixir before walking with bare feet on grass covered with the morning dew. This is likely to increase energy in the physical body. The star also presents to an individual some deeper awareness of relationship to others, particularly individuals of the female sex. The ability to relate to females better will result for either males or females who have difficulty in relating to females.

The civilization associated with this star had abundant energy resources and chose to work with them for artistic reasons by the appreciation of magnificent beauty. The creation of powerful plasmic forms was available to them. The star was able to detach a portion of itself. This was in an orbit near the planet and gained closer proximity with each orbit. A powerful energy at the fourth dimensional level created a powerful resonance between the center of the detached star and the center of the planet. Eventually this was created as a stable connection and the secondary star melted away pouring all of its energy into the planet, energizing it powerfully and deeply for a period of about 250,000 of your years. The development of this civilization took place during this long time period. Mid-point in that time it was seen that more energy might be useful for certain of the art forms, and a direct tap to their sun was made, a very easy matter at such point. No longer constrained by the usual third dimensional aspects of gravity, time, or distance, further energetic taps were easily made, and this without any harm to the sun. The educative process took many leaps so that conscious direction of such powerful energy forms were intertwined with their consciousness. This would be very difficult to achieve on Earth because of the high energy levels involved.

This appreciation of the natural beauties and energies that are available to them has led them to investigate such energies in all of the various planets that deal with such beautiful natural forces. Earth is one of these with energies that tend towards the material in the expression of such energies through the flowers, the beautiful scenery, the various plant and animal forms, and of course the Earth's crust herself in the way it makes the various beautiful formations of mountains, valleys, rivers, and so on. This appreciation of such art by these beings is that which is transferred to humans as they would work with this star. Many times this will simply attune them to their own connection to these beautiful energetic forms. These forms are a natural direct expression of the Earth's own love. These forms do not have the purpose of a doing or the accomplishment of a particular goal. These are forms that have within them their own inherent majesty, beauty, and art. The living process of being is brought out in all people in working with such forms. So there is a natural tendency here in appreciation of Earth's own majesty and beauty to attune to these deeper forces in oneself.

In the dream state some individuals are drawn to their Sun. When you go into the Sun you naturally witness such forms of nature. These can be solar flares which are many thousands or even hundreds of thousands of miles in length. But at a deeper level these are the forms that also govern the creation of certain genetic and biological materials including the dance of the DNA that is created in the formation of the zygote. There is also in the awareness of these forms the understanding of higher-dimensional reality because the electron densities, magnetic field densities, and electromagnetic spectral densities are so high that these naturally give rise to warping of time and space, and creation of temporary gravitational effects. All of these things are those which have been played with in the past. Some of these were worked with in Atlantis for the development of energy technologies and a studying of such.

The star is of some encouragement here as these beings understand the underlying principles. This is a direct knowing of the energetic force itself which says: "I am, and I dance with this beautiful presence." It is this dance which then becomes the form that is visible in these things that take place over long periods of time as in the movement of the Earth's crust, or short periods of time as in the creation of a beautiful being, a hummingbird, a flower, or an awareness of the movement that human beings can create within themselves. The appreciation of this, the deep awareness of it, and the sense of continuity that is created within beings as they become aware of this principle, is what this star is broadcasting to Earth. This is the essential nourishing characteristic of the yin principle as defined through Chinese understanding of the Taoist principle of yin and yang. Here it is a principle that seeks to express because it knows itself through that expression and because the expression itself is so beautiful.

On Earth this must naturally have the form that intertwines with other forms. You are in a place where there are creative forms happening all the time amongst all the different people, but also amongst the natural forces of living beings and the natural forces of physics. You would consider these forms graceful because they naturally flow in a way that intertwines and coordinates these forces so beautifully. There are also principles that are being established at a creative level that will proceed and make their way known on Earth in a few hundred years. These are the principles that lead to the development of new life forms, new forms of communication, and new forms of art. These are principles that guided

Lemurians deeply in the past and are principles that are not so much consciously available to people now. It these principles that the star seeks to encourage appreciation of within people at this time. We do speak of this as the star for the civilization has utilized this star as a broadcast center of such energies as have other stars and civilizations.

Caph (Beta Cassiopei)

[m 2.26] **Blue-white subgiant, 46 light years. Pulsating variable with a period of 2 hours and 30 minutes.**

With Caph there is a correspondence to mental body functioning. An enhanced ability to transfer ideas into consciousness will be noted. Telepathy will be strengthened and the ability to accept telepathic impulses will usually be enhanced. Regular utilization of this elixir or meditation upon this star will give people better ability to express in writing some of the images and understanding that they have gathered. Better ability to bring ideas into focus and express them clearly will be noted by most people. This is a good star for writers.

In working with such creative pursuits as writing, many times the energy flows are stressed within the individual in a cyclic way. These correspond to brain rhythms very similar to those which occur in the sleep state. For most individuals in the sleep state they will move through cycles which relate to rapid eye movement for the generation of dreams and related activity, then move into deep delta for deep attunement to the collective unconscious and awareness of soul purpose. This simple cyclical nature of the creative process as it occurs naturally in sleep is symbolic of what occurs in creative writing. Individuals who wish to understand this better would be strongly urged to use Caph. This is for bringing one's own awareness into words by a deeper attunement to the inner creativity. Writer's block may be assisted. People who have ideas and wish to bring them into form may also be assisted.

The other thing that is generally assisted is where mental body functioning has been too highly stressed in the individual. Many times individuals with this as a tendency will be noted to have triangular faces with the larger part of the triangle on the top. Also you may find that such individuals will tend to have difficulty in the feet, knees, lower leg, or calf. Such individuals are advised by acupuncturists or holistic healers to attune to the Earth, to bring more energy into the feet, and to deliberately do things that will bring the physical form into balance. This is correct and very helpful. But what is the person to do with the mind in the meantime? It is important that the mental body be a part of this process and thus be able to take energies that are as if held there and release them to the emotional body, the aetheric body, the astral body, and most importantly to the physical body directly. This is very helpful for individuals who know why they are attracted to such mental body functioning and know how to balance physically. So in addition to other things that would help the body physically, there can be benefit with such individuals in utilizing Caph.

There can be also for some people a sense of all of the pieces of a puzzle suddenly falling into place. This elixir can be helpful for private investigators or detectives. This can also assist individuals who are seeking to understand very difficult matters such as the understanding of nature or science or some important concepts that one is seeking to learn or teach oneself. It is a way in which energies available to the mental body become crystallized and then are able to transfer into consciousness easily.

There is a civilization associated with Caph with some direct lineage and connection to beings from El Nath. They are also aware of a large group from the Andromeda galaxy and took part in a powerful seeding program that took place there a long time ago. It was perceived that the naturally occurring fluctuations in energy of Caph were helpful with the development of their own awareness, healing abilities, and ultimately, the peacefulness of the civilization. This cycle took place approximately once every five and a half months. They saw that making this cycle go faster would be of benefit for their development. Over a period of several thousand years this was stepped up in vibration until it is at it current rate of a couple of hours. This cycle is likely to grow shorter and shorter in length over the next few hundred years. This is because of the continuing development of this civilization. It is a way in which they are as if increasing their own vibration by attuning to the vibration of the fluctuation in intensity of their star.

Wei (Epsilon Scorpii)

[m 2.28] **Yellow giant-subgiant, 70 light years. Has a strong presence of calcium.**

This star can enhance hands-on healing energy in people. The practitioner of Reiki, various forms of massage, acupuncture, or acupressure will do well to utilize this star. The energies that are transferred are largely those already available in the person's development; thus they simply are able to be more consistent and apply these energies more regularly than they have before. Some energies from past lives served as a healer, energies of one's guides that have direct healing capacities, or unconscious energies that might be available only under stimulating circumstances, will all be more clearly available to the healer. This energy may proceed easily from the heart center as well as from the hands of a person who is doing such healing work.

Many individuals will seek to tap or draw upon some of their own deeper energies with such hands-on healing techniques. Some of these may be energies that they need to understand or learn about. Some of this may be past-life information. Sometimes this can be taxing or difficult for the individual and bring them to a place where they don't easily accept what they are able to do in the most positive aspects of the healing. This sometimes leads to expectations, which gets in the way of any hands-on healing work. An energy channel becomes established as they grow and learn and are able to work with these powerful energies. This channel can actually reduce and become more limited because of subtle or unconscious fears, or from the person's own physical body being drained or in some way affected by this energy.

The calcium in this star can remind people that it is possible to create better structure in their bodies. There is also a reminder here of strength in many different ways. Part of this is from the natural vibrations of this star. Wei has some ability here to stimulate in the unconscious the natural tendency of the body to work with these materials. Calcium metabolism is really more dependent upon silica than most people realize, and as a result their undue attention on calcium is only at the manifesting end of this process. It is not so much for the ability to absorb and work with calcium that this star is helpful, but rather with the structure to utilize energy to allow these things to move through a person.

This star can help attune people to past lives related to healing. Sometimes small pieces of these past lives may be remembered in the period of preparation, in the training time, or in the time of initiation for many hands-on healing disciplines. Many times there will be powerful deep recall of the past lives where such healing went on. They may be able to understand and feel and know some of these ways in which they had decided to become a healer and came to understand of how to work with higher guiding forces.

The beings from this place have worked with time travel extensively. They have understood it as an important means of communication and travelling through space. As a result of their awareness of this it has come to their understanding that what humanity needs now is healing and that people are able to create this healing but sometimes have this ability taxed within themselves partly because they are unconscious of past lives. This energy is directed to Earth at this time by this civilization to help people become aware of their own internal structures, the way in which such healing energy can be made available, and of how their own past lives can be of assistance to them in dealing with such healing forces at this time. These beings therefore see that by increasing the light from this star, there can be an attunement of individuals to this deeper healing. A powerful healing of the race can occur as a result of this. This will eventually lead to people letting go of the need for learning lessons through disease.

There are many techniques that certainly are affected here. This is not the same as the work of Morning Glory flower essence in the attunement to the healing process itself, nor is it the same as Sirius, which would tend to emphasize the transformational quality as part of the healing. Here it is an attunement to the underlying energies which are the very basis from which these techniques come. All hands-on healing techniques will be affected, including many that have yet to be described or discovered. The technique called Omega now being taught in the United States is one that has been directly seeded by these beings and is the one that is to be affected even more powerfully than Reiki, acupuncture, massage, and related activities.

Scheat (Beta Pegasi)

[m 2.3–2.7] **Yellow-orange giant, 200 light years. Irregular variable similar to Betelgeuse.**

This star has some remarkable opportunities in working with people at this time on Earth. The ability to transfer energy to the crown chakra is enhanced by this star. There is some additional contact with higher level spiritual energies in the way of sudden inspiration, visionary states, as well as deeper awareness of interconnection to the galaxy, to other beings, or to past lives. This awareness can come quite a bit out of time or simply manifest in the way in which it seems to be appropriate. The ability to understand the law of cycles is enhanced as the individual can come to understand cycles that are far greater in magnitude and scope than they are used to in their usual waking consciousness.

This star can bring a sense of opportunity to people. Individuals would do well to utilize this star who recognize that opportunities may be available to them, but who are unable to work with them as they come and thus miss these opportunities. Scheat can significantly enhance the ability to recognize the opportunities, to understand the higher aspects of them, and to draw these opportunities in quickly.

This star can assist individuals who seek greater attunement to God. This would not be God as created by religious institutions or particular dogmatic ways of thought, but as you understand God for yourself in a personal way: your own inner awareness of higher reality. This often is something that can be very stimulating or something that changes what is happening inside your body or changes certain ways in which you see yourself. To understand this—to feel it, to know it, and to allow it, to actually welcome it—is an important aspect of the crown chakra. What is being created here is an attunement to a civilization that is basically in alignment and harmony with the awareness of God on all levels.

This star can influence astral travel states by making these more spiritual and more able to assist the individual in their own evolution. These experiences can become more concentrated in the sixth and seventh chakras to assist in the transfer of spiritual information and experience back into the physical body.

In Atlantean days there was an object launched into space similar to your understanding of a satellite. This was done through an energy vehicle; it was not a physical satellite as you understand it. This allowed an energy from Atlantean times to proceed towards this region, as it was perceived as an energetic place. This was actually as if in response to a request from the civilization associated with this star and nearby systems and energy that was available at that time to the Atlanteans on many different levels. Some of these levels of energy worked with the Atlantean ability to perceive and understand the nature of spirit, the nature of psychic attunement, and the awareness of God. This came as a powerful burst of energy to pour itself out into space in a short outburst of technological innovation towards the end of the Atlantean period. This business of attempting to make a connection to others generated some amusement as well as some honoring and respect for the technologies that were available to the Atlanteans. The star responded. It was as if the civilization saw that a beacon of light established between their area and the Sun's area would be of some benefit. But it was also seen that the real ways in which this would benefit humanity are yet to come, and these are slated to occur very soon in their most powerful manifestation.

Individuals who have had Atlantean lifetimes may find that they are able to access this a little more easily by utilizing this elixir or meditating upon the star. These individuals may also be able to waken their connection to these higher spiritual forces. Those who are having a little bit of trouble with this time of great change on Earth and wish to see the larger picture by attuning with cycles to see how things unfold appropriately will do well here. This was because in that time of Atlantis there was not only that energy asking these beings from so far away to share insight or understanding with them; there was also a question as to what is our future, what is the nature of life on Earth, where has our civilization gone wrong? There were many at that time who realized that there would be difficulties. There are similar questions in this current time of change when people are becoming aware of new possibilities. This time it is not necessary for humanity as a group to pose such a question or send an energy vehicle out into space. The answers are already being poured into you and all you have to do is open to them.

For individuals who wish to attune to higher vibrations by a powerful stimulation of the crown chakra, there will be some benefit in combining this star elixir with Jelly Opal, White Diamond, Lotus, Silversword, Xenon, and Krypton elixirs. This combination can be applied directly to the top of the head and there will be some benefit and some sense of change for about half the people who try this. This can be repeated over a one month period for maximum benefit. It is best if this is done at night or in a darkened place. There are individuals who have certain patterns of baldness that begin on the top of the head. Sometimes this is not simply male pattern baldness as associated with testosterone, but rather some deeper awareness of this higher spiritual reality that is not being accessed by the individual. Hair growth will improve for these people when they would use such a powerful combination dropped on the top of the head.

Dscubba (Delta Scorpii)

[m 2.34] Blue-white, 600 light years, 4 stars.

Dscubba can bring into clearer focus the many aspects of one's past behavior. This can bring into focus unconscious judgments and how they interrelate to one's current life, to each other, and most importantly to beings who have stood as important aspects or important symbols of various characteristics in the past. The interaction with small groups that presented energy of a difficult nature to a person can be overcome and worked with more consciously by use of this star. This can include interaction with cults or brainwashing where some of these techniques utilized were largely unconscious and the person involved had little understanding of what was going on at the time. To a lesser extent, information can become more available about relationships or interactions with groups that caused unconscious difficulty from past lives.

Use of this group of stars can bring many people a deeper awareness of their very nature and what they are attempting to balance. They may be able to see that their life has real meaning. It may seem that the old ways don't fit very well and the new ones don't seem to make very much sense. What usually comes out from this is the reason one has been attracted to new ways of thinking and new ways of understanding oneself. This can be a willingness to understand and release judgement.

Judgment is a difficult matter for people. They may require it in their own development in order to understand their potential. When you understand as much as you can about the nature of judgement and your connection to it, choice appears in your life almost coincidentally. You begin to attune to choice more, not necessarily understanding why. You may realize you have made a choice towards a path that requires judgement. Most people on Earth will struggle with judgment at some point in their lives. For people who are attempting to release judgment, understand and work with deeper levels of forgiveness, and understand their ability to coexist with others, there comes a time in which the awareness of the judgment is crucial to their own moving forward. This is a very important time for most people and usually will occur in their lives a minimum of three times. Each one corresponding to a higher level of consciousness, a deeper awareness and acceptance of themselves, a deeper level of forgiveness of others in the world, and forgiveness of God. In their awareness of what transpires as one moves through this process, it is important to acknowledge judgment as it is and to see what it did for you and how you were able to grow by it.

Sometimes this group of stars can be helpful as a reminder to people of how interaction, relationship, and awareness can be balanced and at the same time bring a sense of harmony. There is within these four stars a fifth. This is not a star in the usual sense but a very powerful point of light. The light tends to be absorbed and reflected back by those other stars. It pours its light out into the galaxy in areas of energy transmission beyond the electromagnetic. When this reaches Earth there is a general acceptance of the energy and it makes its way into Earth as if to create a state of powerful balance.

In addition to the body, the mind, and the soul, there is also the awareness of the collective unconscious as a fourth and important reality. These are all held together by two facets. One of these is the conscious way in which you are able to establish judgment by deliberately seeking a balance with logic, meaning, and understanding. The other facet is purely intuitive, where without judgment there is simply an acceptance of what is. This can allow that very same energy that might be seen as an obstacle to pour through as a tremendous source of inspiration and information. The collective unconscious is the awareness of what the lifestream of humanity is all about together on Earth. It is as if in attuning to the collective unconscious, a greater awareness of oneself and the possibilities in the world begins to come forth. This is so important in working with a group. When individuals begin to attune to each other and understand the nature of who they are, often they will unconsciously begin to unlock many aspects of the collective unconscious. This can often to lead to difficult situations where past karma or a need for power in a group dominates. With this star's influence, perhaps some individuals will become aware of the opportunities to release judgment and find a new harmony amongst each other. This will be very helpful to prevent cults, dogmatic expression of religion, or difficulty at an unconscious level from getting started in the group.

When you begin to look into the depths of this, you begin to see how the energies from this star group can change the way in which people relate to each other, to themselves, and to the collective humanity. These are complex matters because of many years of patterns that are essentially unnatural to the very nature of the human condition. It is not necessary to create judgment, nor is it necessary to create separation. Ultimately it is the karmic purpose of this energy of the star group to find its way into somebody somewhere to show how this uniting can take place for an entire race. This energy has birthed a Christ-like being to unite and to show new attitudes and new shifts in possibility in several civilizations. In some cases these beings were able to cause changes in the societies of their own worlds. Therefore there is also some benefit in including this elixir for use with children, particularly very young children. It could be added to water used in a baptism ceremony. It could be utilized as part of a remedy when children are fighting by combining it with Walnut in the Bach flower essence tradition.

Merak (Beta Ursae Majoris)

[m 2.37] **Blue-white, 60 light years.**

This star significantly influences the ability of an individual to transform expressive energy in a power-based system into energy that they can work with in a more conscious fashion. This would be a balancing influence for individuals who are accessing the deeper levels of consciousness in which they understand inherent freedom as it is held in check in a society based on domination. There is generally a small connection available at a conscious level to the expressive energies that tap into the nature of existence and power in a person's life. Meditation upon the star or utilization of the elixir of this star will assist in making this much more conscious and increasing this capacity. Although this can be directed in self-expression, it may be especially useful for those who hold power in some level of denial in themselves. This can include individuals who find themselves in leadership positions and politicians of all kinds.

This is very important now because systems are changing. You have a society where there must be domination in order for there to be forward progress. This has been accepted as a natural tenet in your civilization for many thousands of years, and yet it is completely unimportant in the grander scheme of things. Motivation from fear is not the only way to create the energy to get things done in the world. When there is an awareness of the necessity for shared awakening, this can actually be a more powerful motivator for forward progress.

This energy for shared awakening is stimulated now when expression takes place. Expressive tendencies from music, art, writing, or awareness of movement, or even through scientific breakthroughs or discoveries, touch deep places in yourself. These are connected to the collective unconscious, to your reason for being here in the first place, to your awareness of God, and many other innately human capacities. Merak can encourage this potential to motivate society based upon spiritual unfoldment, deeper communion, the awareness of God as a rallying force, and the willingness of people to make love an important part of their lives and of their Earth. These beings from Merak have known of some of the magnificence of your art on Earth, and in an attunement to this have seen of this universal shared principle. As this principle is shared more powerfully, people will have more choices and will more likely see that they are able to shift their awareness of this in themselves.

Free will must be a very powerful aspect here, so it is not fixed as to how this energy will come forth. It may be through self-expression, through some way of understanding power and domination in their society, or through ways in which they wish to strike out newly and create new forces, new energies, and new awareness. Indeed the results of Merak at this time on any being are fairly unpredictable, but will generally be seen to be a lot of fun. Many people will enjoy utilizing this star and find that various changes happen with them when they take it which will encourage their own expression of who they are and of the more positive influences they are aware of.

People in leadership roles are being stressed more heavily than others with regards to this shift of societal motivation towards freedom, love, and the awareness of God. This is a shift away from domination and the concentration of power in the hands of those who would abuse it. This sort of thing is being encouraged by one's guides all the time, especially when one is in a position of leadership. This is partly because a person asked for this encouragement before coming into this life, and partly because it is what is needed now for the survival of the race. Most people will benefit by using this star because certain inner aspects of their own choices in society will come forth. Using this star will make easier and more obvious to them their ability to influence the political process or assist in helping leaders make their own decisions. There will also be some benefit here to people with insomnia because it will help them understand the power shift happening on Earth. It will help them be at peace about this time of change, understand its purpose, and see that they can also influence this process in a positive and helpful way.

This star can encourage the transformation of the context of power within an individual. If the context is shifted from one of power to dominate into power to create, power to invite, and power to free, then this deeper awareness in a person of who they are and their connection to God and other people is enhanced. Such contextual shifts can be very powerful and can shift tremendous things within a person and liberate all kinds of energies.

Enif (Epsilon Pegasi)

[m 2.38] **Yellow supergiant, 800 light years.**

Enif has powerful characteristics which can create a sense of unity and purpose. This can be well applied in small groups or family situations where individuals are seeking to unify their purpose in order to create the sense of community, family, or the feeling of pulling together towards a goal. The ability to understand and recognize some deep truth or motivating factor in each of the other members of this group will be strengthened in all of those working with this star. There will be little effect if the group is too large in number for you to have a clear picture of who the others are. This elixir is appropriate if it is a large group that you have worked with for a long time or if it is a small group that you have worked with for a short time. In understanding and working with this interaction, ask yourself: "What is the true nature of this person?" Walk in their shoes, so to speak, and understand life from their point of view. This with the influence of this star will assist greatly in this higher perspective. The loving energies in such a group may be better coordinated. The end result may be understood as the cosmic joke that the true nature of their work together is in the process of the interaction between the individuals, and this becomes clearer and more acceptable with the influence of this star.

There were three planets encircling Enif approximately 19,000 years ago that collided. This created many planetoids that were in new orbits very far from the star. The many surviving beings wished to maintain communication with others of their race. As methods of space travel were not available to these beings at this time, they sought communication through the star itself. A deeper attunement to their whole group occurred. Individuals on these 2,000 planetoids had different abilities, and over a few years it was determined that some had a better ability to communicate than others. These became the representative or spokesman for their communities and found that they could establish the maximum degree of communication and awareness by focusing their energy deep into the Enif sun which then poured this energy back out into the whole solar system area and into the individual communities. This was utilized as a communication network.

When space travel was introduced at a later time this technique was enhanced to utilize this star as a communicative nexus for that portion of space. This has been utilized by other civilizations as well. Such a use of the Enif sun as a communication node is encouraged even with Earth people. This ability to link beings together has become a natural part of the development of this star. This beautiful star radiates this energy and strength into all of the galaxy. There is therefore a natural ability for people when working with this star to attune more to each other, to bridge their separateness, and to understand how they can work together and know each other. The natural result felt amongst people will be the awareness of the group as a single entity.

Gertab (Kappa Scorpii)

[m 2.39] **Blue-white subgiant, 450 light years.**

The use of this star can strengthen the connection between the mental and astral bodies. This can help create clear mental pictures for various emotional states. The nature of the hidden emotions comes forth, the ability to understand their true place is understood, and the sense of this is then created as a pattern of energy. This may be perceived in the kinesthetic, audio, or visual modalities. There will be enhanced clarity in understanding it, feeling it, knowing it, and being able to share it with others.

An enhanced ability to release such emotions will be strengthened approximately three days after utilizing the elixir or working with the star. The astral body of the individual will tend to come into a state of temporary resonance which will directly relate to hidden emotions. As these emotions surface, some of the energies are transferred to the astral body where they are understood three days later. The astral body can bring awareness of the emotional body in the pastlife context into consciousness for people. There will also be some attunement to the astral realms in a fairly harmonious and connected way.

This is established because the beings associated with Gertab have primarily worked with methods of translocation that utilize astral bodies. These astral bodies do not usually interfere with those of humanity. This star can benefit individuals who wish to learn to work with translocation of the astral body. This is not the same as astral travel, for you are able to actually disappear the astral body in one place and reappear it in another very, very far away.

There have been many instances where beings from Gertab have acted as guides or helpers for people on Earth who are working with emotions or the astral body. Many times what is necessary in order to move through this is a dissolving of an emotional block. Such an emotional block can be from a pattern that the person is not aware of on a conscious level. Bringing energy into the emotional body to observe this pattern, to understand it, to shift the context into which it is created, or to work with it in any way that brings form and consciousness into the person will be of benefit. These beings from Gertab have seen how new information from the astral body can be of such benefit in promoting this change.

Phecda (Gamma Ursae Majoris)

[m 2.44] Blue-white, 80 light years.

Phecda can heighten certain of the sensory aspects of psychic awareness. Touching an object while under the influence of the star elixir may assist some individuals in attuning to their own psychometric gifts. This is an ability here to shift vibration while maintaining some contact with the physical. This vibrational shift is one that takes place entirely outside the domain of the conscious mind. What is needed for appropriate psychometry is a state of emptiness where no special thing is focused on, and then an object is introduced into one's awareness. Sometimes this is aided greatly by going outside of the visual or auditory context through which one usually draws information. Fingertip sensitivity, the ability to draw information from inanimate objects, and the ability to absorb and work with information from various sources that are physical in nature but entirely non-verbal, will be accentuated and assisted. There will be deeper awareness of molecular vibration for many people.

Some of the seeding of the raccoon has been under the domain of some the geneticists from Phecda. By increasing sensitivity in the fingers and hands, the raccoon might eventually come to some deeper intelligence and awareness and a healing capacity for others in the animal kingdom. The raccoon is an important symbol for people at this time. In studying the raccoon and the great sensitivity in its hands, one can understand that human awareness of the sense of touch is certainly at a mid-point of its evolutionary development. Human geneticists may eventually utilize some of this information and awareness of the powerful characteristics of sensitivity of the raccoon to bring this into people. This would not necessarily be by direct genetic transfer, but by influence of genetic structures through mental body processes.

The beings on the sixth planet of Phecda have developed the sensory organs and sensory nervous system far beyond that which you can understand. They have come to understand and associate themselves closely with touch. Part of the reason for this is that much of their civilization has developed underground and they have come to rely on the sense of touch. In their awareness of other civilizations, they saw that reliance on the visible sense, on the audible sense, and other senses including the telepathic sense, were not sufficient for a complete awareness of their environment. Many delegations of beings from Phecda have been sent to other civilizations throughout the galaxy to train them in greater touch sensitivity, which resulted in greater awareness of their environment.

Imagine for a moment that the same sensitivity of the human ear is applied to the skin surface for the entire body. The ear can detect the motion of a single molecule of air. This would give you some inkling of the nature of the beings from Phecda. These beings can be fully aware of what is all around them. This awareness includes the subtler levels of vibration such as the aetheric, the magnetic energies of the movement of the aether, and the awareness of the light forces as they move through a being. The distinct advantage here is relatively equal awareness of the entire spectrum of electromagnetic energy from cosmic rays all the way through radio waves. As a result of all of these various forms of awareness of energy, these beings have an ability to observe and understand in ways that are beyond human comprehension.

It was seen by the encouragement of Pleiadeans that there would be benefit in some of this awareness coming into humanity. The big question was how this awareness is to be accepted and known in people. Psychometry appears to be an interesting way to do this because for individuals who can trust the process, they can produce information that does not seem to be anchored or referenced to anything conscious, and in this way as if prove some of these underlying psychic principles in ways that are a bit more physical and acceptable to many people. At this time there is a general encouragement for people to simply accept the gifts they already have, and this is one of the reasons the energies from Phecda are limited to this awareness of the fingertips and psychometry. In the future there is likely to be a great increase in all of these capacities in people.

People are attuning to sensuality in ways in which the psychic functioning that is essentially psychometric in nature is activated. There can be an attunement to subtler energies perceived at the skin surface during sexual activity, during sensual activity, or during activity of massage or closeness. These are communicative pathways between people that are likely to be affected and assisted greatly by this elixir or meditation on this star. Sexual functioning can be enhanced and a deeper sensuality or awareness of their own body function can take place. A deeper attunement to their environment by physical means may become available to people.

Alderamin (Alpha Cephei)

[m 2.44] **Blue-white subgiant, 50 light years.**

This star has the capacity to bring some energizing of the mind's ability to influence the physical body. By utilizing this star elixir or observing the star you can increase the ability to visualize your own physical body more clearly. The creation of images of changes to be brought into the physical body that appear to be in alignment with other things in your life will be enhanced. Individuals who are seeking to change the characteristics of their physical body for greater health, body building, or shifting various characteristics such as losing weight or gaining weight will find benefit in utilizing this star. You create the image first and then you invite into your life the various characteristics that can assist you in creating that image in physical form.

This star has many other characteristics that are of higher frequency than most individuals will be able to attune to. In states of deep meditation it may be possible to attune to a pulsation in the movement of aetheric fluidium through the physical body. These pulsations can resonate with other vibrations. By attuning to various rhythmic patterns that relate harmonically to the Earth resonance frequency, powerful states of channeling of Mother Earth can take place. This is a state in which actual energy transfer to the Earth, as well as from her, can take place. Further applications of the energy of this star extend into many areas that will likely unfold in the future.

Aludra (Eta Canis Majoris)

[m 2.46] **Blue-white supergiant, 2,500 light years.**

This star can be of some benefit in combination with such things as Gold elixir that stimulate the heart energy and awareness of it. Individuals who are dealing with physical difficulty in the heart as a result of coronary difficulties, energy blockages, arterial blockages, heart murmur, or various heart-acting viruses will do well with this star elixir to stimulate and access more energy in the heart region. The natural ability of people to awaken and strengthen the heart is an important characteristic now on Earth and important for humanity's own development. Most people will benefit by utilization of this star in some form.

The capacity to understand and work with conscious expression of love will be enhanced. There will be deeper connection between the third eye and the first, second, and third chakras for the projection of such love energy into the mental spheres. This is a characteristic some of the Pleiadean beings have studied. Some of the energies that the Pleiadeans have tapped into in order to broadcast some of this awareness have utilized this star's energy directly, and have influenced it. The first time this occurred was 718 years ago. Therefore the light from this star that would be directly related to these experiments has not reached Earth. However the thought energy proceeds instantaneously and is connected to the essential energies of this star. One of the purposes of this experiment in Pleiadean civilization was to eventually share the results of this with Earth people. This may allow a deeper coupling of energies not only between the civilizations but between people so that they would understand different aspects of this higher love themselves. The Pleiadeans have utilized many stars for this purpose but this is the first one chosen and therefore is the one with the strongest ability to create this in individuals.

In attuning to this star you can to some extent harness its broadcasting ability. When you have a concept of some aspect of love in your life that is conscious and clear that you wish to share with others, utilize this star in meditation or as an elixir to allow the sense of this to expand. Be aware of the third eye chakra and see the energy pouring from the forehead, perhaps even imagine it blue in color. As this energy expands it carries on it waves of this love within you.

Now because of the nature of wave function, what will be naturally drawn back will be energies of great value and assistance in your own development. As energy is focused, concentrated, and worked with, there must always be a return effect. This is in some ways the basis of the Hindu saying that the smile you send out returns to you. It is not just a matter of positive karma here that is being dealt with. All beings are actually connected together by this love at the fourth dimensional level outside of the usual constraints of time and space. When you look at it from a third-dimensional level, you see that you are separate from that place where that love is to land. Because you are one, this energy is available to you as you send it out.

Sabik (Eta Ophiuchi)

[m2.4-3.0] **Blue-white binary, 70 light years. Two nearly identical stars, variability due to eclipsing.**

The energy of these two stars can work with certain of the dualistic aspects in humanity. These are closely intertwined aspects that relate to acid/alkaline balance at the physical level. At an emotional level this can relate to the perfect combination of the energies of love and sadness. At the third chakra level this can relate to the ability to project and receive power energy. The understanding of the perfect balance of yin and yang may become available. The way in which these come about will be very individualized. This star can aid people who are struggling with understanding how this balance is created in themselves and what it means to them.

The energies of these two stars are shared together beautifully. This double star has the capacity to balance, to create bridges, and to radiate these energies. What makes Sabik unique is its ability to project this as a continual questioning. These stars are moving through a cycle of understanding right now that takes them as deep as is possible for them into communication with the Sun, with the Earth, and directly with people. Most stars work on a vibrational level that does not allow them easy access to thought patterns such as those of humanity but rather must be constrained to communicate with other planetary bodies. In seeking to understand itself and to work with all of the aspects of what it means to understand separation, Sabik has sought out awareness of societies throughout this galaxy and others, into other dimensional levels, and even other universes.

You might wonder then with the power of such a star, why it does not simply combine and allow itself to become one. This is because it has recognized the inherent benefit in separation into the yin/yang polarity. This imbalanced state leads to awareness of separate capacities that can then be combined at the appropriate time. It has not come to any decision about this and therefore remains in a state of observation. By its natural ability to understand and work with balance, this star system makes its information available to all beings that it observes. So as it is observing humanity it is also providing information to humanity. Information cannot be provided from a star in the sense that it can from a civilization, a book, or something that might be written down. This must be something that affects people physically, affects their conscious processes, or works with their vibrational energies on some level.

Where this star can focus its assistance for people especially now is in working with balance between acid and alkaline, between male and female, and between inner and outer. This can have a powerful assistance at a physical level as people may be able to observe this shift in themselves. This can be combined with other therapeutic techniques such as the use of acid/alkaline balancing substances, the use of other vibrational remedies, the use of what has been termed the Rife Beam-ray technique, and other technologies for destruction of such infections as Candida. Even certain side-effects of drugs used for battling AIDS and other powerful degenerative diseases that upset the acid/alkaline balance will be assisted. The vibrational aspects may be brought into greater consciousness for the people involved. In dealing with this internal balance, each person must eventually find their own way that is unique. Anything that can aid in the visioning, understanding, and acceptance of this unique point of view will be of great value.

Izar (Epsilon Boötis)

[m 2.4–2.7] **Two yellow giants with a small companion star containing various metals, 110 light years.**

The energy of these stars relates to the electron balance on each side of the cell wall. In most people this will be observed and felt in the balance of potassium and sodium in the way in which this relates to emotions and the water in ones body. This is much more than physical. The higher characteristics dealing with the ability to manifest energy in the world and to absorb energy in the world will be influenced in a most positive and beneficial fashion by these stars. Some individuals have difficulty in the transformation of inspirational energy into physical energy, and this eventually manifests in one of the various forms of Chronic Fatigue Syndrome. A synergistic effect is usually observed in utilization of this star with other modalities of healing and assistance of CFS. In working with these other modalities there is usually little attention on this channeling of energy. It is as if the soul energy is not easily transformed and balanced in the being. As a result, at a mineralogical level potassium and sodium will cause difficulty for the thyroid and adrenal glands. The vibrational characteristics of these minerals are not easily observed when balancing takes place with nutritional supplementation. The influence of this star will be quite beneficial as individuals can understand that the energies of God that they transmit in the world and the energies of the world nurturing and loving them that they turn into the energy to love God can create a balancing effect in their breathing cycles. Their respiration is affected, but even deeper their heartbeat is affected and there is an instantaneous balancing of potassium and sodium in the physical body.

Many of the neutral metals that are found in this star system come from the smaller third star. These are liberated by the action of the larger stars and as a result are observed spectroscopically as coming from the whole but in fact are generated in the smaller star. This is of some importance because these energies themselves are symbolic at a vibrational level of the capacity of potassium and sodium to liberate, to release, to create a natural balance, and ultimately to cause the proper utilization of water across the cell wall membrane. This is precisely analogous to the action of the two stars that then work with the balancing principle between them to allow the generation of an energy that is helpful but which comes at its source from something that is shared. This energy can help individuals to create their own internal balance through the appropriate use of minerals of all kinds in their bodies, and especially the way in which potassium and sodium are so crucial to proper functioning in the physical body.

People have manifested in physical bodies to understand and work with the capacities of the physical nature of being. Physical substance is utilized and stressed in order to develop this conscious awareness. Physical substance therefore carries into consciousness vibrational attributes that influence very powerfully one's own development. Those substances that have the maximum effect will be those that are utilized most extensively in the body. The primary substances are oxygen, water, and at the subtler level, aetheric fluidium. Light has so many different characteristics that it is really not appropriate to consider it as a single substance. Aetheric fluidium is so beautifully influenced by magnetism. The water is so beautifully influenced by consciousness, by thought, and by all sorts of vibrations. Oxygen itself is so beautifully influenced by emotions and the way in which people are able to work with breath.

Then at the next level will be all of those substances largely metallic in nature used to build the physical body itself. Of these, the first ones to influence would be potassium and sodium. Next would be the influences of silica, calcium, chromium, copper, manganese, and magnesium. In the balance of sodium and potassium, all of these other processes are changed. The correct utilization of oxygen, pranic force as then developed with oxygen, as well as water and its ability to transfer vibration, and the ability of the body to create its own magnetic fields and interact with aetheric fluidium are all powerfully influenced. Sodium and potassium, as creating the balance across the cell wall membrane, influence these processes very deeply. This is a fairly easy matter to understand electrochemically because of the way water interacts with potassium and sodium in an electrical balance across the cell wall. This is only a small part of the picture because wherever there is electricity there is also magnetism, wherever there is water there is a transference of vibration, and wherever there is the utilization of water there must also be the utilization of oxygen.

When potassium and sodium are available more appropriately and correctly in the human body, many physical body processes are affected quickly. Many times individuals who have had excesses of sodium will find that there will be benefits in bringing very well-absorbed potassium into the physical body, usually from herbs, a liquid form of potassium, or perhaps potassium orotate or potassium ascorbate. These benefits are felt immediately. There is benefit in utilizing Izar elixir in combination with potassium supplements, especially with those in liquid form.

Some of the issues of balance itself, understanding give and take, water and its ability to transfer vibration, these things are naturally a part of this balancing process with potassium and sodium. There is a direct influence on such secondary effects as uptake of oxygen and utilization of prana, and the uptake of water in the utilization of vibration. A deeper nurturing can take place with a deeper attunement to God-like forces which are inherently balancing. It is as if the physical aspects attune one to these higher aspects rather than the reverse.

CHAPTER 7
★★★★★★★☆☆

Third Magnitude Stars

Tsih (Gamma Cassiopei)

[m 2.5] Blue-white subgiant, 200–600 light years. An erratic variable which ejected a cloud of matter seen on Earth in 1937.

Within the center of this star a doorway has been opened to the collective thought forms of the civilizations associated with this star. These energies are projected throughout the universe. These are being created in an erratic pattern because this civilization has understood the true nature of chaos. Much of your recent studies in mathematics on Earth have revolved around the science of chaos. This is still very much in its infancy mathematically. Individuals who wish to understand how chaos is applied in their life and work with these energies in a more direct fashion or individuals who are studying this for pure mathematics or understanding of the universe would benefit by utilizing this star.

The awareness of energies that can come into your life with great irregularity are significantly assisted by use of this star. This can relate to the utilization of peak experiences in a way in which you feel them, know them, and eventually assimilate them into your life. The deeper side of this is the awareness of the higher aspects of cycles that relate to seemingly irregular patterns for individuals. At the highest spiritual level this star presents to individuals the ability to let go of old patterns and come to new ones that are based in nature and in the true essence and capabilities of their relationships. The ability to eject matter—as the star is observed to be doing—is the direct transfer on a symbolic level to this letting-go process.

Gienah (Epsilon Cygni)

[m 2.5] Yellow giant, 75 light years

With the use of Gienah there is the heightened ability to

connect individuals in the beginning stages of relationship. This would be the ideal elixir for those involved in the early stages of any dating or courtship process so that they understand the true nature of their loving vibrations earlier in the relationship. This can prevent some of the later difficulties that often come from the inability to perceive the true nature of the vibration of the love between them. Some of the false images pulled from societal influence, parental influence, or past-life influence will be seen for their true nature early in the relationship. Because most individuals are starved for love in the way in which they are able to permit themselves to receive love and to give it in the world, they do not usually wish any interference. When this loving aspect occurs, they will usually seize upon it with great force. However when this is done there is usually significant unconsciousness associated with it that leads much later to difficulties. Widespread use of this elixir might significantly reduce the divorce rate.

Markab (Alpha Pegasi)

[m 2.50] **Blue-white giant, 110 light years.**

Markab can strengthen the ability to share psychic gifts such as telepathy in a loving way. The characteristics of individuals who have struggled with telepathy will come into greater focus and consciousness so that they can resolve the deeper issues. There is an enhanced ability to travel to remote locations with the astral body and exchange information easily with others at such a location. This is a form of telepathy. The Tibetan ball of light technique will be enhanced. The civilization associated with this star has worked with the ultimate creation of this ball of light technique for travelling purposes, and some of this will transfer to individuals. The power of such energy within an individual will be more clearly known. The real key to working with these techniques is that the energy is allowed to be as powerful as possible.

Menkar (Alpha Ceti)

[m 2.54] **Yellow-orange, 150 light years**

The use of this star can help people to release some of the unconscious connections to others, particularly those made in sleep. The ability to consciously make such connections will be enhanced. The unconscious connections made by most individuals through newspapers, television, or radio will be brought into greater consciousness. This elixir is valuable for individuals seeking to truly understand the media, forms of advertising, and the way in which the media influences people's perceptions of world events. This is a personal process in which people are able to break their ties to authority figures and instead base more of their understanding on their own authority. This may be psychic in nature: drawing impressions and information through their own deeper awareness and a more conscious connection with the events and beings and products involved.

Zosma (Delta Leonis)

[m 2.57] **Blue-white, 80 light years. Contains ionized magnesium, iron and titanium**

Those who understand leadership and charisma may reach a point of deep introspection where they may be in a position of more fame than they wished, more exposure to the public eye than they felt was appropriate, or an awareness of themselves in a leadership capacity that brings them to a place where they must reconsider who they are. There is usually a point of deep uncertainty that may not be observed outwardly. The time period in which this occurs for the individual will be well modulated and assisted by use of this star.

This elixir can be taken at various times during the day when the person is moving through such a crisis point. They may find that their awareness of themselves shifts. They may be able to see more easily through other people's eyes the true love and sense of caring by which they are actually able to funnel or channel other people's energies. The true leader is one who is not directing from their own point of view, but guiding the energy from the point of view of the others. One can begin to recognize a joyfulness in such leadership capacity. The gap in consciousness where one sees oneself new and different is eased, and the sense of one's own self is made more clear.

Han (Zeta Ophiuchi)

[m 2.57] **Blue-white, 600 light years.**

This star can bring a sense of deep purpose into one's life. This can bring a sense of connection to one's ancestors and a sense of how one will utilize genetic capabilities better in the world. A better sense of one's life's work and the ability to apply this will be enhanced for most people. This star can bring in some higher spiritual capacities for working with others in a more appropriate way. How to seek out and work with right livelihood will be enhanced to some extent with this star.

Arneb (Alpha Leporis)

[m 2.58] Blue-white supergiant, 850 light years.

This star has some capacity to energize the aetheric to mental body connection to enhance visualization. At the current time the energy of this star is more concentrated in the upper body. This star can assist individuals in visualizing and working with energy transfer into the heart for clearing of arterial obstruction, working with heart disease, and other circulatory difficulties associated with the upper part of the body. The energies of visualization can as if burn out, heat up, and cause to become fluid the obstructions in the physical body.

In mid-point of the next century we see many opportunities for working with these energies in ways that will bring greater awareness of the future and a psychic ability to transfer healing energies.

Giena (Gamma Corvi)

[m 2.59] Blue-white giant, 300 light yeras.

The use of this star can bring some additional emotional psychic sensitivity. This can be helpful for psychiatrists, psychologists, and others who wish to be sensitive to others who have lifestyles or ways of approaching the world very different than that of the therapist. A therapist may wish to bridge a gap to a person of a completely different economic or social class, racial background, or upbringing, or someone who appears to have significant powerful karmic overlays as in the case of individuals who feel compelled to change their gender. In working with such individuals, the therapist would do well to utilize this star. They can have deeper insight into themselves and into their emotional connection to the client, and in this way come to understand the issues involved much better.

Zubeneschamali (Beta Librae)

[m 2.5] Blue, 130 light years. One of the "lunar mansions" or "lunar stations" in Chinese or Indian astrology.

This star has the ability to guide your understanding of how unconscious energy is to be applied in the world. This can be useful in guiding how you will map out this ability to work with the unconscious. This star can assist individuals who are seeking greater understanding of unconscious patterns to share with others, or those working in a group to understand their own patterns. It can be combined with Zubenelgenubi and with Luna elixir for understanding unconscious attributes. This combination can bring forth deeper awareness of the past lifetimes as they have worked with ancient patterns that you are repeating now.

Some of the energies of the civilization associated with this star have to do with the creation of certain states of mind which can tend to deeply influence one's unconscious reactions and behaviors. These states are utilized by extraterrestrials associated with the Zeta Reticuli system for control of individuals. A similar energy is available in the consciousness of most people to bring this into a more conscious form. This star can be used when you are seeking to understand your relationship with such negative extraterrestrials, when you wish to bring forth various buried patterns, or when working with assistance in hypnotic release of such patterns so that you have deeper conscious awareness. You may have experienced a very difficult dream state and woken quite aware that various unusual happenings may have occurred during the night, but you cannot remember what happened. There may be a deep emotional scar associated with this so that there is an unresolved anger as if you don't even want to think about it, and when someone else brings it up there is an emotional reaction. This sense of uncomfortableness can be eased by the use of this star. Deeper awareness of what occurred and the truth of it can be enhanced without the emotional entanglement and difficulty being so difficult. This would be one of the elixirs that a hypnotherapist would have on hand to use with clients when such extraterrestrial involvement is part of what they are working on with that individual.

Ascella (Zeta Sagittarii)

[m 2.61] Blue-white giant and a subgiant, 130 light years.

Some deeper awareness of correct use of speaking capacity will be made available for most people. The way in which your words create certain thought patterns in other people will become clearer by using this star. The effect of your speech on others will be better understood. This effect may be one that you have internalized unconsciously and can now bring into greater conscious awareness. This star can enhance the ways of creating greater joyfulness by speaking. At the highest spiritual level, this will enhance the use of healing sounds with other people. There can be also release of past-life awareness in which there was misuse of sound, voice, and the Law of Speech (bringing ideas into form by speaking them aloud). This release can create an emotional shift. This star can enhance awareness of these emotions moving through the person and help ease these emotions.

Iota Aurigae

[m 2.64] **Yellow giant, 250 light years. Contains nonionized metals.**

With use of this star some additional physical strength may be transmitted to the individual and the person receiving this may find that it is easier to communicate it to others. Several processes of communication with children will be strengthened. When the issue is, "Do as I say and not as I do," the individual involved may have a hint that there is some small iota of understanding missing in their own communication with his or her children. The understanding that the individual involved is unable to accept is usually made clearer. Because the mixed message is largely unconscious, the child is unable to work with it. Instead of asking a question of the parent, the child transmits behavioral difficulty. As a result the interaction between the parent and the child simply becomes more unconscious. The star elixir can sometimes help the parent in understanding the true nature of the communication as it was originally intended, and adding strength to it.

Graffias (Beta Scorpii)

[m 2.65] **Blue-white group of three stars, 600 light years.**

With these stars the signature has precedence since no civilization is directly associated with this star arrangement. Emotions associated with one's family situation that may be buried or difficult to access can be brought into greater focus. The use of synchronized dreaming between the children and the parents in a family will be significantly enhanced. Use of this star system is recommended in times of emotional stress and difficulty for the family such as often occurs with illness or the teenage years. In bringing to focus some of this energy, sometimes what will occur is greater clarity in the family situation and enhancement of communication. One powerful issue may come to light in a new way in which you can understand it quite differently. It is best here if possible while under the influence of this star system to focus on that one issue. Bring it into the dream state. Allow the deeper unconscious images associated with it to come forth. Some of the discomfort that might otherwise have been associated with this blockage will be lessened so that it is more comfortable and easier to work with and talk about.

In the adoption process there is also some benefit noted in working with this star family. The ability to understand the true nature of these relationships at an emotional level will also come forth.

Sheratin (Beta Arietis)

[m 2.65] **Blue-white, 44 light years.**

In working with this star individuals can develop a deeper awareness of how they are able to transfer the powerful energy of change into their current life. These are accumulations of unconscious energies developed from repeated pastlife involvement with change. The unconscious aspects of the Law of Progress can be brought into consciousness. Using this star alone before falling asleep at night is of great benefit in bringing these pastlife attributes into greater awareness. This can be of great benefit because it gradually eases the need for rebirth. This star can be of great benefit combined with any sort of Buddhist practice. Many times the underlying goal of these practices is the cessation of rebirth. In an awareness of the powerful energies associated with this star, the person may come into harmony with the whole idea of cycles of birth and rebirth and be able to more easily absorb and work with the energies from the past. This can come in many different forms, whether emotional, mental, or physical, and can be available to the person even at the level of the astral body.

There can be benefit in using this star when selecting a key or doorway lifetime for exploring other past lives. From that lifetime it may be easy to work with other past lifetimes or lifetimes that came after the doorway lifetime because there are direct and powerful ties between the individual and that doorway lifetime. In a working with such an energy the star can be beneficial in allowing easier contact with the doorway lifetime.

Unuk (Alpha Serpentis)

[m 2.65] Yellow giant, 60 light years.

This star has some properties that are similar to that of your own Sun. It has an ability to provide additional energy of leadership and concentrated awareness. The true understanding of leadership for some people will come into their consciousness under the influence of this star. There can be deeper awareness of their own physical capacities and some assistance in sports. The ability to receive love of a non-personal nature such as adulation, admiration, and respect will be emphasized. One can have a deeper sense of peace about certain personal problems where respect or assistance from others is an issue. Some soothing of the emotional body and release of stored emotions will be noted for many people. The physical processes relating to melanin and melatonin will be assisted. Some individuals experience depression in the time of year of maximum darkness, especially the period around December 21 in the northern hemisphere. This light-related depression will be somewhat eased by use of this star.

Theta Aurigae

[m 2.65] Blue-white silicon star, 150 light years.

The utilization of this star elixir at this time will be of great value for many people in their transformation of energy from the third to fourth dimension. This star can assist individuals who are having trouble with "grit". The traditional associations with silica are the deeper aspects of real strength such as the ability to say no. Individuals who are working with silica at homeopathic level for any purpose may have this elixir added and derive direct benefit. At the higher level this is a way in which the transformative characteristic of silica will be enhanced for many people. This can strengthen the process of utilization of silica in the physical body. Silica represents transformation for many reasons. At the physical level this often involves transformation of calcium. This elixir will be of great value for individuals who are struggling with calcium-related difficulties including osteoarthritis, osteoporosis, or the mending of broken bones. If at all possible, silica should be present in the diet in small amounts. Silica can be provided through horsetail herb, and it is best taken for a week and then not taken for 3 days.

The spiritual characteristics that are enhanced for individuals by this star can be of great value for many people at this time. This is a way of finding courage and strength in the resolute understanding of their own beliefs as relating to their conception of God, the universe, and these higher spiritual characteristics. Atheists or agnostics will benefit by using this star. People who are struggling with actually using or applying these higher concepts in the world will also benefit.

This elixir may be useful in reducing some of the effects caused by high frequency emissions (high frequency meaning anything higher than 400 kilohertz). These emissions will be noted especially from computers. You would utilize it by placing a few drops of this elixir on the outside case of the computer itself. It will have little direct effect on the computer monitor. The environmental safety devic order that can be associated with this will also benefit from this elixir.

Beta Corvi

[m 2.66] **Yellow-white giant, 95 light years. Contains ionized and neutral metals, with a strong presence of calcium.**

This star can enhance the ability to shift ion balance in the physical body. This can enhance the interaction of several hormones and neuropeptides in the brain. In combination with the herb Ginkgo Biloba there will be some acceleration of the ability to transfer information for better memory, better thinking process, and deeper levels of consciousness in which various aspects of the unconscious and the superconscious are made more clear to the person. This herb, when taken at the 24% concentration, has remarkable abilities in the human body. Many of these reach a cellular block, and the star elixir or meditation on the star can help a bit with moving through that block, thus making the action of this herb more effective. Enhanced mental functioning will be noted as various logical or intuitive problems are worked with. The best use of this herb in combination with this star is for intuitive understanding or deeper states of consciousness when channeling or working with energies from other sources. Individuals could also use this for the programming of what could be termed a cosmic computer or reading of the akashic records. This is fairly difficult for many individuals because it often stresses nerve synapses and the ability to transfer information within one's conscious roles.

Ruchbah (Delta Cassiopei)

[m 2.67] **Blue-white giant-subgiant, 90 light years.**

This star can enhance, particularly in men, the understanding of states of grace and the ability to work with the acceptance of love. Some ability to move more gracefully will be noted. Individuals who have been working in areas of physical body perfection where grace is important as in the sports of tennis, gymnastics, horseback riding, swimming, and various decathlon and related Olympic functions will do well with this elixir or meditating on this star for bringing greater fluid motion into the physical body. This can extend to subtle levels, in particular where individuals are involved in processes such as choreography, where they need to have a vision of how the dance will work. Though dancers will be assisted, they have usually focused on these deeper ways of grace in physical form and do not need the breakthroughs that this star can provide. There are women who have difficulty with grace and perhaps feel a stronger tie to the masculine side. If they wish to develop the feminine a little more and the graceful states associated with such female energy, then this star or elixir would be recommended. At the highest spiritual level there is deeper awareness of God's grace and the way in which karma is shifted out of deep love.

Muphrid (Eta Boötis)

[m 2.69] **White binary, 30 light years.**

With use of Muphrid there is a balancing in relation to what you wish to do creatively. Thus you may feel better about art or about music. The balancing can take place in the expressive side, but it can also take place in the side that observes or is at one with art. Individuals who are seeking to expand their own horizons of what they accept from others' creativity will do well to utilize this star. It is as if they can see with new eyes or receive new energies in ways they had not previously. An example would be when a new art form is shown to you that you find difficult to accept as artistic or creative, and others involved feel strongly about it in a positive way. You will do well to work with this star if you are feeling some resistance to accepting it as true creativity and you wish to observe this and work with it more easily. Similarly, if you are an artist working in this new form and wish additional assistance and energy, the star may be of some assistance.

Media (Delta Sagittarii)

[m 2.71] **Yellow giant, 70 light years. Contains nonionized and ionized metals, and titanium oxide.**

Use of this star can provide greater spiritual confidence and strength when individuals are uncertain about the best way to proceed in working with spiritual concepts and ideas. This star can also bring deeper understanding of your relationship to other people, and how they are there to expose you to their spiritual ideas or their point of view. This can be of benefit for people who are working with new spiritual ideas or attempting to assimilate ideas that are developed in relationship, as in a marriage between two persons of different spiritual persuasions or interests.

Lesath (Upsilon Scorpii)

[m 2.71] **Blue-white subgiant, 450 light years. Contains nonionized helium; ionized silicon, oxygen, and magnesium.**

The unconscious ability to influence physical body processes in the utilization of energies for healing will be influenced by this star. At a deeper level this can influence the physical transference of substances into the blood stream. This can create better absorption, but more than this is the activation of various elements that are usually found in the body but not well utilized. This activation is enhanced and supplemented by the energies from this star. There can be enhanced circulation as well as strengthened physical functioning. This can bring insights based on unconscious concepts and beliefs or long-buried ideas. The inner healing processes may be strengthened, but some degree of counseling or emotional release would be necessary for these to be ongoing in the person. There can be great value in sharing the influence of this star for a group of individuals who are looking for a common goal, who wish this to be a part of physical form in animals, plants, or people.

Delta Ophiuchi

[m 2.72] Yellow-orange giant, 95 light years. Most this star's energy is broadcast in the infrared region. Contains titatium oxide and neutral metals.

Meditating upon this star can provide some additional stimulation and deeper awareness of the third eye. The stimulation with infrared light can be valuable for opening the third eye. The infrared light that is received from this star occurs at a much subtler level. This is inherently spiritualizing and will generally awaken most capacities of the third eye. Those abilities with which the individual is able to work with best will usually come forth. Thus it will give visions of the future to one person, deeper awareness and insight of healing capacities to another, and increased telepathy with a third. The use of this star can be combined with the use of krypton in the light bulb device or other device for stimulating the third eye center as we have described in the book *Other Kingdoms* through our channel Maurice B. Cooke in Canada.

Tarazed (Gamma Aquilae)

[m 2.72] Yellow giant, 350 light years.

Deeper power in one's heart may be noted in working with this star. It is a little difficult to predict exactly which line this will travel, the physical, the emotional, or the spiritual. It will depend on which of these are least developed in the person, so there is usually good reason to utilize this. As the heart becomes stronger, the ability to share love with others may increase. The ability to clear the heart of negative aspects of physical difficulty may increase. This star may enhance the ability to transfer love in a healing sense, the ability to understand the soul love, and the ability to bring universal love into greater consciousness. Which direction this will take will depend on which of these are at the lowest ebb in the individual.

This is well combined with Gold elixir for individuals wishing to create a deeper expansion of their awareness of heart energy. At a higher spiritual level, there can be telepathic transference of some loving capacities. This is of benefit for people who wish to see that their vibrational transfer has been received or has somehow affected another person. Some benefit may accrue in relationship from both parties taking a combination of Gold, Tarazed, and

Venus elixirs. The combination of Altair and Tarazed in meditation or elixir form can help one have the strength to develop an inner love of what one's task is about.

Zubenelgenubi (Alpha Librae)

[m 2.76] **Blue-white binary, 65 light years.**

This binary star influences in a very positive way those aspects of close relationship where individuals have given over their will to another being, yet recognize that, paradoxically, the other being has also given over his or her will to you. Individuals may be able to find a peacefulness in their relationship by balancing forces that may be negative, aggressive, or those causing great disruption in their relationship. Use of this star can assist people in finding an inner harmony and an independence. They may understand that the closeness of the pair-bond relationship is only to symbolize what is potentially possible in the relationship of all beings with God. This star can also assist the relationship with one's spirit guide or the relationship with the soulmate or twin flame (which usually extends into subtle realms and is not manifested in the physical).

At a higher level, the influence of this star is primarily karmic. You may begin to recognize karmic patterns and see how they are able to cause you to interact in a relationship in certain specific ways. The essential factors of the karma may become clear and you may begin to understand more about the motivation for something. For example: "I do this because I know it will save me, change me, assist me; and yet as I look into my world I see no basis in fact why this behavior or action really does help." These are indicators of such karmic imbalance. The use of the star at such time can be quite valuable to bring people to a place of deep acceptance of themselves and at the same time show them the inner purpose of these behavioral aberrations or difficulties. As these are understood, you can then nurture or love yourself in a way that more easily releases the need for the creation of these behaviors in the pair-bond relationship. Intimacy is therefore assisted and the ability to communicate in your relationship is strengthened. All of these ways of working with this star will tend to relax and ease some of the energies with regards to relationship but also bring forth new concepts and ideas.

Porrima (Gamm Virginis)

[m 2.76] Blue-white twin stars, virtually identical. 32 light years.

The use of these stars can create a powerful balancing of the ability to be effective in the world, combined with the ability to learn. The awareness of this balance within individuals for the purpose of learning can affect left and right brain balance, but generally will be around apprenticeship and working with other people for learning new information and new ideas from them. Utilization of this star provides a deep learning as if there is an apprenticeship, a companionship, an absorption, a oneness, and then a release so that the learning takes place in a powerful transfer.

In Atlantis this binary star was utilized for the development of crystalline technologies for the receptivity and transfer of information into a crystal and then into a person. This was done utilizing the light from this binary, the elixir, but most importantly by journeying to Porrima in one's mind. The two individuals wishing to transfer information and knowledge via the crystal imagine themselves in the midst of the star system, perfectly balanced. Then the crystal appeared between them. As each would touch opposing faces of the crystal, the information was transferred.

Iota Orionis

[m 2.76] Blue-white, three stars, 1,700 light years.

This star can generate greater insight into ecological action, various ways of dealing with money, various economic situations one may find oneself in, as well as those things that have long lasting impact on the world. This is an excellent elixir for individuals involved in various forms of ecological or politically motivated ecological change, those individuals who wish to see correct action on Earth, and those who wish to more fully understand the magnificent long-term mechanisms involved in the Earth's own existence.

This ecological awareness is an important lesson for the civilization from Iota Orionis. This message pours from this star to them and to all other beings who can be aware of it. The star is sometimes able to project a sense of sadness or mourning because of the enslavement of the civilization on the fourth planet by the entities from Eta Draconis. As they move through their periods of difficulty, they will likely see this ecological awareness as the ultimate answer, and from this derive ways in which their planet will eventually become quite uncomfortable to those who would enslave them. As a result, approximately 100 to 150 years in humanity's future, contact with these beings is likely. An awareness of how their struggles yielded softer technologies may be of benefit for humanity and others. Until that time however very little in the technological realm will likely be available to individuals working with this star.

Cheleb (Beta Ophiuchi)

[m 2.77] **Yellow giant, 100 light years.**

This star can stimulate the love center to enable communication with other people that transcends verbal or visual modes. Some strengthening of auditory modes of communication, particularly through song, will be enhanced. This is specifically directed at the connection between voicing what is in the heart and the ability of other people to receive this.

The civilization associated with this place has a great deal of interest in Earth at this time but have also created some specific barriers; they are not to intrude on your consciousness, much less directly intrude on your civilization. One might wish to attune to this star to help dissolve certain blocks in one's character, such as blocks to powerful emotion, or past experiences where one has a block to memory. This star can also assist when there is some difficulty with creating deeper intimacy with others where sometimes it feels as if a wall is created around oneself. These would be good symbols to indicate the use of this star.

This star can increase cellular activity, and create a better balance of minerals across the cell wall membrane, especially the balance of sodium and potassium. This will be enhanced with well-absorbed water containing minute quantities of well-dissolved minerals.

In the future this star may have some application in interstellar diplomacy. This star elixir can strengthen the ability to communicate aspects of love to other races. This will be between people and those beings who have perhaps gone beyond the understanding of Earth beings or are on a par with such understanding.

Rastaban (Beta Draconis)

[m 2.77] **White giant, 400 light years.**

There are multiple influences from this star which can be

useful in dealing with inner conflict and with trying to sort out ideas that do not necessarily make sense or that do not fit well together. It may at first seem that you are only adding energy to the difficulties. This will eventually sharpen the contrasts and highlights between the competing ideas and allow you to take a higher form in which you are able to utilize the approach that works best in your life. Then what may also emerge from this is an attitude in which there is laughter or separation from the competing ideas, and then you do not take the entire issue so seriously.

The civilizations that have existed in this star system are not native to the area. Those had been killed by a race of powerful reptilian beings some 650,000 years ago. These remnants of the original civilization still remain and have influenced civilizations that have lived there. Some of these have lived in peace, others in war, others in enslavement, and others in mastery. Because of this frequent change from one civilization to another in some of the planets associated with this star, there have been many powerful interconnections that eventually resolved most of these conflicting ideas.

Kornephoros (Beta Herculis)

[m 2.78] **Yellow-white giant, 110 light years.**

This star can enhance healing processes derived from mental energy. These can involve genetic change. By continued meditation, various genetic structures can be subtly altered and eventually come into a place of greater harmony with the being's lifestyle, developmental process, awareness, and desires. This is a slow and subtle process by comparison to other techniques, but once in place it can hold better than most other techniques.

The star emits a burst of radiation at the aetheric level that may eventually be picked up or received by finer-tuned instruments than you currently have available. This burst occurs every 3.3 minutes and influences slightly some physical body processes in humans. This influence is one that tends to preserve genetic structures. If the meditation on change in genetic structure can take place so that it intercepts at least three of these intervals—meaning that you meditate for at least 10 minutes—you will more powerfully and beautifully enhance this process.

The idea is to specifically see new genetic structures formed in the physical body as having their source somewhere in your thought forms. This can be directed through a particular chakra that you feel is most well-stimulated at that time, such as the heart chakra or the third eye chakra. See that chakra as active and influencing this process. This process takes place in your imagination at a microscopic level. Imagine entering into the DNA helix, unwinding it, and finding a gene to heal. You then create the shift as you imagine it in color form, sound form, or light form. In your imagination re-compress the helix, put it back in the cell, and see it begin to replicate. To have fun with these ideas and to play with them will assist in the process.

At the highest level, it is simply a way of welcoming the form of the change that you wish to come into you in whatever way appears to be the best. This means you love the change, you welcome God's energy as it moves through you, and you breathe that change into your being.

The mental functioning enhanced by this star can bring new ideas into your understanding about the nature of the body, the universe, ecosystems, the biosphere, or mankind's problems. This is a useful star also to work with when you are contemplating and looking at these larger issues. The civilization associated with this star has moved to extreme levels of mental development, and along with several other civilizations, is waiting for humanity's development to influence them.

Cursa (Beta Eridani)

[m 2.79] **Blue-white giant, 65 light years.**

This star has a capacity to increase endurance and strengthen the ability to do work of a mental nature with many individuals. Some enhancement of thinking process will take place. Physical stamina will be enhanced where concentration or direction of the energy flows in the physical body by the mind are necessary. Any sort of physical action where danger is involved can be influenced by this star elixir in a positive way. When working with biorhythms, individuals may find that a coordination of the valleys or switch-points between two or more cycles would be excellent times for utilizing this star. The coordination of physical and mental rhythms into some place of difficulty might be averted by the use of the star.

The beings involved with this star have shared most of their energies with their planetary system and sun and have improved its longevity as a result. Because of this, this sense of patience may also be transmitted to some individuals who work with this star elixir. This star does not directly enhance patience, but when someone is involved in a concentrated pursuit which combines mental and physical, they may begin to understand patience better as a direct result of the elixir.

Cor Caroli (Alpha Canum Venaticorum)

[m 2.8] **Blue-white, 120 light years. Magnetic spectrum variable with strontium, silicon, and chromium.**

This star will tend to influence the ability of the aethers to affect the person. There can be a natural thinning of the aethers and a lessening of the negative influences of ELF waves, negative vibrational states of the Earth from geopathic zones, and magnetic field disturbances from electric power lines and video display terminals. This star can also be of benefit in the absorption of inert gas energies. The aetheric vibrations of group interaction will be enhanced and so utilizing the elixir of this star in a group could be of benefit. Some slight enhancement of the absorption of chromium will be noted. Some lessening of the negative effects of radiation will be noted. The frequent accumulation of radioactive strontium 90 in the physical body can be of detriment, and the ability of the body to excrete this material will be enhanced. It would be wise to utilize this star with other substances that have been seen as valuable for reducing radiation in the body, in particular sea vegetables and to a lesser extent such substances as miso, carrageen moss, and sodium alginate.

The civilization associated with this system has technological ideas to transfer to humanity at a future time relating to space travel by manipulating gravitational fields without the use of toxic substances. This can be of great benefit for humanity. Individuals who are contemplating such new techniques in space travel will do well with this elixir.

Kaus Borealis (Lambda Sagittarii)

[m 2.80] **Yellow giant, 60 light years.**

The civilization associated with this star is an outpost of

certain entities of great power and positive regard for Earth (what you might call love, though they certainly have no concept of this). This decentralized civilization has its point of maximum concentration near the precise geometric center of the galaxy, but also connects to many of the positive civilizations that have a high regard for service that are distributed throughout the galaxy. Acting as an outpost of this civilization, this star is a gatherer of energy and translates this energy deeper into the center of the galaxy for communication with other galaxies.

A deeper sense of perspective and a deeper understanding of how one fits into humanity's purpose may emerge when an individual would meditate on this star. A more practical result of utilizing this star is an understanding of correct vocation, right livelihood, and the ability to work within one's path and to get back on the path should a person have wandered from it.

Individuals may recognize the sense of connection to other stars and to the universe. This may increase their sensitivity to the vibrations of other stars. People may be attracted to other stars, but when they meditate on them they notice little result. This process of attunement can be shortened if meditation upon this star is done first. Then usually for a period of a few months when you meditate on any other star you will know within a few moments whether it is appropriate. If the star is not appropriate, you may notice a slightly negative feeling, a sense of some compression, or some difficulty or coldness. When you meditate on a star that is appropriate you may notice immediate expansion, some gentle assistance, some warming, or other such positive sensations. These sensations are enhanced to some extent by this star. This additional sensitivity comes primarily due to the function of this star as a transmitter of energy, vibration, and information for the center of the galaxy, other galaxies, and other civilizations.

Vindemiatrix (Epsilon Virginis)

[m 2.83] **Yellow-white giant, 75 light years.**

This star can strengthen resolve and the ability to follow through where other individuals are involved. People who work together can gradually discover a common goal. You may find that there are resistances and struggles with accepting that goal as your own. For instance:

"It isn't what I thought of myself, but what the group thought of." Or: "If I work with this, will I be tied to this group?" By utilizing this star, you may discover the ideas that formed the initial inspiration. This can assist greatly in deeper modes of apprenticeship or learning between the individual and the group, particularly where what you are learning is not fully known at the outset. This star can be a beneficial influence for research groups involved in a cooperative creative process where the end result is unknown.

The civilization associated with this star has worked with the bringing together of energies from other civilizations in the creation of new ideas and forms that were eventually returned to such civilizations. These may act as beneficiaries for human thought in the future with the energies of love and the ability to work with such. Because of this, some technological ideas from this star may also be available to some people. When scientists or those involved in technological processes would meditate on this star, they may find new ideas coming into consciousness over the ensuing three day period.

Zeta Persei

[m 2.83] **Blue-white supergiant, 1000 light years.**

This star can help individuals feel some deeper relaxation around fear of war, battle, and violence. This star can assist individuals who have experienced themselves as a warrior during past-life therapy and found this warrior state of consciousness to be very difficult. They may feel some willingness to see the truth of what war is about—that it is a war within oneself that one is also creating as a reflection outside. With the influence of this star, it may be easier to create a dialogue between the two parts of a person—perhaps seen as shadow self and light self, perhaps seen as the fear-based self and the love-based self.

Part of this is due to the willingness of the beings associated with this civilization from Zeta Persei to rebuild their civilization at regular intervals as a result of the destruction from great wars. They eventually decided that peace was far more important than fighting, and many differences amongst them were eventually put to rest. This took place about 5,000 years ago. They then began to question the use of their extensive technologies for making weapons. "What can we do with all of this stuff?"—might be an equivalent. On Earth you are now faced with this as well, what does one do with all of the implements of war, once one is willing to set them aside? Certainly it is a great and important symbol when they are simply destroyed. But these beings recognized that in the creation of a powerful beacon of peace, these energies might have some benefit to other beings somewhere in space. This powerful light is repeated at regular intervals. Another one of these will reach Earth about April 7, 1997, and at such time some additional brightness may be noticed coming from this star.

Algenib (Gamma Pegasi)

[m 2.84] **Blue-white subgiant, 650 light years. Cepheid variable.**

The ability to transfer information from one subtle body to another as modulated by the mental body is directly affected by meditating on this star or working with the elixir. Creative visualization as well other forms of visualization are directly stimulated. This can mean visualization of another's idea, imagination by revery, or creation of new ideas when reading something. Stimulation of such ideas can also take place via other media such as video or movies, whereas creative visualization is largely self-generated. All of these are enhanced as the mental body is able to more easily direct the flow of energy and information within all the subtle bodies.

When a visualization is created through the mental body to connect the aetheric body to the physical body, there will be a consequent flow of energy. The energy will at first flow from the physical body to the aetheric body. The visualization through mental body energies will then create an intertwining effect and the combination of information and energy will take place. This energy will then flow from the aetheric body to the physical body in the specific form that was visualized. The ability of the mental body to modulate and work with this is an important part of the healing process.

Visualization is an important part of the healing process, even when healing is done through what would appear to be allopathic techniques such as various drug substances or even something as clearly allopathic as the setting of a bone. This is usually unconscious. Visualization cannot be ruled out even in double blind studies. This is because the doctor involved, the person who is creating this study, the people funding it, and others associated with this study have at least some unconscious connection to the various individuals involved. The use of this elixir or meditating on the star will tend to enhance the healing process and make it a little more conscious for most people. Where visualization is directly utilized, healing can be significantly speeded up by the use of this star.

The energies for this work primarily at the mental body level. The civilization associated with this star is relatively dispassionate and uninvolved in most of the other affairs of this galaxy. As they are dispassionate, these beings are equally available if their energies are correctly utilized. It is possible that about a thousand years in mankind's future, contact with this civilization will take place and significant enhancement and expansion of the mental body in all humans will take place.

Tau Scorpii

[m 2.85] **Blue-white, 300 light years.**

The use of this star can help people develop a sense of courage. This sense of courage may open them to remember deeply buried feelings of an emotional nature from their past. Some of these may even form as clear pictures of past lives that will immediately give rise to some information about the lesson of that life. There may be a release of this energy when the life lessons were difficult or dealing with negative emotions. This elixir may help some individuals continue working with the information. Some inner building can take place. There can also be a deep sense of forgiveness for oneself and an awareness of where these patterns may be repeated in the person's current life. Some of these patterns will be more easily altered as a result of this insight. One can easily get immersed in all of the insights and details, and forget that it was the courage to look in the first place that brought forth this insight. Taking the elixir or meditating on the star again will help bring this sense of courage in immediately.

The individual working with this star may note that it takes about three days for an effect to take place. These are taking place at astral body level, thus connecting to the past lives. The usual recommendation would be to meditate on the star or take the elixir and then do it again three days later while working with the insights as they come in and you are attempting to make them a little more concrete and understandable.

Some stimulation of the astral body and some ability to bring energy from astral levels into physical form may be noted with use of this star. Some release from suicidal tendencies may be noted for individuals with such tendencies.

Pleiades: Alcyone (Eta Tauri)

[m 2.86] Blue-white giant, 400 light years, the brightest star in the Pleiades. Other major stars: Maia, Atlas, Taygeta, Electra, and Merope.

Alcyone and Electra and Merope all are homes of the civilizations of greatest value and connection to Earth at the current time.

Alcyone as the most important of these can provide a significantly enhanced ability to channel from extraterrestrials in a balanced way, and to perceive the correct place of contact with entities from other planetary systems. There can be an ability to establish extraterrestrial contact from channeled data, deeper understanding of the ways these worlds touch your world, and the ability to utilize this information appropriately in one's life. Alcyone can also enhance the ability to perceive spiritual truths that may be shared and understood as universal principles.

Merope will bring a greater ability to coordinate these principles in one's life, perceive universal law, and understand the correct ability to affiliate with the other lifestreams on Earth, particularly the animal kingdom.

Electra will govern the ability to coordinate with the plant kingdom. Individuals working with Electra may discover inner telepathic abilities, utilize these more appropriately in the world, and understand their true significance. Electra can create deeper states of meditative calm and oneness with cosmic principles and universal laws. The awareness of these universal laws as a thought form of love, assistance, and awareness is enhanced with use of Electra.

Sigma Scorpii

[m 2.86] Blue-white giant, 571 light years. Double star, one of which is slightly variable with 6 hour period.

This pair of stars can help individuals become aware of how past-life patterns affect the physical body and the expression of emotions. Because of the variability of these stars as they relate to each other, some people may experience deeper awareness of such cycles.

The civilizations associated with these stars have projected their awareness of cycles in themselves into their stars, which has influenced the variability of these stars. The speed of variability has been gradually changed by them depending upon their phases of development, moving through periods of much more rapid fluctuation and periods of much more infrequent or irregular fluctuation. At the current time there is a transference of such energy to many beings in this galaxy and also to some beings in the Andromeda Galaxy. Some of this energy is available to individuals on Earth.

This binary can attune individuals to the ways in which the cells absorb water better under certain conditions, such as the time of day or the things eaten or drunk. This star can also affect many other rhythms of the body. Those who study the body clock as described in traditional Chinese acupuncture may have better attunement to such cycles.

Past-life interactions will also affect body cycles. Many times individuals will find that certain times of the day are far better than other times for doing past-life recall work or for becoming aware of powerful influences from the past. For some individuals this will be a split cycle where for about twelve hours of any day there will be an attunement to darker energies, past lives of some difficulty or darkness; and for the other twelve hours there will be an attunement to pastlives of greater light and deeper awareness. It is usually wise to look into both. The use of this star elixir can assist individuals in fine tuning the process and becoming more aware of which of the cycles they fit into as they do such work. It has often been recommended that people become aware of their past lives in some way. If this does not seem like something an individual might want to do, there still is benefit in the use of this star elixir because that individual may then seek to understand how the rhythms of creativity or communication in their own life might be influenced by past-life experiences, whether they know it consciously or not. The way in which these come cyclically in the diurnal/nocturnal cycle will be made clearer by the use of this elixir.

Delta Cygni

[m 2.5] **Blue-white subgiant, 110 light years, binary.**

Some strengthening of the ability to understand the Law of Karma will be enhanced in people as they become more future oriented. With this star the forward-looking avenues of karma are accelerated. Thus you can understand the consequences of your actions, understand cause and effect, more easily derive the choices to be at cause, and know the difference between your reactions and your actions in the world. You may be able to express this understanding to others.

At a higher level, many new avenues may open for individuals who have looked at this and found that a better way of expressing their deep awareness of the law of karma is not through the mind or verbalization. With this star there may be an acceleration of energies in dance. Individuals who have come to some deeper contemplation and understanding of this important universal law may discover an ability to dance. This can enhance the ability to express through dance, to release karma through dance, and to understand the actual dance of karma in their own way through dancing. This is not quite the same as trance dancing, but is somewhat similar in that the dancing takes place in an altered state. This is a human translation of a more magnificent and far-reaching energy, and other individuals may translate this energy in other forms. It is possible here that a deeper inspired state as a result of working with this energy will take place for many individuals and they may at least appreciate dance more and find that their ability to observe cause and effect in their own life is positively enhanced as they are involved in dance, even in such a peripheral way as just watching it.

The three civilizations associated with this star have each moved through many levels of awareness and understanding to a place of timelessness in which their understanding of the laws of karma are extremely different than yours. As each civilization has moved through this, the residual lessons of this have remained with the star. These energies are vibrated from the star as a beacon of clarity and love for all of those in the universe who would need those lessons or need to understand them a little better. Such beings have left this system but saw that they could leave behind some of the keys and stepping stones to deeper awareness and understanding for all beings who wish to absorb such understanding.

Epsilon Persei

[m 2.88] **Blue-white, 700 light years.**

A generation of vibrating energy that can be attuned to other vibrations can take place in the sixth chakra center in the human body as a result of the influence of this star. This is recommended for individuals who wish to concentrate more energy in that center. The sixth chakra is located at the approximate geometric center of the skull. Vibrational energies can be created at the sixth chakra that can have useful healing abilities. The awareness of this energy for healers can stimulate their own creative processes so that some connection with another can take place. This connection can be one at a purely physical level if awareness of the information coming into the person is then brought into some personal form and then sent down the hands. Individuals involved in massage, reiki, acupressure, and related hands-on healing techniques can benefit by use of this star if they are wiling to receive intuitive guidance and understanding and bring it into clearer and more powerful form.

This star can also enhance the ability to transmit telepathically. This can be useful for teachers who wish to communicate difficult concepts. This is done by remembering the feeling associated with the concept that is to transmitted as well as the actual ideas.

The star transmits an energy that has been nourishing to the various life-forms on the planets around it. These include intelligent life-forms but also life-forms akin to your animals and plants as well as biological entities such as viruses and microbes that exist in the Earth environment. This nourishing is somewhat similar to the effect of sunlight transformed by chlorophyll and related substances by your plants and the beneficial impact of sunlight on various other entities.

Pi Sagittarii

[m 2.89] **3 stars, one of which is a yellow giant, 250 light years.**

Approximately 27,000 years ago, these stars were located a far greater distance apart. The civilizations amongst them had made contact and communication amongst each other and learned of many different ways of working together and knowing each other. These civilizations were able to bridge their sciences together. As a result of this a project was launched which lasted approximately twelve years, at which time powerful energies of mutual attraction and repulsion were utilized to bring the stars into much closer companionship. This allowed far greater communication among these civilizations. Eventually the interchange of DNA coding and genetic material was utilized for a cooperative cross-seeding of the many races of these civilizations, as well as among the various other life forms that might be understood by you as plant, animal, and mineral that worked with these beings.

Atlanteans attuned to this star group and the great revelations that were made there. They noticed these three stars moving closer together, and knew full well that these were not planets. As a result of this, some of the information from these civilizations was transferred to the Atlantean civilization to be used for experiments with genetic coding. This was a case of a little knowledge being a dangerous thing. Although it was primarily an inspiration that was transferred and not that much direct, concrete knowledge, still a certain karmic debt was incurred by these beings from Pi Sagittarii when those in Atlantis misused some of this information for the production of misshapen beings who were hampered by great difficulties in neither being animal or human.

So these beings from Pi Sagittarii have sought amongst their many tasks to rectify the situation to some extent. This group of stars will assist individuals who wish to contemplate and understand their own genetic coding, their connection to their own DNA, and the awareness of their own lifelines through the physical body. They may be able to understand their heritage and genetics, as well as their awareness of how these things could be changed by them more consciously. These stars are broadcasting an energy to Earth that is specifically filtered to affect the three important levels of existence: one affecting the spiritual side, another the physical side, and the other that which relates to thought, feeling, and communication. In understanding how these things tend to work together, these stars will help people become aware of the great power that is imparted by genetics.

At this time it is important for people to look at this information in all kinds of different ways so that they come to their own decision about this. It is likely that even in as little as 10 to 20 years hence, people will have more and more awareness of their own genetic encoding, and how they can influence this in their children in the time immediately before conception, during conception, and during the first and second trimesters of pregnancy. This is not just for the improving of physical conditions, but for the producing of offspring of higher capacities, greater intelligence, more love, deeper psychological attunement, and most importantly, more psychic abilities. These stars as a group will increase this consciousness in many people. It tends to be a spiritual energy by its very nature. These beings from Pi Sagittarii are very carefully filtering the energies that are made available to people, and it will only do good. But it is important to realize that it does tend to empower people's choices all that much more. We would certainly strongly suggest that should there be family history of birth defects or such problems as Down's syndrome in a child yet to be born, that this star elixir be utilized by the father, the mother-to-be, and even by others in the family—especially in the time before, during, and immediately after conception—with a clear and strong visualization of the great health, strength, and innately well-formed capacities of the child to be.

Gamma Persei

[m 2.91] **Yellow giant and a white star, 113 light years.**

This binary can help people attune to the symbols of the body. This will enhance the understanding and use of foot reflexology and iridology. This binary will also enhance the understanding of the symbols of the ear, and the ability to affect the body by massaging the ear.

The beings from Gamma Persei understand symbols deeply. They deliberately manifest these symbols as a conscious coordination of masses of beings deliberately moving and working together for the creation of a single consciousness. This is a bit difficult to describe but is a bit like imbuing large masses of protoplasm akin to brain tissue with conscious functioning and allowing them to interact and work together. These beings from Gamma Persei are not particularly interested in space travel but are aware of the many other possibilities of existence and consciousness in their universe. They are projecting a sense of encouragement and strength to Earth so that people can attune to the structures they have already created.

The primary structure your consciousness is creating is your individual body. Therefore there is some benefit in attunement to this binary star when one wishes to understand physical processes more clearly and powerfully, the lessons of disease, and how these reflect in the physical body through the various systems of representation as found in the feet, the hands, the ear, and the eye. This elixir may be valuable for a woman wishing deeper communication with her unborn child because of the deeper attunement to the symbols that are shared between the mother and her unborn child. This will work best in the second and third trimesters of pregnancy.

Gomeisa (Beta Canis Minoris)

[m 2.91] **Blue-white, 210 light years.**

This star has a capacity to increase the awareness of an individual's connection to groups. This will include any group a person puts their attunement upon, such as community, past-life groups, or groups relating to political activities or larger endeavors of all kinds. This star attune individuals to energies associated with specific group endeavors. Gomeisa can be combined with the globular cluster M92 for some strengthening of awareness of the soul group.

The civilization associated with Gomeisa has been through seven important phases, and in each of these phases a deeper awareness of larger and larger groups was an important part of their development. As result of that deeper awareness, they were able to establish communication on multiple vibrational levels between various planets in their solar system, between their sun and many other suns, as well as between many beings of different levels of sentience. There can be a lessening of judgment in people as a result of this awareness that the star is broadcasting.

Meditating on the star may also attune you to all stars and bring you a slightly higher awareness of the purpose of the stars in your life. This is a rather gentle influence. The highest capacity of this energy is to create communication between the soul group of humanity and other large soul groups. This is not specifically directed at any star at this time. We see the possibility of groups of emissaries coming from Gomeisa to bridge between humans and other civilizations, particularly those whose destinies appear so intertwined with humanity's destiny, such as Pleiadeans, Sirians, and other groups that may appear in the future for humanity.

Deneb Algedi (Delta Capricorni)

[m 2.92] **Blue-white binary, 37 light years.**

This binary can enhance the ability to work with patterns and cycles that are related to practical environments. This can strengthen the ability to make predictions based on past performance. Some aspects of the underlying cycles may become clearer for individuals when they work with this star. This is a way of predicting the future based on a careful study of patterns and how they move through various cycles. The individuals who work with this are astrologers, economists, and historians. After they have observed and worked with most of the information available and understood these cycles, they may become very quiet and enter a state of emptiness. This emptiness often becomes filled with new ideas and better intuition as to the correct course of events.

Individuals working with the stock market for attempting to predict trends might do well by utilization of this star or elixir. Individuals who seek such ways of making financial gain will usually limit their capacity for deeper understanding when the money gets either very good or very bad. When they lose a lot or gain a lot of money, they will begin to jettison some of their deeper spiritual ideas. Their ability to understand their own patterns and how their patterns are evolving can yield the bigger picture. The spirit, the understanding of life, and the understanding of these cycles as applied to all of humanity with themselves perhaps as an example are much more important than the monies involved. This can sometimes be useful for individuals who have been burned by stock markets, commodity markets, or various related financial institutions. They can often then feel a little better about their work and understand the bigger picture when utilizing this star.

Entities from this star system were able to project some ideas of practical form and wisdom into the Atlantean culture. Much of these ideas were rejected by the Atlantean culture but still remained as possibilities for people to work with later.

Tejat (Mu Geminorum)

[m 2.92] Yellow-orange giant, 150 light years. Irregular variable with a cool surface temperature.

This star can gently and easily increase the ability to bring spiritual ideas into clear and expressible form as mental concepts and direct ideas to be shared with others. There will also be a stimulation of the seventh and eighth chakras, so these ideas may come when least expected. There may be greater patience with abilities that do not seem to form patterns in the usual sense. Various cycles such as biorhythms and astrological rhythms will be easier for people. They will be more patient with themselves having utilized this star or its elixir. Individuals may also find that it is much easier to express what they have learned without judgement. They can simply allow the ideas and what they symbolize to fall where they may so that others might absorb them and work with them.

The technique called first thought will be enhanced. This is a psychic technique where when you wish intuitive guidance, you ask that some vision or idea come in. You then deliberately look for the very first thing that you receive. Sometimes having this open state where you are fully aware of all of the thoughts can be held when you meet someone for the first time or are involved in some new activity. What you receive may often appear to be unrelated to current activities, to your usual mental processes, or even to the person or situation that you are involved with. The later thoughts may judge this or cloud it over or make it seem less important. Use of this elixir can extend the first thought period slightly and make this a little more available for many people. What may come forth is an awareness of this not always being the way you want it, but the way the universe wants it.

There is the sense sometimes when working with this star that there is a pattern in things but the pattern is not obvious. Indeed the expansion of the universe does not take place in the steady way that you think it does. This cannot be observed from within the universe. Those beings who have studied this and worked with it found that only by utilization of energies within their star could they come to a deeper understanding, since the star as microcosm of the universe was working with such an energy. This civilization came to a place of great understanding of the true patterns of the expansion of the universe, but the star burned out. This caused a great deal of difficulty, partly at a karmic level and partly what you would consider sadness amongst the beings involved. They had to work with energies in a new way with other beings in other civilizations, but they left a remnant of their deeper awareness within the star. In a limited sense, this star's variability tracks the expansion of the universe. This may be the pattern that is not obvious but which somehow becomes more intuitively accepted by individuals when they work with this star or its elixir.

Sadalmelik (Alpha Aquarii)

[m 2.93] **Yellow supergiant, 1,000 light years.**

A gradual accumulation of the awareness of group interaction and group energy takes place unconsciously for most people who regularly interact in any group situation. The use of this star will gradually improve one's ability to bring the energies that are unconscious into better focus. Often in such groups there are many things left unsaid which people together are a little afraid to speak of. This star will give them a little more strength to say them and likely give them the trust to hear such words and in this way share all that much better in a group.

At a higher spiritual level there is a deeper awareness of the very important transcendent step of moving from individual or personality based consciousness to group consciousness. The awareness of how this shift takes place within people can be enhanced by utilization of this star. Group interaction is enhanced. Anyone who is involved in the creating of a community would certainly do well to utilize this star.

At the highest spiritual level there is an attunement to an energy that is coming from this star into Earth to simply encourage this ability to make this shift to group consciousness and to understand group interaction at a very much higher level. Various high capacities of spiritual telepathy that bring messages of deep clarity can improve, and an ability to understand this and put it into form will generally be strengthened.

Some people may feel frustrated with the inability of a group to maintain its focus and ideals. Its very reason for coming into existence seems to change with time, and this is difficult for the founders or those people who are involved deeply in such a group. Taking this elixir at homeopathic level 12X will improve the situation quite a bit. This can allow people a deeper awareness of the ability for a group to change while remaining in alignment with their original founding principles.

There is also likely some benefit in utilizing this star for individuals studying the Constitution of the United States or the documents being drafted around the world for the setting up of new states or countries. This will enhance the understanding of the group interaction as brought into form through the words.

This star can stimulate the throat and third eye chakras. The mental body is strengthened. There is also some better assimilation of vitamin D.

The energies of this star were focused into the United States in its birthing at the time of the Revolutionary War. This was the energy of creation of a powerful group force amongst the founders and the delegates to the first Constitutional Convention for the development of the process of government and the writing of the Constitution. This was a very deliberate way in which the understanding of this could be made very simple and poured as if in a beautiful light into the Earth from this star. The civilization there had understood the great benefit of this so that people here on Earth would eventually find the way in which this evolves out of a mere paper document to a true embracing of principle of group interaction. This is to pave the way for eventual communication between these beings from Sadalmelik and Earth beings in a way that is not frightening to Earth beings, for their physical appearance is very different than that of humanoids. However this race does have only benevolence in mind and love for people of Earth.

Matar (Eta Pegasi)

[m 2.95] **Yellow binary, 360 light years.**

Matar can be helpful in parent/child relationships, especially when children are moving through behavior of modelling. This occurs often unconsciously in the child from the ages of four to seven years. When an individual who is an adult is aware of difficulties incurred in that age period during their childhood, there is benefit in utilization of Matar for deeper attunement to those difficulties. Matar will be especially helpful when you imagine recreating your childhood in a way in which you pour the resources of love and help into that child as you imagine him or her going through those experiences and seeing that perhaps the experiences can be changed so they come out right. Negative experiences can be converted to those with positive feelings. Experiences where there was little understanding or learning can be converted into those of greater knowledge and awareness.

This star elixir will assist individuals who are counseling children, counseling parent/child relationships, and those counseling adults who are dealing with inner child issues. This will be felt more by the client taking this elixir, rather than directly influencing the practitioner.

This star elixir will have some effect on the astral body, as the deeper awareness and development of the astral body occurs from the ages of four to seven.

Those who find it difficult to sleep at night because of very vivid dreams caused by astral traveling or out-of-body experiences, might do well to use this elixir to have deeper awareness and conscious control of those experiences.

Nihal (Beta Leporis)

[m 2.95] **Yellow giant, 113 light years.**

Nihal can help people relax certain standards of racial prejudice, thus making it easier to absorb and work with information available from other cultures. The civilization from Nihal has gone through a powerful xenophobic period and has only recently begun to accept the awareness of other beings and their possible contributions. This has not yet resulted in a direct beaming of some of these capacities to Earth, so the effect of this relaxation of various xenophobic ideas in people will be subtle but continuous. Attunement to this civilization from time to time over the next few years may yield to people deeper insight and awareness into their own processes of accepting all of the various faces of humanity.

Al Nasl (Gamma Sagittarii)

[m 2.97] **125 light years, very close companion star. Al Nasl is the closest visible star to the center of our galaxy.**

Al Nasl is acting as a focalizer or refractor of the energies that originate in the center of the galaxy. Many of the previous comments concerning Nunki and M13 with regards to representation of the center of the galaxy are also true for this star. The primary capacities that pour from the center of the galaxy are the energies of the angelic realms, creative forces, and the energies to manifest other galaxies. These energies are modulated by this star to some extent. But of course when an individual is utilizing the light from that area or gazing into that area, one will not only be receiving the energy of this star but of the background energies from the center of the galaxy.

In addition there is a powerful capacity to perceive and understand the truth as it is manifested through this star. This can allow individuals deeper insight into their own patterns and help them to release such patterns where they stand in the way. Al Nasl can also be very helpful at a physical level with speech impediments. This binary will also assist an individual who has difficulty in public speaking, or who has a poor ability to hold one's own in an argument or a debate. Al Nasl will help an individual understand their own position. This deeper awareness will usually make it easier to listen carefully and actively to someone else. In addition to these capacities, there can be a tendency in some individuals to speak truth in ways that hurt, and this can be somewhat reduced by the use of this star.

Blue Tourmaline gem elixir and Al Nasl elixir can be a powerful combination for throat problems where there is a difficulty in communication, particularly around some issues difficult to speak about for an individual. There may also be some assistance with throat cancer, larynx cancer, and lung cancer where it is related to issues one has difficulty speaking about.

Epsilon Leonis

[m 2.99] **Yellow giant, 340 light years.**

This star can enhance appropriate emotional expression. This star will assist psychological techniques for emotional clearing and for the enhancement of communication with other people. There is deeper awareness of how other people see you. At a higher level there is an enhanced ability to create an emotional bond with someone else that can lead to a telepathic communication as if then you are able to see yourself emotionally through the other person's awareness. With the eyes of the heart, you see the other person more clearly; and through his or her heart, you see yourself.

At a higher spiritual level, this star can attune individuals to a sense of empowerment that can be shared amongst all people using the energy of the heart. This is not so much an energy of unconditional love as it is an energy of communication that recognizes the common bond that all people share. This bond is an energy of contact, telepathic communication, and emotional awareness which can allow individuals to lead others in effortless ways, do this in a way in which such leadership is easily accepted, and in which other people are empowered by the work itself. This star is therefore recommended for individuals who seek such higher capacity in leadership and assisting others.

The civilization associated with this place has no particular interest in Earth at this time. However they have recognized over the eons the necessity of communication and attunement to other civilizations and other vibrations. In a sort of move of sympathy and compassion, they allow some of their energies to assist people on Earth with their own intuitive development and deeper awareness of many capacities within themselves. So what you will recognize from these beings is a sense of empowerment that they send towards you—effortless, loving, and with no specific direction.

This star can also assist individuals who wish to attune to some of the techniques of non-attachment, which are occasionally suggested by various spiritual teachers from India, although the westerner Jack Schwartz also speaks of such matters. This business of non-attachment can be enhanced somewhat by the use of this star. Non-attachment is an interesting term, it belies what is really going on, which is the empowerment of processes within the physical being that go far beyond that individual's usual capacities. This star will enhance the sense of such empowerment, deeper communication with higher-self energies, the awareness of the true self, and the interaction with others, all of which are usually required for the development of true non-attachment.

Dabih (Beta Capricorni)

[m 3.06] **Binary, 130 light years.**

This double star is fairly stable and produces a continuous shadowing effect as the revolutions take place. This shadowing effect causes individuals who attune to this energy to have different aspects of their being brought into form. For the main thrust of this, the more spiritual side of life is made available. But then as there is this shadowing, there is a sense within of putting this into form and making it practical, real, or understandable. This gives way again to the spiritual. This is a cycle that has been understood for many hundreds of thousands of years by the three civilizations that have existed on planets that encircle this binary. These beings have projected different forms of this to Earth over time.

What is occurring now is a projection into consciousness of the practical idea of putting spiritual ideas into form. This is preventing most individuals who would seek spiritual awareness from separating from the world. The way of the householder has replaced the way of the ascetic monk as a primary mode of learning and understanding in the world. This star would be good for those individuals who feel a tendency from their past-life interactions or their current life situation to want to get away from the world to develop themselves spiritually or who seek to isolate themselves to meditate or find places of peace and calm. They may begin to understand the great benefits of utilizing others in the world to mirror their own spiritual development. They may also begin to recognize that there is an inner part of their spiritual awareness that can come out in the world in a practical way and be applied appropriately. This is truly a principle of integration. As a result there will be for most people with knee difficulties some improvement. There is a natural tendency for people to accumulate difficulties in the knees when there is difficulty with this integrating of the spiritual and the practical.

For many people there will be an improved sense of belonging. This can be a feeling of being able to merge with society and do what is needed, but then being able to easily detach when necessary. This can gradually lead to the development of a clearer internal frame of reference. Combined with Fomalhaut there can be a reduction of the hold of addictions on people because of these underlying principles.

Dabih will stimulate the minor chakras in the feet, particularly the point Kidney 1. The fifth ray is made clearer and stronger for most individuals.

Sadalsud (Beta Aquarii)

[m 3.07] **Yellow supergiant, 1,100 light years.**

This star can create peacefulness in the interaction amongst all women and men by increasing the female part of their understanding. The male mind can open to its female aspects and in this way relate better to women. Women are able to better express and share the very nature of what it means to be a woman. This star may eventually be able to work with these energies in large groups; for now it is simply in small groups or in one to one relationships.

This star can also strengthen the physical aspects that relate to the female aspects of one's own development. For men this can create a better balance of hormones in the physical body and reduce the tendency towards male pattern baldness or other difficulties related directly to an imbalance of male and female energies. In women, the use of this star can reduce hair grown on the body by gradually creating a physical balance that yields a better ability to visualize the female principle coming into form at the physical level.

At the highest spiritual level the individual may be able to accept both male and female halves and be able to communicate this very easily. People may understand that the truth of this intermingling of the sexes is to be the evolution of a new way in which the soul's energy is better expressed, as the soul is not personality based in either male or female concepts or precepts.

There is some strengthening of the root chakra and of the genital region. A conduit of energy can open between the root chakra and the throat chakra. This can be empowering or helpful for individuals wishing to express various aspects of their own understanding of male and female.

Zeta Tauri

[m 3.07] **Blue-white shell star, 940 light years.**

The civilizations associated with Zeta Tauri have departed the star. Much of this star's life-giving properties towards such civilizations have ended. The star has the capacity to project some of the past awareness and memories of these civilizations. Much of the life associated with this star is slated to change in a few thousand years, a relatively short time in the life of a star, as it enters into a new period of change and transformation itself.

The signature of this star has to do with individuals who are willing to break out of past patterns and come forward in ways in which they have not been seen before. This star may be able to make available important energies that are held deep within a person and not acknowledged in his or her life. Sometimes what blocks this is a particular emotion. When this is a very personal emotion that is not easily dealt with in a group context, therapeutic context, or in the context of assistance or inspiration by other people, this star can be especially helpful to make this emotion clearer for you. If it is your pain that you cannot face, this star can make it easier to face the pain, release it, understand its source, and forgive yourself. Thus, this star can be helpful in encouraging individuals to look at their own sources, work with these levels of inner energy, and make decisions about how this is to be shared or revealed in the world. Some individuals who are imbalanced with regards to extraversion or introversion will find this star is helpful for creating a higher balance of these qualities.

Scat (Delta Aquarii)

[m 3.28] **White, 83 light years.**

Scat can encourage people in their tasks when they need to

delegate or to form a group interaction that goes on to delegate others. This is especially helpful in research projects or the teaching profession where interaction of clear hierarchy is an important part of the work, an example being graduate studies under the auspices of various professors. Such academic relationships are often made a little more acceptable to the people involved by work with this star. There is also an ability here to accept and release some of the naturally occurring difficulties that are produced by bureaucracies. The ability to pierce through the veils created by bureaucracies is improved. Thus individuals seeking to move through red tape to accomplish their goals appropriately may have insight and understand how the group interaction has created such red tape. At a higher spiritual level there can be a telepathic concordance between the people involved in such research projects or between those in a bureaucracy who would seem to oppose you and your progress. Various new ideas may come forth from this in the dream state.

At the highest spiritual level there is a shedding of fear. This can produce a deep willingness to become one. This is only for those who are already open to such ideas, perhaps having studied Buddhism, Taoism, or other forms of understanding this oneness amongst people.

This star can stimulate the heart chakra and the minor chakras in the palms. The astral body is soothed. For those who seek to use the astral body for deeper communication in the dream state, a natural strengthening and more healthful sleep will take place.

Fourth and Fifth Magnitude Stars in the Zodiac

Giedi (Alpha Capricorni)

[m 3.56] An optical double, two unrelated stars. Giedi 1: [m 4.55] supergiant, 1,100 light years.
Giedi 2: [m 3.56] giant, 116 light years.

These stars have an excellent capacity to work together for people. At the closer star there has been the development of a civilization over a long period of time quite aware of Earth and the things that people on Earth are trying to learn together. Beings from this civilization have been guides and helpers for many of the spirit guides of philosophers, scientists, politicians, and certain inventors who have sought to bring some of their energy into form to make things available, practical, and real for others.

Much of the energy that pours into Earth to allow this as space travel and as an overshadowing of spirit guides is through the action of the further of the two stars. Beings on that star have ascended through multiple dimensional levels and reside in the center of their star. They are able to project their energy as a generally nurturing and sustaining influence both through the closer star, and directly into Earth. This creates a natural acceleration of such energies.

These stars can bring two qualities at once. There can be an underlying sense of who they are and that they can go forward. The other quality is a willingness to express oneself and to bring this into form. This combination can be useful for expressing something when there are blocks against it or where one might have some fears about this. There will be an acceleration of the willingness to share what is being spoken. As the speaking takes place there can be a feeling that one is doing the right thing, that it is time to speak of such matters, and that these things need to be said. This can easily flip into the reverse where you listen carefully and although what is said is critical or judgmental or difficult to hear under normal circumstances, you are able to hear it and extract from it the part that allows you to care for yourself and understand things a little better.

This willingness to express things in the world has been of tremendous influence in bringing ideas into form. But this willingness to allow this as a nurturing has allowed individuals to take this to its logical conclusion. For things to be really practical there needs to be more than just the expression of it or more than just the completion of an idea. There has to be the willingness to go forward with this and to allow it to be nurturing to the one who invents it or shares the idea.

Petra (Eta Piscium)

[m 3.72] **Yellow giant, 450 light years.**

This star can increase the ability to remember past lives and release sadness associated with them. This can also be of great benefit with individuals who are suffering from a tendency towards addictive principles. The unconscious aspects from past lives can be made much clearer, and a willingness to accept these truths and to move forward with them can be enhanced. Sometimes with this star there can be a clearer memory of past lives of negative impact, and an ability to feel these things and release them. This tends to be fairly self-correcting so we see no danger in individuals using this star bringing into action some of these pastlife negative memories. There is a deep awareness within this civilization of the addictive principles. Some of these have been learned from the bursts of energy that pour from Fomalhaut. This is another star that combines well with Fomalhaut. However here the tendency is more towards the awareness of patterns that may extend over many past lives.

There can also be a deeper awareness in the person of being fully aware and able to be. This star is excellent for individuals suffering from insomnia or people who have trouble concentrating because they are juggling many things in their minds at once. This star can create deeper peace by releasing the feeling that struggle is necessary to create change.

There can also be some increased sensitivity in the physical body, and this sensitivity will nourish the person rather than harm them or distract them. This star can assist individuals who experience increased sensitivity when they are fatigued. They may be able to release some of the fear to such sensitivity. This can increase their ability to let go of the things that stand in the way from the past such as toxic materials, toxic ideas, or even toxic memories.

This civilization has worked for a long time with balance of the things that are negative and those that are positive. This energy can be very helpful for individuals seeking such balance deeply in themselves and who are willing to accept their own responsibility in looking into such matters.

At the highest spiritual level there is some deeper awareness of how transition can change not just oneself but how it will affect other people. Often you have come into this life to deliberately release those past lives where addictions were an important part. To do so means transition, transformation, and a deep change that can indeed be exposed to others. Your ability to bring into clearer form your awareness of this and your own acceptance of who you are can often benefit others.

There is some stimulation of the astral body here and it is wise here that this star be used when one is feeling ready for such things as astral travel or dreams of the past. It is also helpful to use this elixir before meditating when it is quite bright outside so that the astral body remains rooted in the current location.

There is some enhancement of absorption of carbohydrates utilized by the physical body as the basic building blocks for muscles and adenosine triphosphate.

El Tarf (Beta Cancri)

[m 3.76] Yellow-orange giant, 217 light years.

The use of this star can create better communication in a family. This may especially help individuals attempting to communicate with those between 13 and 20 years old. This can also help these young people communicate with the rest of the family from their own perspective.

One of the reasons for some of the general alignment symbolically with the constellation Cancer is because of the influence of the civilization associated with El Tarf. Long ago in the early development of this civilization, these beings lived only the equivalent of 20 years in Earth time. These beings developed a deep appreciation of life and an awareness of how things change. They are one of the few civilizations that have worked with reincarnation. They began to recognize the power of reincarnation very early in their development. When people use this star there can be a deeper attunement to one's past lives, but it will tend to be in the phase of life associated with the teenage years.

These beings understood that their greatest strides forward came towards the end of their lives. Though they attempted to extend this lifetime, they were unsuccessful for a long period of time. This gave rise to new sciences and an understanding of biology. Eventually they broke through this impasse and ended all reincarnational cycles. When they did so a great burst of energy was found which they utilized for the seeding of other civilizations and the helping of many others. They are able to rekindle this burst of energy and pour it into the Earth region every week or so. This energy will be very helpful for those who are struggling to understand their own maturing into adulthood. This civilization came into adulthood permanently and is able to broadcast this as a sense of peacefulness and security.

At a higher spiritual level, some of the natural telepathic abilities are made clearer and more conscious by the use of this star. Some children in the time near puberty may become involved with such phenomena as poltergeists or various unconscious forms of mind over matter. These psychic abilities may be made much clearer, more conscious, and more available if that is appropriate for the person. These may become unavailable if it is important that they turn away from such abilities.

At the highest spiritual level, this star can create a natural bridging between parents and children in the times of meditation.

This star can stimulate the sixth chakra and the minor chakras in the elbows and the arms. There can be an opening of love in which all the chakras interact and interrelate with the heart chakra.

Nashira (Gamma Capricorni)

[m 3.8] **Yellow-white, 109 light years.**

Some of the effects from this star are a bit subtle and muted because the civilization there has had some direct influence over Earth in the past and of late has pulled back and reduced some of this influence. At the present time this star is good to utilize when you wish to have the ability to see the whole picture of what is happening on Earth: politically, economically, and geophysically. This is very difficult to create with only the mental body. The emotional body alone is also insufficient. This star will encourage in a gentle way the combination of faculties needed for this larger perspective.

Gamma Piscium

[m 3.85] **Yellow giant, 125 light years.**

With use of this star there is a deeper awareness of the ability to create bridges. These abilities may already be in place, but are often unconscious. This inner sensitivity is made clearer, and the ability to bridge telepathically to other people will become clearer for most people. There may also be an enhanced ability to bridge to other places, other star systems, and other beings.

In their ascent to other dimensional levels, the civilization associated with this star decided to root themselves all that much more deeply into their own planetary system. Space travel is unnecessary for them because they can allow communication by this ability to create bridges. Thus the bridging between people, as influenced and enhanced by what these beings project out into the universe, is not telepathy in the truest sense. It is not a way of the mind coming into form as you connect to someone else, but rather a bridging of souls. With such a bridging there can often be a deep sense of past memories, an awareness of possibilities for the future, and an awareness of interaction on many levels.

We would strongly recommend this star be utilized by individuals who are seeking deeper commitment in their relationship. This elixir can be helpful taken just before such as marriage or just before contemplating such things, as well as just before deliberately seeking to conceive a child or deliberately making large and important changes relating to commitment in a relationship. This bridging can be a little more conscious for people. It will also allow some of the worries and blocks to dissipate and more of the inner strength between the people to be made available. Where individuals may have different ideas about how to proceed, this can be helpful in finding a way of compromise or acceptance of the best way to move ahead.

This star can stimulate the nadis (energy channels) in the fingertips. Individuals who are already involved in bodywork may find that it is a useful elixir to use with their clients. This elixir can be added to massage oil as long as there are no toxic materials and the oil is kept in a light tight bottle.

Mesarthim (Gamma Arietis)

[m 3.9] **Double star, one of which is a magnetic spectrum variable with a strong presence of silicon. 148 light years.**

These two stars are in close communication. Although some people using Mesarthim will notice a left/right balancing and male/female balancing, the primary characteristic of this binary is the understanding of the process of creation and destruction. Destructive principles must generally be employed before constructive principles can be welcomed—a clearing away must occur before building can take place. In finding the correct balance between these many individuals will have deeper insight into their own personal karma and what they have come here to learn. Thus, an enlightened karmic perspective is enhanced by the use of Mesarthim. There is also a deeper strengthening of courage within the individual to make their own path through the debris or chaff of life into the place of creativity and power. When there is a clear imbalance between these destructive and constructive forces, these stars will help bring a person into a better sense of balance and a deeper awareness of how this balance can be created in their lives.

Many times individuals who seek to create do so on top of foundations that lack the correct features for the construction of that which they wish. Therefore the organizations, projects, or tasks which they are attempting to create fail because they lack the correct foundation. The use of Mesarthim can be helpful at an early stage in organizations or when working with energies relating to construction. This can be in the creative stage when one is simply brainstorming; it can be in the stage when one is writing out ideas or circulating proposals; or it can be at the stage when one is simply bringing an idea into form with other people. But the key here is that Mesarthim assists the individual who is strongly oriented towards the creative urge to recognize what must be moved away first so they can proceed with the creativity.

Mesarthim will also assist individuals who find themselves in destructive patterns over and over. However most individuals who are so strongly involved in such destructive patterns that they are really creating a lot of difficulty in the world will not be attracted to such as vibrational remedies. So for such individuals it may be possible as a friend to recommend this elixir, or to take your friend out at night and point out the star.

Mesarthim can assist with technological understanding of the vacuum. People who are coming to a deeper awareness of this may be strongly influenced by this star to come to understand it in themselves. This is a way in which the absence of much actually creates a very powerful potential, and this is a concept now recognized in physics as the zero-point energy. Individuals who wish to learn of such, for instance by studying the writings or papers of Hal Putoff or other individuals involved in such work, would do well to enhance their understanding and mental capacity in working with such by the use of Mesarthim because it embodies some of these underlying principles.

The combination of Mesarthim and Pollux elixirs can heal emotional aspects of the will by creating a balance within the individual. There is a certain synergism between these two stars, as the will must relate to some aspects of physical existence. The cells will also be strengthened with this combination.

Alrisha (Alpha Piscium)

[m 3.96] Binary with strong metallic lines, 130 light years.

A balancing of this time of transition into Aquarius can take place for many people with use of this star. People who may be afraid of technology or who do not understand how to work with it will find that some benefits result in utilizing this star as many of these technological things are metallic. There can be an awareness of how change takes place for people in a way that becomes much more comfortable and much more assimilable, particularly for older individuals. Individuals who fear the future will find a soothing response from this star.

At a higher level, the purpose of this star is to unite generations where individuals have a common goal of the awareness of the possibilities ahead for humanity. There cannot be any delineations by saying certain ages should take it or not take it. This elixir is for any individuals who feel left out of the activities of a younger generation, and who see these activities as very different from their own principles. For anyone who utilizes this elixir there can be a deeper awareness of humanity's progress and a willingness to let go of old patterns that don't fit.

At the highest spiritual level this star can create an awareness of how people interact with each other and let patterns stand in the way of their deep feelings and their real forms of communication. This is an addictive process where people have been willing to accept the old ways rather than seeing the new ones. Where there is an age difference, a gender gap, or a big difference culturally, this bridging to shift this pattern and perceive more of the truth through someone else's perspective will be strengthened.

This star may improve the utilization of choline in the brain. This elixir may also assist in Alzheimer's disease.

Asellus Australis (Delta Cancri)

[m 4.17] White giant, 217 light years.

This star is one of those strongly affected by the burst of energy from El Tarf and has developed forms of communication in its own way. Some of these energies have been extended through the many kingdoms of life and the civilizations that have existed on the third, sixth, and seventh planets revolving around this star. This has allowed these civilizations much interaction with animals. Some of this energy may be available as a way of helping people. People might use this star along with El Tarf for communication between teenagers and animals. Some way of relating to teenagers through animals has been discovered as a powerful means of creating better bonds and a better sense of self. If you can command a 1200 pound horse, you may have a little more trust in your own self; and this is certainly true for any teenager.

Communication with the animal kingdoms and to a lesser extent the plant kingdom will be enhanced for most people. This will especially apply to mammals and their ability to share their needs with people. This will work best with animals in the wild or animals who are non-domesticated; a bit less so with domesticated animals relied upon for food and their own abilities to interact with people such as sheep, pigs, cows, and horses; and even less influence with domesticated animals such as cats and dogs. The closer to the wild state, the more the influence. People may become aware in a very personal way how the family of humanity can combine with the family of animals. They may recognize their own ability to communicate with animals and trust it a little bit more.

The third chakra is strengthened and the eyesight is somewhat improved. The ability to correctly utilize Vitamin A in the eyes is improved slightly. This elixir can balance the production of antihistamines and may assist individuals suffering from allergies to animals.

Acubens (Alpha Cancri)

[m 4.27] **Yellow-white, 99 light years.**

In this star you see some of the more generalized tendencies of Cancer that have a symbolic effect on people such as a willingness to express and work out family issues, to understand the nature of the home, and to create this more clearly. There is some general influence here with better understanding of the subtle forces involved in creating a home, such as through the Chinese art of geomancy known as feng shui. Individuals studying feng shui may do well with this elixir; though working with any of the stars from the constellation of Cancer will assist here to some extent.

Asellus Borealis (Gamma Cancri)

[m 4.73] White, 233 light years.

With use of this star there is some strengthening in the dream state of the ability to perceive your direction with your family and how things are to work themselves out together. The ability to nurture others is strengthened. This star can assist individuals in professions that rely heavily on such nurturing abilities, such as nursing, child care, or teaching younger children. These professions can be stressful and there may be a tendency to overstep one's own boundaries of what is healthful and useful. The difference between empathy and sympathy for people you feel such nurturing toward can be made a little clearer as a result. Continued use of this star elixir for anyone involved in such professions that rely on nurturing would be valuable. Family relationships will not be stressed as much by the drain of energy into the work situation. A common example of this is the nurse who helps her patients to the maximum but is unable to assist her own children and family to the degree that is needed. A better balancing of this will usually take place with the use of this star.

This star can strengthen the minor chakras found in the shoulders and chest, and create some enhancement of energy in and out of the energy centers adjacent to the heart found in the pericardium. The endocardium is also strengthened. The ability to utilize niacin, thiamine, and Vitamin B6 are enhanced slightly.

CHAPTER 8
★★★★★★★★☆

The Brightest Stars in the Far Southern Hemisphere

Canopus (Alpha Carinae)

[m -0.72] **Yellow-white supergiant, 230 light years.**

Canopus is a powerful radiator of the light of generosity. This light can encourage the interchange of loving acceptance and service between beings. Beings that have been associated with this star system have helped to seed Earth and many other systems in a direct attempt to create this sense of sharing amongst beings. It is not a sharing based upon barter or a willingness to receive, but one based on awareness of the principle of giving itself. Individuals who are seeking to create communities based on service would benefit by using this star. There is also a sense of gentleness and power combined that can be the roots of healing for those individuals who have been given too much responsibility or too much power and have used it to make mistakes in which others were harmed.

Canopus has participated in the sharing of information, technologies, and awareness between civilizations. This star can connect beings to past and present technologies from this galaxy for various forms of healing, space travel, interdimensional shift, and the appropriate creation or destruction of matter. Some of these energies and technologies may become more available to people as they become aware of this star.

Rigil Kentauris (Alpha Centauri)

[m -0.27] Yellow, 4.3 light years, similar to the Sun, and a white dwarf companion.

This is the traditional beacon for individuals on Earth who contemplate space travel. This star system has several planets. One of these has been utilized for retransmitting the vibrations to Earth which can create awakening. The other planets have been utilized by many different beings. This star system is currently in a state of some unrest. These planets are being used as a jumping-off point for beings from both the Draco and Zeta Reticulli systems, as well as Arcturus, Aldebaran, and by the Pleiadeans.

It is useful to reognize that space travel is inherent in your own capacity. Use of this star can be helpful for those individuals seeking to engage in space travel by conscious meditation or in a guided visualization. This awareness is important for those who seek to understand how to know and commune with the other beings that may make themselves apparent to the people of Earth in the future. These beings from many different places commingle in this one approximate astronomical area. It is an important bridge between the Earth and various other vibrations. Most of the energies received from the star will be beneficial. There can be an attunement to how space travel will be done in the future and an awareness of how this can be done with greatest harmony.

There is a planet in this binary system which radiates a sense of questioning. It is approximately equal to the Pleistocene era in Earth's own evolution. This is a planet filled with greenery. Experiments based on chlorophyll are being done by many of these beings, in the hopes that this planet might be utilized for development of intelligent life. Should there be massive destruction or cataclysm on Earth, this is the planet that will most likely be chosen as the place to take Earth people to.

Most of the planets are in a stage of non-development, a period of gentleness and awakening. Habitation of these planets by these other beings we have mentioned is only a temporary imposition, not likely to last more than a few hundred years. It is yet to be seen what will happen with this star, so when using this star elixir there is also the sense of increased potential in some individuals. It is as if they know anything they might choose to do can be done, so they can welcome many opportunities and venture in many different directions.

Achernar (Alpha Eridani)

[m 0.5] blue-white subgiant, 73 light years.

This star has the capacity to increase the mental functioning needed for the ability to work in multiple dimensional understanding. This can be helpful for some individuals who not only seek to understand the relationship of mathematics and science to the everyday world, but who also have a concept of the limitations of science at the current time. This can be helpful to individuals who have blockages to science and mathematics in themselves, assisting them to bridge these blocks. This star is helpful for individuals who seek to teach science and math to individuals of an artistic bent.

There is some cross-over of left and right brain activity. But most of the energy given to the individual using this star is from the transformation of higher energies: first into light, then into thought, and then into conscious awareness. A deeper ability to consciously reach specific brain wave states is likely to result from using this elixir. This can be helpful for individuals working with biofeedback to achieve particular states.

Hadar (Beta Centauri)

[m 0.6] Binary: blue-white giant and subgiant, 190 light years.

These two stars have an oscillatory pattern that projects an energy of aetheric shift into the universe. Most of these energies have to do with the subtle level characteristics of powerful intergalactic elements, and not with the civilizations that have worked with this star system. This aetheric shift is utilized by some individuals in other systems when they are learning to shift dimensions. Use of this star can significantly increase some people's ability to shift dimensional forms easily.

Use of this star can give a person a greater ability to perceive the fourth dimensional level. This can assist telepathy, various psychic abilities, and the ability to correctly perceive and work with patterns. People may be able to accept the interpenetration of time and space. It can also assist them to shift their own vibrations, so they can better absorb such nourishing and sustaining energies as light, sound, and energies of vibrational interaction between themselves and others. Use of this star can assist individuals who wish to understand such matters as walking through walls or moving objects in ways that have not been done before. This star can be very helpful for creating the significant vibrational shift that allows them to transcend the physical qualities of the universe into some of the fourth dimensional qualities. This is because Hadar is broadcasting a vibration which is continually shifting between the third and fourth dimension.

As viewed from Earth, there is a black hole in approximately linear juxtaposition very far behind this star system. This is modulating the energy of Hadar that comes to Earth. The energy that is received on Earth is not clear enough to create the transition that is needed. It is one of the things affecting the transformation on the Earth. The Mayans understood that there would be a vibrational shift on Earth centered around 2012 or so. One cause of this will be that the energies of this star system will no longer be affected by this black hole. The energies of Hadar will be more available for people who wish to make this transition from the third to the fourth dimensions.

This star assists individuals who are using love to change their vibrational characteristics. The energies of love are so important and so necessary for human evolution. In the past, some beings have used this vibrational shift without love. By humanity remaining in the influence of these energies confused and changed by this black hole combined with the energies that are available from the nature of life on Earth, it was hoped that people would come to understand that love was an important characteristic for creating this interdimensional shift. To make this shift, most individuals will need the energies of caring, compassion, association with their fellow men and women, trust, and free will. All of these things together combine to make a loving vibration, which is directed and guided by humanity. When this star adds an accelerated ability to shift into fourth dimensional awareness, this loving vibration of humanity will be magnified and transformed from the third to the fourth dimension.

Acrux (Alpha Crucis)

[m 0.9] **Blue-white double, subgiants, one is rapidly rotating, 220 light years.**

Acrux can create an awareness of how Christ's light can coordinate with other people. The being acting as the highest Christ and the energies associated with that being have utilized these stars as a repository and a place for replenishment and strengthening.

This star has an ability to reverse chronic illnesses in some individuals. In dealing with chronic disturbances, certain patterns often need to be understood better, and these patterns can be seen more clearly with the influence of this star. The rapidly spinning star can shift the spin within an individual. These spins take place at subtle levels in the permanent atom and in the most important core nerves in the brain. This star can shift the orientation of these spins in many beneficial ways.

The civilization associated with Acrux has allowed a sense of fair play to come into humanity's existence. This is an influence over games of skill. Some of the seeding ideas for the game of chess came from this civilization. These things may not seem to be directly related. But there is a relationship in the sense that this spin, this Christ energy, and this awareness of fair play is focused on humanity's current phase of evolution. Humanity has reached the point of perfect attunement for receiving the beneficial energies from this place and this civilization. For some individuals working with games, the sense of competitiveness and inner strength can become an awareness of love, compassion, forgiving, seeing it all as a game, and being able to have some perspective on it. This is also helpful in dealing with many conditions of seeming hopelessness or difficulty on Earth.

Becrux (Beta Crucis)

[m1.3] **Blue-white giant, 500 light years.**

This star can create a sense of a deeper forgiveness. There can be a deeper attunement to food substances. This star can be used to ease the transition to a vegetarian diet. This can also be applied to animals when they wish to make a transformation to a vegetarian diet. Becrux can strengthen the gall bladder and kidney meridians, which will allow individuals to correctly utilize some of the most nourishing aspects of foods. A sense of purpose may be imparted by feeling this willingness to be nourished by one's life and by the food. This may create an opening to the heart's highest aspects, and a willingness to receive Christ's light in its own way. It is as if food is made that much more pure and clear by this starlight. The preservation of foods may be possible when utilizing this elixir.

Gacrux (Gamma Crucis)

[m 1.6] **Red giant, 220 light years.**

Use of this star can accelerate movement through life

changes. This can assist when one has to deal with significant phases of growth in relationships. This could be a parent dealing with a child who is going through certain rather difficult stages of early growth. It could be a time of learning difficult new things at one's job. It could be a temporary period of anxiety between the partners in a relationship. When this star is utilized to influence these changes in relationships, individuals will experience a gradual lessening of tension, a gradual awakening of energies between them, and find a love of relationship itself. Gacrux elixir will combine well with Venus.

But more deeply and importantly, for the individuals involved, this star can provide insight into the relationship, which can let them ease off on some of the struggle. Sometimes this will catapult the individuals into releasing emotions, only to discover a deeper love between them.

Beings from this star system influenced some of the animals on Earth, in particular horses and dolphins. Part of this was from genetics, and part from a general love. The sense of love and companionship that is felt between such animals and man remains as a living legacy of some of these energies. Individuals who are attuning to these animals may also wish to utilize this star for deeper insight, understanding, and awareness of the viewpoint of the horse or the dolphin.

Avior (Epsilon Carinae)

[m 1.7] **Binary, 330 light years.**

This star can accelerate healing processes that are electrical in nature. Holding the hands about half an inch away from the physical body and moving them slowly over the body can create a tingling sensation in many individuals. This interaction between the hand of one and the skin of the other creates a gentle electrical field of primarily DC potential. Avior will increase this healing electrical field, primarily with the practitioner but also to some extent with the client. Healing energies at high vibrational levels can be utilized to modulate this DC potential. This is equivalent to a capacitor, which is able to create a DC field across its plates, and also transmit AC by modulating or changing those DC potentials. This occurs from person to person in a healing modality that can best be absorbed through the skin. This healing interaction can assist such skin problems as eczema, acne, or the release of oils or toxic substances through the skin.

Individuals running their hands over their own body can create some of this electrical effect. The polarity will generally be stronger when one person is male and the other female. This polarity effect can also be created between two individuals of the same sex if one of them is homosexual. This is because the sexual orientation of an individual will effect the electrical relationship between that person and the one they are working with. Therefore these ways of healing can be just as strong with such individuals.

This star can also enhance the ability to dislodge negative thought forms. A person who has worked with this star will easily be able to use this energy to sweep away another person's negative thought forms.

Beings from this star have developed techniques of space travel based on high voltage devices which surround their ships with a powerful field. This electrical field can cause problems in all sorts of electrical devices on Earth. Because of this, their visits to Earth have been reduced, and they are exploring new forms of transportation not so damaging to the electronic devices on Earth that are so sensitive to high voltage. Nicola Tesla was influenced by ideas from this civilization. He was able to receive some direct guidance and assistance with some of his work towards the later part of his life.

Miaplacidus (Beta Carinae)

[m 1.8] **White giant, 86 light years.**

This star has the concentrated ability to assist individuals to open the third eye, and connect it with love. This bridging is a potential which will gradually come into focus over the next 300 years. Individuals who align with this star only once in this life will find that in the next life this combination of the heart and third eye will be easier to work with. At that time there will be more attention on the ability to create form, wisdom, and understanding that combines beautifully with love, compassion, and receiving of the true essence of another person. In preparation for their next lifetime or the one after, the use of this star now will be of tremendous benefit for bringing the person into alignment with this potential. One would need to use it only once for most of its effects. If individuals do make it into the Southern Hemisphere, it is strongly recommended they seek out this star and gaze at it for 10 or 15 minutes at least once in this lifetime. This is one of those stars whose particular prominence will not be felt directly for some time yet.

At this time this star is creating a general overshadowing influence for a greater awareness of what is sometimes termed heart-mind in Japanese psychology. To some extent, this star is influencing individuals born in Japan. In their journeys to the Southern Hemisphere, people from Japan working with this star may find that their ability to communicate with other Japanese is enhanced.

Atria (Alpha Trianguli Australis)

[m 1.9] Orange giant, 55 light years.

The combination of the physical, mental, and spiritual aspects is a lifelong lesson for people. The ability to see this lesson in yourself and others will be enhanced by this star. This gives not just perspective and understanding, but an awareness of how you fit into the world and into relationships with other people. It can lead you into an understanding on many levels of the very nature of life on Earth and in the universe.

This star is projecting important transformational ideas into space at regular intervals of approximately 65 years. A wave of these is due to come to Earth in May 1997. This will be a time of scientific transformation, new ideas in philosophy, and new energies of healing and learning. These ideas may be felt as individual inspirations that will not be immediately known on Earth. Those using this star now may be inspired with ideas for combining these many aspects. But in May 1997, many individuals using the star will discover that insight and ideas flow much more powerfully.

Consciousness and choice about how to work with creative ideas may be felt by people using this star. This star is useful for anyone involved in creativity, wishing to teach this to others, or who depend upon it for their own livelihood. They can understand this process and even it out so there are not so many peaks and valleys, but a steady flow of creativity in one's life.

The beings associated with this star have focused for millennia on balance, in the fourth to fifth dimensional sense. This balance is primarily focused upon a geometric structure. It could be termed a dodecahedron if it was translated into the three dimensional universe. It is an inverted series of vortices that interpenetrate the third, the fourth, and the fifth dimensions. In working with this structure as an important symbol for their civilization, these beings have developed a means of space travel that allows them instantaneous transfer from one place to another. They have deliberately kept Earth off limits to such modes of transportation. This is open to change in the future. As individuals learn about the transformation from the third to the fourth dimension, it is possible that humans will naturally rediscover this in their own way. Some of the technological ideas to be presented to Earth in this time ahead may concern these ways of transportation.

Al Suhail (Gamma Velorum)

[m 1.9] **Blue giant, 500 light years, Wolf-Rayet star (carbon type); one of the hottest stars: doubly ionized helium, highly ionized carbon, oxygen, nitrogen, and silicon.**

A powerful vibration of consciousness pours out from this star. There were races of beings existing millions of years ago who embarked on a pattern of learning by traditional organic means, utilizing brains, carbon-based substances, bodies, and the rest of which you are familiar. They were able to create a dynamic support structure in their solar system in which they could multiply to a tremendous extent.

The problem of overpopulation eventually yielded a new solution. Because their lifespan was so much longer, the oneness sought amongst these beings was known in ways much deeper than are available to beings on Earth. They developed their culture to become deeply interconnected and aware of each other. They saw that, by fusing the organic materials at the same time they allowed a transition into another dimensional reality, they would provide themselves with a significant quantum leap in their own conscious evolution, a tremendous difference in their awareness of themselves. At the appointed time, coordinated with all of the highest galactic and astronomical observations (which relate to what you might term cosmic astrology), all of these beings pitched themselves into the center of their star all at once.

Because of the tremendous population of these beings, this created a great shift in the star: it was snuffed out. But this was desired. As this took place, there was a tremendous shift in their consciousness as all of these beings evolved together. And when this occurred a tremendous light burst forth, a light of creativity and awareness. It was an energy that would eventually make its way far out into space to form a galaxy of great light, knowingness, and understanding. The star's light was transformed. The organic matter itself coordinated with the tremendous evolution in consciousness so that this star would radiate much more powerfully than before. It was actually as if the star were burning on consciousness. The substances in the star interact in a whole new fashion, so that consciousness itself is the basis of the light from this star.

They left behind a residue in this that is broadcasting a message to other beings about what is possible. From the choices these organic beings made, it was undestood that the possibilities were infinite. One race can create a tremendous energy which can form a galaxy and can cause tremendous change. This star is radiating an energy saying that all possibilities are available.

These energies were very important in humanity's early evolution. Often the earliest Lemurians drew upon their meditation and awareness of the stars. In the Southern Hemisphere such beings were able to absorb and work with the light from this particular place for the idea of what was possible. At such time the star was much brighter than it is now, though it is likely that it will move through a very slow cycle, where in a few hundred years it will become bright again. This will be because this star is observing and working with some aspects of humanity's own evolution.

What the civilization left behind for Al Suhail to broadcast is an energy that can be tremendously encouraging and empowering. This can be helpful for those individuals who need this great empowerment to create new opportunities in their life. This can lead to an ability to see the higher context, a greater application of universal law, and a deeper awareness of what they can actually achieve. Thus Al Suhail can also be helpful in times of loss or grief. Al Suhail will have its greatest effects where the highest and best is being drawn out of people.

Delta Velorum

[m 1.9] White binary, 75 light years.

This star can have a gentle influence on individuals who wish to understand the resistance which occurs when there is movement between two boundary conditions. This can be extremely helpful in sports, particularly sports involving movement through water. To a lesser extent, this star will assist individuals working to understand aerodynamics—how the resistance of air can be used in the design of automobiles, airplanes, and rockets.

In the future this star will be of great importance for humanity. Working with this star will create a sense of peace so that movement from one place to another will become a little bit easier.

Peacock (Alpha Pavonis)

[m 2.1] **Blue-white binary, 300 light years.**

This star influences change in the DNA for beings from a number of other stars. People on Earth can use this star for constructive visualization of change in the physical bodies of animals, plants, and people. It is helpful for those who wish to visualize such change occurring before it actually happens in the physical body. Over time, this star will influence the changes that come through creative visualization at the family level, and later at the societal levels. This star will influence the ability of individuals to create these societal changes in physical form. Under the influence of this star, there can be deeper assimilation of iron and vitamin B6 in the physical body.

Al Na'ir (Alpha Gruis)

[m 2.16] **Blue-white, 91 light years.**

This star can enhance the wave phenomena which is formed by creative endeavors which involve movement. A wave phenomena is created by the resonance between the audience and the person doing this work, or between the performers who do it together. This is in relationship to stage acting, music, and other forms of live performance. These activities are enhanced by creating a coupling phenomena. The oneness that is shared can allow self-consciousness or fear to dissipate from the performers. The audience will be able to make a transference into the minds and hearts of the characters, receive the information being shared, or more easily perceive the essence or source of the music itself.

When this wave phenomena is coupled with the visualization of a vortex of energy connecting the audience and the performers, this may create a powerful energy that can remain over long periods of time. Because of this, there is some benefit in this star elixir being applied to the environment by spraying it into the air or putting a few drops on the floor or furniture. This would create a gradual enhancement for the physical location, destroying certain lingering negative thought-forms, and enhancing this vortex so that the energy of creativity would linger in such a place longer and more powerfully.

At times in the past, the civilization associated with this star has created what would be received and understood on Earth as vibratory works of art, which encompass all the forms of art as you know them. This pulsation of creative energy is transmitted throughout a number of galaxies. You would perceive this art form as a combination of visual aspects, sound, sensation, telepathic communication, and sense of smell—all at once. Thus, the star elixir is of some benefit to those seeking creativity in various forms.

At the highest spiritual level, the star, particularly when one meditates on it, can give one insight into the resonance phenomena that is created during a performance between oneself and certain higher aspects, particularly the link between the God-self and the highest self, or even the link between God and the soul. In this way, an individual may understand why he or she is working with the performance arts or other artistic endeavors, and more easily learn the lessons from these experiences at a deep level. There is no direct enhancement of creative ability. It is not as if the ideas already there will come through better. It is more that you will understand the process of performance, become in resonance with those you do it with, and in this way understand yourself better.

Lambda Velorum

[m 2.2] **Orange, 220 light years.**

Individuals working with this star can receive aspects of wisdom that are on the border between what is within humanity's capacity, and what is just outside it. Many extraterrestrial civilizations have worked with various forms of mental energy. These mental energies must impart more than knowledge, because knowledge is insufficient for the guiding of any civilization. Wisdom must be incorporated to create an awareness of God and of spiritual levels. The beings associated with this star have worked with these energies for millennia. They have understood wisdom by directly studying and working with it. They have realized that working with wisdom involves free will and patience. They have also recognized that this entire process could be speeded up by additional amounts of love, which is one reason why they make this energy available to humanity so powerfully now.

This energy can assist people who are integrating the knowledge they have, putting it into form, and coming to understand it in themselves at a deep level. The influence of this star can also benefit individuals who wish times of deep quiet, in which their knowledge transforms to wisdom, not at a conscious level, but at a superconscious level where the knowledge is simply awakened into patterns of light, energy, or love. This star can also be helpful for individuals seeking to make the transition from old, knowledge-based systems, into systems in which wisdom is necessary to guide others.

You could say that the civilization associated with this star has "been around." They have understood patience so deeply that their perception of it is beyond the grasp of humans. It is like the patience that pours into a crystal. Therefore there can be some benefit in applying the elixir to a crystal that has been cleared and then programmed. This will allow the crystal to be more in a state of harmony and resonance with the person who has programmed it. Crystals are inherently very patient in the way they present their information and understanding. Sometimes this transformation of knowledge into wisdom can help to project such an energy between a person and a crystal. This process will work best with crystals that are easy to program such as the various forms of quartz, rutilated quartz in particular.

Many of the primitive peoples in the Southern Hemisphere and other places on Earth have had opportunities to work with this star by gazing at it. Certain amounts of wisdom were imparted to tribal elders in the past. They would use this star to impart a vision to the restless young members of their tribes. The elders would work with this star to translate this energy to imbue the younger ones with a feeling of patience, quiet, and calm. The younger ones might not recognize the wisdom, or perceive it in a way that they could make real, but they had the feeling of it, the sense of it, and that was often enough.

Beta Gruis

[m 2.25] **Red-orange giant, 270 light years, slight variability.**

This star projects an energy that can transform acts of aggression or violence into a willingness to accept peace.

The energy produced from this star can counteract the rather negative influence of the planet Mars. This star can project an energy that allows people deeper insight into aggression, allowing people a deep change in themselves, and will help them find a peaceful place deep within. Sometimes this inner peace is necessary to alleviate sleep disorders. This star can assist individuals who experience in their consciousness as they are falling asleep visions of violence or harm to others, or those who have feelings of shame as if they are doing personal violence to themselves at an emotional level.

This star has the capacity to affect the way in which violence is created in the natural kingdoms. The most highly evolved of the various carnivorous animal species on Earth may be able to receive from people a new thought form of a deeper, peaceful coexistence. This thought form would then be projected into the shared soul of each of these carnivorous animal species. This will change these animals. Over a period of several generations this will create genetic changes that will make such violent action unnecessary. The natural evolution of the planet is in this direction. What is not understood is that this transition can be created very simply by people with the use of thought forms. Individuals have experimented with this already with dogs and cats, and have found that vegetarian natures can be created in such animals. This star may even eventually influence carnivorous plants. This can even be extended more deeply into life, all the way to the level of coexistence with viruses and bacterial microorganisms. The full understanding of these microorganisms is not available to human beings at this time, though it is hoped that this star may influence this process at some point in humanity's future.

The beings who have lived on the second planet from this sun have understood these processes of violence and peace very deeply. Their planet has an eccentric orbit, quite far away from the sun. This slow orbit has allowed them long periods of time to prepare for the increase in temperature that occurs when the planet is closest to their star. It was found that the heat could be transmuted and stored so that many of the energy systems of the planet could be run from this energy. However, the variability of the star also perturbed the planet's orbit and many of these storage systems failed. These beings learned to cooperate just to survive. Eventually, this led to a way in which the perturbations of the star and the orbit were both used to broadcast what they had learned.

Aspidiske (Iota Carina)

[m 2.25] Yellow supergiant, 750 light years.

This star is located near an artificially created portal that allows rapid transport from one place to another. Approximately 187,000 years ago, this was a relatively small black hole. This is no longer the case, as it has been transformed. The transformation sucked the light (in the X-ray and ultraviolet regions of the spectrum) that was available from the black hole, drawing it back in. The civilization worked with it to create an artificial portal very similar to some of the natural portals that are found throughout the galaxy. This was accomplished through an awareness of tremendous speed and movement. This enhancement of speed and communication was the result of the way time and space were folded in the star's vicinity, and then changed by the beings who worked with them. These beings used their energies to create a stable energy vortex between their home star and this created portal. In exchange, it is as if the star asked that the energy of this communication and transportation be shared somehow with the worlds that needed to understand higher functioning.

It is likely to speed up the capacities of all aspects of brain function in various beings. Whether or not they have brains in the organic, carbon-based system as you do, it is the idea of consciousness that matters. As a result of this energy, interconnectivity will be enhanced in the brain cells of individuals using this elixir. The 24% concentration of Ginkgo Biloba can also be helpful for brain enhancement. When this star elixir is combined with Ginko Biloba, the substances in the herb will be better taken into the physical body.

It is possible that the starlight from Aspidiske will increase computer function. At first, such computer function will be discovered as having capacity for self-learning capabilities in massively parallel systems. This is a new use for this elixir, but is in line with the understanding of primitive systems evolving into greater consciousness through rapidity of thought. Increasing the rapidity of thought is very similar to the way in which computer programming takes place successfully, so computer programmers will likely benefit greatly by this elixir.

Menkent (Theta Centauri)

[m 2.26] Orange giant, 56 light years.

The civilization there has radiated messages of hope to many other civilizations.

Now, there is a natural encouragement by this star to other stars, to focus a little of their attention on receiving the messages of love, understanding, and awakening that are projected from the Earth. When you wish to send a message out into space, to send an idea to someone far away, or a telepathic communication in which you are not hoping for an answer as much as intending that the message will be deeply received in someone else, use this star. It would be like a message in a bottle, sent outward, with an energy of hope, understanding, and joy created within your own consciousness. This visualization may be helpful when using the energy of this star. When the bottle is received in the right hands, it almost explodes with the energy of powerful joyousness you have sent.

The beings associated with this star do not have a specific purpose in their interaction with the Earth. They simply are an encouraging factor to the other civilizations that do see such promise and assistance available from Earth.

Zeta Puppis

[m 2.27] **Blue supergiant, 2,400 light years. One of the most luminous stars in our galaxy.**

This star is a powerful nexus, trading point, and a communication and storage facility for many civilizations in this galaxy. It is also able to transmute energies deep within its core that project outward as a network that connects many other stars. A natural resonance is created between the Sun and this star, and the energies of other galaxies sometimes pour into the Sun through this resonant link. In this way the Sun is able to feel more at home in the universe, and more able to understand its purpose.

Using the elixir or meditating on the star will help people feel more at home, more aware of their interrelationships to society, and ultimately to their entire Earth and ecosystem. This star can be especially helpful for individuals who seek to learn about other civilizations on Earth, people perhaps forgotten by time and the constant progress of mechanized western civilization. This can include primitive peoples, individuals in unusual religious sects, or individuals whose understanding and thinking has been passed over by the mainstream.

The star itself is a powerful one to meditate on when working in realms of astral travel. There can be benefit in meditating on the star before falling asleep. Although the star elixir may have some of the same capabilities, it is only effective if one can at least be aware of where the star is before one falls asleep. Then, imagine yourself journeying to this star as you drop off to sleep. As a nexus point, this star can be used to go to other galaxies, to the center of the Milky Way galaxy, or to various star systems you may be aware of but cannot contact easily in the astral travelling state.

Gamma Centauri

[m 2.28] **2 nearly identical white giants, 110 light years.**

These stars can make it easier to create a balanced polarity in the physical body. The Earth's magnetic field is what establishes and maintains a balance of polarity in people. Individuals who have experiences in journeying off planet Earth, such as astronauts, cosmonauts, and so on may benefit from this elixir if they have difficulty in re-attuning to the Earth. Individuals who find shifting their polarities to create a polarity balance in themselves difficult to achieve, may benefit by the star elixir or meditating on the star.

Here especially there can be a strengthened balancing between left and right sides of the body. Though this seems to relate to the brain function, it is the overall energy connection between aetheric and physical body that is significantly enhanced. Other therapies will also be assisted by this elixir, such as polarity balancing, utilizing of magnets on the feet, methods of massage that naturally bring the left/right balance into greater form, as well as methods of physical movement, such as t'ai chi, chi gung, or other forms that deliberately seek to balance left and right.

Some individuals may have a deeper awareness that the soul is beyond gender, and connection to the beyond-gender state of all people will be found with this star. This can be very helpful for men or women who have resentments or difficulty in regards to the opposite sex, or with the societal suppression of the buried side of their gender natures. The buried side of the female might be the the way in which expressive purpose is not acknowledged or worked with sufficiently. Resentments, energies trapped in the unconscious, and various denied energies may come also to the surface in a way that is helpful, beneficial, and insightful for people using this star. This can improve relationships where deep attitudes of resentment are based on the mere fact that the person in the relationship is a man or a woman, and thus represents all men or all women. These resentments can be released, and a feeling of greater closeness created. The overall pictures of gender will be made more available, conscious, and easy to deal with. This can be helpful for individuals who seek to create certain forms of societal change in regards to these matters.

Ankaa (Alpha Pheonix)

[m 2.39] Orange giant, 93 light years.

This star strengthens the ability to survive, and has an ability to create a powerful change in the physical body. Stuck kundalini energies can be released with this star's influence. Individuals involved in bodybuilding, or processes that greatly tax physical strength will also benefit. The influence of this star can bring energy to the surface, so that this energy is more easily understood and channeled into various physical activities. At a higher spiritual level, there is a sense of purpose. The purpose itself may not be defined, but there is the sense that such a purpose is really there. It will become clearer to people that the transformative states individuals are moving through collectively do not interfere with their own personal transformations.

The use of this star can bring clearer vision, both internal and external. This means both clearer energy for the eyes, as well as clearer strength at an internal level for the creative visualization process. There may be benefit in adding this elixir to various eyebright (euphrasia) mixtures to benefit the physical eyes, either in eyedrops, or taken internally. The influence of this star will help the body to accept this herb's energies.

The civilization associated with this place has been transmitting a simple idea to Earth for many centuries: "You have the ability to change. You may move ahead as you choose. Do not be afraid." This provides a sense of empowerment which can lead to transformation.

CHAPTER 9

★★★★★★★★★

Deep Space Objects

SECTION 1: GALAXIES

Andromeda Galaxy

Nearest spiral galaxy, 2 million light years away.

This galaxy's influence enhances the ability to understand the long-term purpose of humanity's evolution. This includes the ability to recall one's past lives as different life forms, such as dinosaurs. In some cases these remembered lives are extraterrestrial.

The energy of Andromeda primarily relates to the understanding of the early incarnations of humanity as the Himalaya mountains. These lives are important aspects of one's being. The Himalayas exist as the Rock of Gibralter for understanding the influence of mountains on human awareness. The Himalayas have existed in so many different ways for very long periods of time, and indeed were the first little pokings up out of the sea of hills and eventually islands and mountains in the early phases of Earth history before humanity ever appeared in any form and animal life was unknown. In this way they are the first to bring some sense of separation or difference between the land and the sea, and were the ideal repository of consciousness, though in a primitive form, of humanity as a group. Their great height at the current time is related to humanity's need to understand its own history. For people to understand themselves, they must look with symbolism and awakening in their consciousness to who they have been. Because of their height, people will be atracted to them and learn about them, and in this way learn about themselves. It is partly to do with Elohim influence that these mountains symbolize so much spiritually for humanity.

Working with the energy of Andromeda can also enhance the ability to perceive the overall picture. The understanding that an individual may fit into a larger cosmic scheme is brought into greater awareness and consciousness. This can help one to feel a part of the cosmos and a part of universal thought and understanding.

Andromeda's energy has the ability to bring the physical body into a state of balance and alignment with oneself and others, which may result in an internal state of balance. Awareness of the love principle contributing to the soul's evolution, and ultimately to God's evolution, is brought into consciousness with this energy. This results in most of the things we have mentioned above.

The energy of this galaxy can be attuned to directly by individuals when they are not involved in the thinking process, as when they are receiving this light through dance, music, through meditation, movement, or even sleep.

A number of individuals from Earth have had a chance to visit Andromeda. In some ways Andromeda is a mirror of many aspects of the Milky Way Galaxy. Andromeda's central energy in some ways is a mate to the energy located in the center of the Milky Way Galaxy. Because of this innate affiliation, certain capacities that might be ascribed to yin and yang exist at a galactic level. Many individuals who have had difficulty in understanding what it is to exist on Earth or even in other civilizations associated with the Milky Way have had direct past-life experiences within the Andromeda system. Individuals who have some attunement to Andromeda, because they have seen a picture of it and feel moved by it or perhaps have gazed upon it in the heavens at night, will do well with this elixir and may find past memories of long journeys to other places, other times, and other people.

Much schooling of individuals to some understanding of what it means to be involved in the Milky Way system has taken place in the Andromeda system. But very few individuals are natives of that place, but rather they have come here to experience Earth and retain some memories of Andromeda because at times, when the going was very tough here, they could have a shifted perspective, a new way of working with things by a brief visit or a fairly brief lifetime somewhere in the Andromeda system. Because it is a system just like the Milky Way, there are many capacities there, many things that go on, many planets, and several of these mirror Earth's development on some levels. But there is in general with such planets some inability to welcome great radical change, as change as such has been destructive enough in that place. So therefore it is a little different; it is somewhat associated with periods of relative inactivity, peace, a feeling within oneself of a gathering rather than of an expression.

Globular Cluster M13 in Hercules

1,000,000 stars, 25,000 light years.
Ancient globular cluster.

At this time the energy of the Hercules Cluster is the same as that of the center of the Milky Way Galaxy. This energy can help people develop a deeper awareness of the love and assistance of the angelic realms, as well as the governing principles of those beings who have directly influenced the formation of the Earth. The ability to receive God's wisdom is strengthened. Although this can be done through channeled states, it is more in the realm of religious experience. The death experience, and those difficulties associated with it, are eased for the dying person as well the loved ones who are around that one. The birth process is somewhat enhanced, particularly when it is clear that an entity of an evolved spiritual nature is being born. The child and the mother, the father, and their loved ones can benefit by meditating on the Hercules Cluster or the elixir from this cluster.

Awareness of one's reincarnational cycle across many lifetimes is enhanced and strengthened. An ability to understand humanity's relationship as a whole to other civilizations of extraterrestrial nature will also be more available, but it will be from the point of view of the common good, the common purpose, the common alignment between these civilizations and humanity.

Those channeling the beings known as the Elohim may notice a deeper attunement to these beings with the use of this globular cluster. It will also be easier to release the energies from such channeling. The Elohim are the beings of powerful creativity for this spiral arm of the galaxy. They might be understood as a perfect balance or a blend imagined as a three dimensional yin/yang or a magnificent moving of male and female in a dance. Yet these energies are those of powerful creativity which have been utilized to bring into form many solar systems, including the Earth itself. As these energies have an influence and a power associated with high degrees of intelligence and cohesive activity, they are the primary arm of God seeking to know God's self. As a result they will influence much of that which they have created only to a limited extent, allowing their creation to find its own way. Yet when individuals would attune to the energy of such creativity, its essential informative capacities are available. These are usually stepped down through levels of intelligence of other guides who can access the information in various capacities. Thus it is usually more beneficial for individuals to work with the information through beings such as ourselves or our guides before they would access the Elohim directly.

The Large Magellanic Cloud (in Dorado)

190,000 light years. A companion to the Milky Way Galaxy, it may have a spiral structure.

As often takes place when dealing with these larger objects, there is such a preponderance of information available it is a little hard to sift through and pull out what is most appropriate. Imagine for a moment that you were far away from the Milky Way, and you wished to know what the message of the Milky Way was. So many of the stars that we have discussed combine their various properties, and the energy made available is then very confusing. But there can be an overall picture that emerges.

With the Large Magellanic Cloud, this combination of energies involves a sense of movement into other realms or other dimensions. There can be a sense of spaciness or difficulty with focusing of one's energy when using this elixir. This is a small side effect. Individuals who are seeking less practicality, a deeper sense of visions and spiritual awakenings, or ideas that might not have to be rooted, will benefit from using this elixir. Creative inspiration and ideas for works of art will also be encouraged. Individuals who tend to spaciness or difficulty in concentrating would not do well to use this elixir.

A deep sense of shift can be felt. The powerful vibrational aspects of a majority of the civilizations in this place are working in relation to higher dimensional transformations. The majority of these are transformations between the ninth, tenth, and eleventh dimensions. Such energies sometimes have certain capacities of love associated with them that individuals on Earth might find helpful and encouraging in their own seeking of the vibrations of love.

However the tendency here is more towards an awareness of the creative states necessary for the creation of stars, and the powerful vibrational energies that can shift galaxies, universes, and awareness on many levels. This is therefore an energy of some depth, and can have long-lasting effects. We see that it might be well to have the various tools of good grounding also available, such as Hematite or Neon elixir. These grounding tools can be a bit helpful for individuals on the Earth, should they use the elixir of the Large Magellanic Cloud and not be able to recreate their more practical experiences easily.

There are many people who read about these matters of creativity, visualization, spirituality, and so on, who wish to have direct experience of this. But they find that their practical natures stand in the way, that they are very grounded in comparison to the other "spacy New Agers" they come in contact with. Using this elixir or meditating on this place would be strongly recommended for such individuals.

There is a long-standing relationship between the Milky Way Galaxy and the Large Magellanic Cloud. These beings are working in concert with those in the Milky Way Galaxy for the development of the understanding and the perception of vibrational awareness and vibrational shift for evolutionary purposes. However, the direct experiences of such beings are not always available, because the entire galaxy itself is so different than that of the Milky Way. There is such a different way of doing things in the Cloud. But sometimes these energies communicate back and forth. The centers of the galaxies are sometimes in a state of resonant communication, which imparts knowledge and wisdom throughout many of those civilizations in both galaxies which can be aware of these higher energies.

The Small Magellanic Cloud (in Tucana)

An irregular shaped galaxy, it is relatively dust-free, implying fewer old stars. It is connected to the Large Magellanic Cloud by a stream of matter.

A grand coordinated experiment amongst a number of civilizations in the Large Magellanic Cloud have created this galaxy by using their own forces at a relatively high interdimensional vibrational rate, using their own loving energy, and their own awareness of the creative process. This is still an ongoing process, an experiment that they are coming to understand. Therefore individuals on Earth who wish to be involved in rather massive creative projects may do well to use the elixir, or to meditate on the Small Magellanic Cloud.

Using this elixir, individuals can feel a greater patience and strength of purpose in such large endeavors, and have an easier time coordinating with other people in the development of this energy, but it must be used judiciously. We do not suggest a group of beings who are involved in the same project would use this together under most circumstances, unless they are capable of such free thinking that they can bring through ideas rapid-fire, as in an associative consciousness processes, rather than through hard work and logical processes. Individuals who are contemplating such a large project who wish new ideas from entirely different realms not previously considered possible, who feel this creative urge, and can also put up with some of the spaciness that may be felt, will do well to use the elixir or meditate on this place. Otherwise some of the similar energies associated with the Greater Magellanic structure would apply.

Pinwheel Galaxy (M33 in Trangulum)

2.4 million light years, one of our local group of galaxies.

Here are a number of civilizations that will eventually have impact with Earth, though less so perhaps than Andromeda and those found in your galaxy. These beings understand the function of love in ways in which this has been allowed to form a blending of dimensional energies. This may come into form for people a bit later in this century when individuals recognize that in order to shift consciousness and maintain a feeling of compassion for others, a dimensional shift is also necessary. This is a way in which they are feeling very much a part of the Earth and the changes around them and not caught up in emotions such as fear or a feeling of great sacrifice. These things are a little hard to explain at the current time when your society is not under very much stress. As stress increases you will see that the influence of M33 will be of some benefit as the beings there have in their various ways learned of many aspects of this.

By their own evolution, some of these beings have developed technologies that are not machine based but primarily thought form, thought energy, energy at aetheric level, and inert gas based. Such technologies may eventually be available to people and will be seen as having many beneficial effects. Individuals who wish to attune to new techniques in telepathy, hands-on healing, awareness of various psychic matters that have beneficial impact on other people and which are enhanced when feelings of love are present, will generally do well when working with M33 in any form. The elixir itself may be found to increase capacity of heart to heart connection amongst some individuals and may be valuable amongst research groups or individuals who seek to work together when they are seeking to find new methods of communication, and new methods of working together. Those things that were not very helpful in the past might suddenly turn around for them and become more helpful.

Emissaries from M33 have come frequently to Earth in the past and have left some connections. Some individuals may find that taking the elixir before sleeping assists them greatly in astral travel experience, particularly when they have some general idea of the physical location of this galaxy and some general idea as to its shape. As they fall asleep and imagine this, they may be drawn easily to an experience in an entirely different time and place with a very different feeling about matter, energy, and other matters. A large number of individuals in this place have a completely different biological base than you experience here on Earth. This is due to the presence of silicon/hydrogen systems; the hydrogen is primarily found in ammonia-based compounds and ammonia itself. Because of this it is unlikely that a direct visit by the beings in this place to you will be possible. But in an altered-state form, such as an aetheric-level form, this is certainly conceivable. Some of the beings in these various planets in M33 have developed highly evolved forms of moral-based, ethical-based civilizations that will certainly have some beneficial impact on people who are contemplating such things as new forms of government, new ways of service, and new ways in which individuals can co-create communities and work together.

Whirlpool Galaxy (M51 in Boötes)

35 million light years. A quite beautiful open spiral, with a small satellite galaxy attached to one of the spiral arms.

Most of the beings in the civilization associated with M51 are currently in the satellite companion. The message from them to Earth is clear and simple: to take care in the proper use of technology; to have a deep awareness of the balance of nature in working with technology; and to understand that self-governing systems tend to create energies beneficial for humanity, but must be stewarded and cared for.

A destruction at the very center of this whirlpool has created what might be observed as pulsars, neutron stars, and similar phenomena. This powerful energy is the result of technological intervention in natural processes by the various civilizations that worked together many thousands of years ago, to the point where the deeper understanding of working appropriately with such energies became an important part of many of the civilizations in this place. This understanding has formed itself as this inner message to be translated and transmitted to humans.

At a much higher spiritual level, this energy and message breaks apart into many sub-avenues. Individuals with attractions to various technological forms or devices, various ways of understanding the Earth and the correct way to work with self-governing systems, and individuals with their own specific needs, may find that using this elixir will bring more understanding of these characteristics into their lives in ways they had not foreseen. This will allow their specializations to take them further and further into deeper understanding. Using the elixir on a regular basis (usually in a yearly cycle), will help people become aware of the big picture. It can then take them farther than they had thought possible into their specialization, but later bring them back so they do not lose sight of the larger issues involved.

Spiral Galaxy M81 in Ursa Major

There is in general in this place an accelerated view of consciousness phenomena. This does not transfer very well to most individuals. People who find they are on a very fast track, working beyond their capacities at high stress levels, may do well with a homeopathic version of this galaxy, perhaps at the 30X potency. These individuals may find that they can relax a little more easily, perhaps gain some perspective, and then go back to work at the appropriate time.

Some of the individuals associated with this galaxy understand a great deal about consciousness in ways that are difficult to transfer easily to humans. Over a period of time, attunement to this galaxy may provide new insights to those who are interested in understanding the process of consciousness. Individuals who use the elixir of M81 may notice for themselves a gradual change in how they access and work with large amounts of information, as if it increases their information capacity. This is a little different than some of the mental capacities that are perhaps increased by the use of Procyon. Rather it is a way in which the individual is able to work with many kinds of information and somehow see how they fit together a little bit better.

Spiral Galaxy M83 on the Hydra/Centaurus border

8 million light years. Has a high number of supernovas.

The energy of this galaxy can increase the ability of people to change their vibrations and translocate. This is a psychic gift which is not easily developed here because of the aetheric density on Earth. Individuals who are coming to understand the ways in which they can change their location from one place to another by apporting will benefit from this galactic elixir. Some who might utilize this energy might be those who have felt themselves obsessed with the idea of translocation for most of their lives or those who see translocation as a possible solution to the pollution from internal combustion engines. The proper use of apportation will be available during the next few hundred years for humanity's technological development, and will be guided to some extent by some of the emissaries from this galaxy.

Several accidents have occurred in the past in the development of apportation in this galaxy. In order to witness certain interesting galactic phenomena, the simultaneous translocation of large numbers of beings into areas too close to the powerful gravitational fields of various stars occurred. A supernova was triggered in some of the stars. These energies are available for you to see now. Although this happened millions of years ago, it is still causing some difficulty in this galaxy.

There are many different ways in which individuals may come to know the energies from this galaxy. Though the inhabitants of this galaxy are of many forms and have come to understand many things, they have also discovered that direct interaction with humanity would likely not be of great benefit. Thus, they simply present some ideas that can fill some gaps, and assist with humanity's evolution now, meanwhile filtering most of the other attributes from their civilization out of humanity's understanding.

The Sombrero Galaxy (M104 in Virgo)

Viewed edge-on from Earth; there is a dust band across the galaxy's center.

This galaxy represents the powerful ability of many civilizations to coordinate their energies for the creation of multidimensional realities as well as other universes. Use of the elixir made from this galaxy will benefit the understanding of the creative process in general. The true nature of creativity may emerge for people, giving a much deeper understanding.

The ability to draw from many sources in working with creative impulses is very important. Individuals who have blockages from childhood or past lives against certain things they need to learn in order to put their creative ideas into action will benefit from this energy. By bringing the various blockages to these learning capacities into their consciousness, various difficulties will be eased, and their ability to learn these new things will be strengthened. One example would be the artist who needs some math in order to create a particular sculpture or idea in form, but has a block to learning math. The creative source behind his or her work will be enhanced by utilizing this elixir. Then the math may even become something joyful for the artist as he or she begins to learn it.

Emissaries to Earth from Sombrero Galaxy have made their presence known at various times in the past. It is likely that some beings from this part of the universe will come to Earth again soon. This energy will stimulate the natural creativity of people on Earth in a more cosmic way. There will also be some additional energies to draw people together for creative solutions to Earth's problems. A great outpouring of art and understanding will result from a visit from these beings.

One of these visits occurred in the year 1963 to balance some of the difficulties associated with the assassination of President Kennedy. Later there was a powerful outpouring of creative energies. It was as if the Earth called to those who could help to bring this balancing energy in. So emissaries from this galaxy made their creative energies more available to people. This made a difference. Not only was there some balancing of the sadness and difficulty associated with this event, but there was a powerful outpouring of music, art, and new forms of understanding. This continued until approximately 1969 on Earth.

SECTION II: OPEN STAR CLUSTERS

Open Star Cluster M35 in Gemini

2,800 light years. Five hundred stars.

The stars of this cluster are able to interchange and exchange energies, information, and understanding on very powerful and God-like levels which are beyond human comprehension. This exchange of energy and information yields a powerful creation of new ideas and new ways of creating matter and universes. Sometimes this cluster acts as a source point of inspiration in the universe for those who wish to delve into such high orders of creativity and those who wish to understand God. This cluster will benefit those working with the combination of various organized religions in themselves, those working with peak experiences, and those working with spiritual understanding in a very personal way. Most individuals will simply be encouraged to align with higher spiritual principles at a very deep level because of the strong energy and intelligence of the stars themselves.

This elixir will greatly benefit people who are attracted to various meditative disciplines or working with particular spiritual practices, but who are finding themselves unable to do this work easily. Perhaps they are finding it takes a great deal of discipline and do not have very much joy in it. They will thus have the feeling of the great joy inside which would have been theirs if they were able to complete their chosen spiritual disciplines. They may be able to actually be one with those disciplines. In return, their contribution to this joy by writing or sharing about this joy may affect other people. They may have a new vision of their own understanding of this spiritual awakening.

Praesepe Cluster (M44) in Cancer

530 light years. One of the nearest clusters, over 350 stars.

The primary energy here is in assisting individuals to fully accept loss, to release it, and to understand the great gifts of what one does not need any longer. This is a way of surrender and trust in the God-force. At a deeper level, most people will discover that a sense of what is needed created in them, as well as a sense of what is not needed. Priorities can shift to spiritual levels, so the true God-nature of the priorities emerge.

The Double Star Cluster H and Chi Persei

7,500 light years. Mostly young supergiants.

This was once a single structure, and it sought to divide itself for the creation and encouragement of creative forces at the seventh and eighth dimensional levels. This has led to a deliberate polarization and separation in the creation of an equivalent to the male principle (yang) developing alongside the female principle (yin). At the higher dimensional levels this is not related to sex, sexuality, reproduction, or any urges for communication as you perceive it. It is a deliberate focus on specialization over millennia.

As a result of such separation there may be a resonant phenomena available to people when they meditate on the cluster or use the elixir. This resonant phenomena can make one aware of the deliberate separation that one has allowed in coming into incarnation in the first place. This can give some remembrance of past lives and some awareness of the time before birth in which contracts were made with individuals one is yet to meet. It enhances remembrance of the strong survival energies poured into the child. Such things were accessed by consciousness, and made more available in the time before birth, and awareness of such an energy will be increased by the use of the elixir or by meditating on this pair. There will also be a renewed awareness of deliberately allowing separation from the highest self to allow individualization in form. This is the deeper symbolism of the separation of the yin and yang principles.

There is in this pair of clusters a certain resonant energy which you would understand as love. It has many other capacities and components. This elixir can benefit those individuals who seek to love God. They can understand just what that means by recognizing gratefulness, compassion, praise, and the highest aspects of the separation between God and a human being. This is a spiritual phenomena. What occurs during such separation is a deliberate willingness not only to invoke the negative aspects that involve emotion, karmic balancing, and other matters, but the positive aspects as well. By separating from God one can develop a deep appreciation of the one self that is united with God by being able to see it and know it better.

These clusters deliberately separated so that they would come to know each other, and eventually they will be drawn together again. This rather slow phenomena (in cosmological terms) is one that can impart a sense of patience to people who wish to return to God. For individuals contemplating suicide, sometimes a deeper awareness of the deliberate nature of such a separation can take place, which will release some of the energies associated with such suicides. Negative influences associated with Scorpio or Pisces may be eased.

Open Star Cluster M37 in Auriga

4,500 light years, at least 400 stars.

This star cluster has developed certain characteristics of deep intercommunication between the suns. As a result it has the ability to transfer energy into other star systems, and has been valuable for this in times past. Certain planets have used this energy when moving through periods of important growth. When the civilizations on these planets and their stars became unstable, M37 helped create such stabilization. The characteristic energy of this cluster is one of underlying stability. It may be found helpful to create general psychic stability, evenness of functioning, an ability to endure difficult situations for longer periods, and in releasing stress. More importantly, it may be found helpful in conditions relating to psychosis or mental or emotional instability.

This elixir may be especially helpful in children in the ages from 7 to 11 or 13 years old. In this period of time just before puberty, the human child forms many of the important ideals, attitudes, beliefs, and other structures that will be carried into adulthood. Many of these beliefs and attitudes relate to the very nature of stability of form, and the ability of people to intercommunicate and trust each other and themselves.

There are several worlds in this cluster that have developed rather interesting and unusual forms of transportation. This cluster may benefit those people involved in forms of transportation on Earth who are attempting to go faster or with greater accuracy. Some individuals have a fear of moving quickly. They may have trouble driving a car or being able to fly in an airplane. This must be distinguished from a fear of heights or large open spaces, which sometimes is that which leads to a fear of flying. If it is the high speeds or instability that gives the sense of being unsafe in such modes of transportation, then using this cluster would be very helpful.

Part of this is because three of the civilizations from M37 developed unusual techniques of transportation which could give a continuing acceleration with a feeling of great steadiness. This mode of transportation is one that may be available in the future through technology, though it is as yet undetermined whether this will be the primary mode made available to people on Earth or not.

There are a few other stars in this cluster with some interesting characteristics, but most of these energies tend to blend with the main idea of this greater stability, and a greater ability to endure difficulties.

Open Star Cluster M7 in Scorpio

800 light years. Old stars.

There is a relationship here to the early periods of civilizations on Earth. By using this star cluster in any form, anyone looking into such civilizations will be enlightened and given good ideas as to places to look deeper to understand the ways of other civilizations. This includes the Mayan, Aztec, many Native American civilizations, the early Egyptian phase, and even those who would look into early periods of the seedings in Atlantis, Lemuria, and ancient Greece.

This star cluster accumulates data. There is a matrix within it of a computer-like nature, similar to a number of others located all over the galaxies, as well as the one located in the Earth's Sun. All of these tend to accumulate information of various characteristics. Within this cluster is an ability to understand large patterns; this may also be made more available to people when they use the elixir or meditate on this cluster. These patterns relate generally to the main thrust of an entire civilization.

Western Civilization has the ability to coordinate art and science, as well as the ability to deliberately explore and reach all facets of other civilizations in an attempt to assimilate and incorporate them. At this time the ability to assimilate information from other cultures will be enhanced for most people when they use this star cluster. There will be some ability to appreciate other cultures in a historical sense. Some individuals who feel certain prejudices towards other cultures may find this eased a bit by using this elixir or meditating on this place.

At the highest spiritual level, there will also be an attunement to the purpose of one's past-life incarnations in other cultures. This can help one to understand what one is to incorporate and integrate in this life. Individuals who have some difficulty in the left knee may find that when they have tried other things, even physical therapy or various forms of naturopathic healing, and these have not been successful, that using this star cluster will be very helpful. This is because the integrating principle is often represented by the knees, and the left knee symbolizes the drawing in of this information.

This matrix or star cluster does much more and has many interesting capacities. People who are born under the sign Scorpio and have an interest in healing may do well to use this star cluster to attune them to data that can be extracted intuitively in working with other people. This is the ability to attune to this cluster and use it as a computer.

Open Star Cluster M6 in Scorpio

1,300–2,000 light years.

Most of the energies that would have been available from this cluster have transferred to M7. The remaining energies are those of interdimensional contact. This relates more towards guides, masters, and beings who are familiarizing themselves with the interdimensional transferring principles relating to the sixth, seventh, eighth, and ninth dimensions.

This cluster will assist individuals who wish to attune better through channeling or by reading channeled works or other things shared about beings who work at higher dimensional levels. There can be deeper attunement to these higher vibrational forces as they are worked with by such beings. At the subtler levels, beings who are involved in the sixth, seventh, and eighth dimensional transfer use the equivalent of the elixir of this star cluster for their own attunement. By using this cluster you become similarly matched in vibration.

Open Star Cluster M52 in Cassiopeia

3,000 light years. At least 120 bright stars, many young stars.

This star cluster came into maximum power and awareness during the time of the change from dinosaur life forms into early primate and mammalian life forms just before the dawn of Lemurian civilization. It was a powerful influence in allowing that transfer. Individuals who wish for a deeper understanding or awareness of humanity's relationship to primates would do well to use this star cluster.

In this star cluster there is also a deep awareness of the potential within humanity to rebirth itself by forming new areas of life extension, new areas of deeper harmony, and new communities. In its elixir form it can be shared amongst individuals seeking to create conscious communities, communities of deeper interaction, and it will give additional benefits. This is especially true if there is any interaction with animals in these communities, even more so if such animals are related to primates. There is some affiliation to other intelligent animal kingdoms such as to the dolphins, the dogs and cats, and to a slightly lesser extent to other marine mammals and whales, and then to the rest of the animal kingdoms.

Another use for this cluster is for those involved in projects where they must draw from old ideas and put them into new forms. This could involve using long-buried information from the past that may have been altered or changed through history or through the interpretations of those who have written about that information. They will then have a new appreciation of the underlying ideas, bring these into clearer form, and discard the parts that were added or misinterpreted.

In using this cluster, especially in its elixir form, there will be some releasing of tension in the shoulder region and a general strengthening of the spine.

Open Star Clusters M23 in Sagittarius

4,500 light years. 120 stars.

This cluster can enhance the digestive process and other functions of the body to support brain function. A use of this elixir over long periods of time will help to build up memory function and improve the ability of the brain to correctly interpret information on multisensory levels. It can combine well with the 24% concentration Ginkgo Biloba herbal solutions or tablets, so that brain function is enhanced over time with repeated usage.

The cluster itself is a powerful computer which has the ability to link to brain function in many people. Indeed, this cluster has made itself available in the record-keeping of sentient life forms for a long time. Many of these life forms have been able to transfer information into and out of the cluster, where the information resides as a sort of backup memory. This information is available to people over time as they attune to the cluster. This cluster can assist many individuals who seek information about their fairly recent past lives. It can enhance their ability to use this information in order to chart their future courses in life. This can help them to appropriately and correctly choose a job function or new relationships.

There is also some strengthening of the ability to perceive three-dimensionally. Individuals with certain forms of eye difficulties will find this cluster helpful, particularly in those cases where there is little difficulty in the eyes themselves, but there is difficulty at the brain level in coordinating the two pictures presented by the eyes for depth perception.

Open Star Clusters M11 in Scutum

5,600 light years. 600 stars. A dense, compact, spherical shape.

In using this cluster, a deepening of the ability within people to create lasting relationships will be observed, and some strengthening of long-term love bonds will generally be felt. This may manifest as deeper intimacy or appreciation of the partner, but this can also be extended to families or groups. This is particularly helpful for groups that have worked together for long periods of time, or family or personal relationships that have existed for a long time. There will be an added sense of coming together, of newness, of closeness, and an appreciation of each other. At a higher spiritual level, people who meditate together or do any sort of spiritual work together can become aware of new aspects of that spiritual work more easily when meditating on this cluster or using its elixir.

Open Star Cluster M34 in Perseus

1,500 light years. Seventy to eighty bright stars.

This matrix of stars has also been utilized as a computational center. The ability here is to give people what would appear likely to create emotional understanding and the ability to accept one's emotions. But more importantly, it gives one the ability to accept the emotions of others, especially people that one has known in the past who have created powerful messages for one's own development. Many times these are often negative messages from one's parents of judgment or struggle, or difficult emotional aspects of one's own inner awareness.

In coming to a place of forgiveness with one's parents, or perhaps the teachers or others who might have raised you, there are many facets that come into play. The emotions can be felt deeply within the person in such a way that they are easily released, or easily assimilated if need be. Often when one relives an earlier incident, one's own emotions will generally cloud the picture of the emotions which were presented to you by the teachers or parents or others who were involved in the process. Utilizing this cluster and drawing the information about emotional awareness from it may assist one in accepting what was happening at that time. Not necessarily automatically forgiving it, but understanding it and becoming more deeply aware of it. As a result, self-nurturing or nurturing for oneself as a child will then lead to a deeper awareness of contact with the individuals that influenced you at that time. As a result of the influence of the cluster and the awareness of the emotional contact, one may then have emotions about certain incidents. But this time the process will be clear, it will be understood and acceptable. Then there will be forgiveness for yourself, for those who influenced you, and for the very nature of your development.

At a higher spiritual level, what will result is an awareness of all emotional processes and how these can then be changed so that one will improve the situation when one is working with young ones or when influencing other people. In this way one will not continue the difficulties.

In the future, an ability to strengthen the transference of love energy into other beings will be helped, especially across the boundaries of various Kingdoms. For instance, one may become able to love the inhabitants of the Kingdom of the Air, even though they are so different than humans. This kind of growth will be accelerated and assisted by this cluster.

Open Star Cluster M67 in Cancer

2,500 light years. Very compact, with 500 stars. 10 billion years old, it is one of the oldest clusters.

These stars are very long lived. Within this cluster are some of the remnants of the essential formation energies of the universe. These energies are directly related to the underlying characteristics of the universe. It is in the universe's essential nature to continuously surpass each moment of previous beauty. Since you are expanding as part of the universe, you cannot contemplate or understand the expansion of the universe. The true nature of the expansion of the universe can be understood as the awareness of the universe surpassing itself.

This energy can transfer into people in many different ways. The general result will be an awareness of how consciousness of one's roots is expanding and increasing for people. This also relates to characteristics that are not felt through the usual pathways of the intellect or emotions. Thus people will generally become more and more aware over time of geomancy and their awareness of the Earth herself. This can include awareness of the currents of water, ley lines, and magnetic field interactions within the Earth. These are very old things that have been implanted in your very cellular structures. These go way back before the times of DNA implantations or various inherited characteristics. Thus attunement to underlying levels of energy of the Earth's own structure will be transferred from this star cluster.

There will also be a deeper attunement to the purpose of all life. This is not something complicated, but is instead an awareness of God manifesting through all things in life. Some appreciation of the different forms of religions as they seek to manifest this principle will be noted, and naturally a greater ability to manifest religious tolerance. An awareness of the different ways in which religion works will be made more available to people here.

There is an inner matrix within this cluster that has contained within it the oldest records of the development of the universe. Scientists and others who study this, or who seek to understand about the very nature of the universe, would certainly do well to use the elixir or meditate on this place. This can assist individuals who seek to understand the very nature of life itself.

This cluster can assist people who make flower essences, gem elixirs, or homeopathic remedies and are intrigued by the principles involved. This is for those who are not simply looking at the applications of vibrational remedies but who are going beyond them to look at the underlying principles of their work. This can lead to the principles of life itself, that the very nature of the universe is based on vibrations.

Hyades Cluster in Taurus

88–150 light years, the closest cluster.

The energy of this cluster tends to focus into the brightest star, Theta 2 Tauri. Some of the star's brilliant appearance is not due to the star itself but to the energy of the entire cluster focusing itself through this star. This is an energy of inspiration that can brought into works of art, music, dance, and poetry. It can be used as an additional force for civilization or for people to grow and learn. This force of inspiration can be very powerful in times of stress or difficulty for the artist or for the people who would receive what is being shared. The energy from this cluster can be very helpful to people involved in artistic pursuits when a blockage is felt and one needs to have an extra push of energy, a breaking down, or a shifting of perspective. There can also be benefit to people who require more information about art they can use immediately. This star cluster provides immediate energy for people as soon as it is used.

This cluster can attune people to higher levels of artistic endeavor. This can allow them to understand more of the underlying principles so that they may feel for themselves as if they are a part of the art that they are involved in. This energy can assist people who see their involvement in artistic endeavor only to a limited extent. Perhaps they are feeling that the way they relate to their audience or the feelings they have when they are involved in the art are insufficient. They are not perceiving that they are also involved in a much larger process. This is a transference of energy from higher levels into other people and other beings. In attuning to this channeling process of artistic inspiration, all of the energies are quickened and strengthened. This strengthening gives the artist a deeper trust and an ability to be more empty so that they can welcome the higher force energies. This can speed up the entire artistic process.

Open Star Cluster M41 in Canis Major

2,100 light years. Several hundred stars, of varying types.

Beings from Sirius have used this cluster in attempts to receive and study information of a nature that may be dangerous for humanity, and to evaluate whether the information is appropriate for humanity. Although this cluster is very far away, its position is quite perfectly suited for this function. These beings who work with clusters for massive computational techniques are able to evaluate the information, and know that very little of such energy will bleed through from Sirius into Earth. The underlying picture here is one that has been influenced by Sirius over centuries.

Meditation on this cluster or use of this elixir will tend to give people a better ability to work with technology and be more comfortable with it. But it will also tend to teach them what to put their attention on, and what not to. Thus they will develop an affinity for certain areas of technology and just intuitively feel that other areas are not worth pursuing or are in some way negative or harmful. They will know this without necessarily having facts or information immediately at hand, though they may eventually discover those facts later.

The distance of a star cluster from any civilization is not as important to its utilization as its angular distance with relation to those beings that are involved in its use. Thus much of the computations done by beings on Sirius utilizing star clusters are computations that deal with the Earth and with people here. Some of the computations deal with fulfilling requests, bringing appropriate information, assisting with channeling, or bringing data regarding possible futures.

Open Star Cluster M46 in Puppis

5,400 light years, 500 stars.

This cluster has been a place of commerce and gathering for many civilizations in times long past. Civilizations that have lived there and worked with the energies have been able to enjoy inspiring communication with many beings for long periods of time. This encouraged their own development tremendously. Many of the beings there have ascended to very powerful levels of higher dimensional form and have been involved in the seeding processes of distant galaxies.

What they have left in their cluster is an energy of general encouragement and strengthening for people. This can be an ability to integrate information from other cultures or areas that seem very different than what people currently are working with. For instance, this could involve the ability of musicians to absorb and understand an aspect of something very different than they are used to, such as chemistry. A cross-seeding of ideas might be strongly assisted.

The energy of this cluster will help those who are involved in forms of entertainment that have as their secondary function opportunities for people to meet and cross-seed amongst themselves to know each other. Individuals who are involved in networking will benefit from this cluster's energy as well. They can trust that they will be in the right place at the right time in order to bring the right people together so that they may know each other and learn how to care for each other. This energy can also bring inspiration into such networking to assist people in working together in harmony and beauty.

Some of the energies that assisted with the early cultural development in Japan were enhanced by this cluster. Isolation and the need to use minimal natural resources eventually gave rise to principles of harmony and cooperation. This cluster will assist individuals who seek to understand more about the Japanese lifestyle and the current ways in which this lifestyle is influencing the world.

Open Star Cluster M47 in Puppis

1,600 light years, 45 bright stars.

Several of these civilizations became very powerful leaders of other civilizations over time. They utilized the proximity of other stars to form computational matrices that influenced the star systems. This cluster is one of those computational matrices that is quite valuable to other civilizations even now.

Some of the abilities transferred from this cluster are a deep reverence for life itself and an ability to enhance life functioning. There may be some excellent transference of these capacities for people who wish to work with the Devic orders. This cluster's energy is particularly useful in agriculture for the proper utilization of nutrients in the soil, for an enhanced assimilation of these nutrients with any plants, for an ability to work with the development of cross-breeds, hybrids, or new forms of plants.

The elixir of this cluster can be added to various nutrient mixtures for plants, particularly those that are organic in basis such as manure tea, kelp mixtures, or fish emulsion. The plant's ability to absorb these nutrients are enhanced, particularly where people visualize such uptake of the minerals.

There are many other areas where this energy comes into play. This cluster has been utilized by many civilizations that have seeded other civilizations. The information needed to bring the seeding into form was drawn from themselves, from other races, from their own science, and from their own love or capacity to understand. It retains much of the information about how such seeding takes place. Those fascinated by this seeding process would do well to use this cluster appropriately. The main uses for this cluster will take place in humanity's future with the seeding and transference of humanity's highest capacities into other civilizations.

Open Star Cluster NGC 6231 in Scorpio

5,700 light years. Bright enough to be visible to the naked eye, it has many supergiants, with several intensely luminous stars.

This cluster is a powerful magnetic matrix which is drawing energy from many star systems, acting as a transformer, and then pouring the energy back out into the universe. This elixir can assist individuals who seek to understand more about magnetism, magnetic principles, or even the very nature of the aether. It can be added to the vibrational remedies or techniques which are used for bringing energy from the aetheric body into the physical body. It can also be used for people who wish to increase their own ability to understand self-produced human magnetism. This is a magnetic current that is observed to move primarily up and down the spine and across the brain.

This cluster can help attune one to the central focus of an idea by bringing it into a clear and powerful form. When this takes place there will usually be a transformation in one's attitude as to the very nature of the idea and how to use it. This transformed ability will bleed into other things, making them more able to contribute to this one central idea. This can be especially helpful to people involved in science or medicine, where a theory to explain how something works is an important part of the process. One capacity provided by this cluster will be to make this theory more available by condensing ideas to make them clearer.

Especially with exposure to this in elixir form, there will be a tendency in some people to be very closely aware of their heart. They may hear its beating or experience it on some deeper physical level. This is not so much to provide energy of love as it is to make them aware of the central focus of their body's attention. This can be especially valuable for people who feel a little off-center or are unaware of the nature of their heart and what it does. This cluster's energy will also be felt by individuals who have some difficulty in expressing or receiving love. Such people may have difficulty visualizing or imagining energy of a loving nature towards someone else.

Rosette Nebula in Monoceros

This nebula surrounds open star cluster NGC 2244. 5,200 light years, 93 light years in diameter. Two bright stars in the cluster are emitting strong stellar winds.

This interesting structure was created by the interference of the major civilization with the stars themselves a long time ago. This interference caused the translation of huge amounts of energy. This was reduced in its intensity by the coordinated efforts of 171 civilizations throughout a number of galaxies who focused their attention and time on this area for a period equivalent to about 200 years in human conception. This would be similar in some ways to the result of wholesale, widespread use of nuclear weapons on Earth. Much difficulty was caused by the ability of this kind of destruction to cause such dramatic change in the very fabric of space and time itself, even leading to powerful destructive energies released from the stars into space.

It is partly because of observing this unusual destruction and concentration of energies that civilizations involved with Earth know it is very important to prevent such a use of nuclear weapons on a widespread level in the future so that such a massive destruction and great change of space does not take place in this part of the Milky Way Galaxy as well. You have the remnants of this kind of destruction here in the Rosette Nebula.

The civilizations involved in the reduction of the interference the destruction caused have sought to teach the souls that remained after such destruction much about themselves and other beings, without these souls incarnating into the third and fourth dimensions. This has been a difficult process, but was necessary since the inhabitants' natural attunement to that part of space continues, and these beings were unable to manifest at the three-dimensional level, due to the tremendous stellar stresses that are now found in that region of space. As a result, these civilizations have developed a bit lopsidedly. This civilization has need of some of the understanding of the characteristics of love that humanity is working with. Because of this, the beings involved are seeking to assist Earth at times by projecting to Earth people energies of encouragement, happiness, and most importantly a fear of nuclear weapons. This is to help make it likely that people will survive on Earth and be around to teach such beings some of the things they want to know in a few thousand years.

Some of the individuals who would benefit from using the elixir of this cluster are those who wish to understand more about the true destructive capacities of these weapons and who seek to understand their use in past times as in Atlantis or in other civilizations in other star systems. Those who wish to understand how nuclear weapons act as a symbol and a uniting force for beings all over the planet will do well to utilize the elixir of this cluster.

The bright stars within this cluster are the focalizers of this energy. They are also broadcasting a warning beacon to beings that are unable to make an easy transfer from the third and fourth dimensions into higher dimensional realities. To exist in the third and fourth dimensions in that region of space is extremely stressful and very difficult, almost impossible for any civilization. These energies are acting to warn individuals to make such a transfer into higher dimensions. Individuals on Earth who seek to understand the ability of radiation, when fully released and understood, to enable assistance in transformation to higher dimensional levels, would do well to use the elixir of this cluster. This may be difficult for people to reconcile with their own fear of radiation. Both the appreciation or fascination with the radiative process and a fear of radiation as damaging to the human condition, are well-founded. This elixir or meditation on this area of space can allow some reconciliation of these two different ideas.

This cluster is one of those places that is also available to people in astral travel. The very nature of the stellar winds in that area causes a gentle attraction, and most individuals who experiment with astral travel once or twice will go to such a place to experience it.

SECTION III: NEBULAE

The Great Orion Nebula (M42)

1,600 light years, 30 light years in diameter. The brightest nebula, with several small companions.

This group of nebulae is indeed a family in a certain cosmic sense. The development of multidimensional communication and the ability to work with all sorts of powerful thought forms from many civilizations has developed within the creative side of this entity. The Great Orion Nebula has used this energy to create these companion nebulae, which are as if its sons and daughters. This sets an example for the galaxies by showing that it is possible to incorporate the highest and best of many thought forms, bring them into a level of unification, and from this extract the highest creative principle. This is done at a multidimensional level.

This being has had a very difficult task over the last 12,000 years. It draws upon the energies of a number of civilizations that do not seem bound for the evolutionary-scale change from physical to spiritual. It also works with energies from many beings who are indeed on such evolutionary spirals from the material to the spiritual. This entity has been able to extract from this essential life principles which derive specifically from the underlying energy of wanting to grow, to change, and to become more aware.

Meditating on this nebula or using the elixir will increase one's ability to incorporate change and to extract from various thought forms, even negative thought forms, certain aspects that one may find valuable and useful. However these will be different from one person to the next, just as the various forms of negative and positive thought forms one is exposed to are different.

With this nebula there is also an energy that is supportive and life-giving at a very deep level. This life-giving energy is far beyond the usual levels of organically-bound molecular structures intrinsically interwoven into humanity's existence. Carbon, oxygen, and hydrogen form the structures of DNA and physical matter. These elements relate at a vibrational level with how you perceive and work with the very energies of creation, sharing, life, art, and music. The nature of what it is to be a human in form is strongly based on the elements that make the cells. This nebula creates energies far beyond a level bound to any specific substance.

This nebula can be valuable when you wish to bring through creative energy that can transcend the limitations of the artistic media within which you are working. This can help you to understand the particular art form and reach the creative essence. The result of this is unpredictable because something which is not in a form that you have common access to will produce results though the path of least resistance in your being. This path may be quite surprising to you. This nebula is also valuable for surprising insights and unusual points of view.

The Ring Nebula (M57) in Lyra

1,900 light years. Very hot central star. Doubly ionized oxygen gives this nebula a green color.

In three-dimensional space, rings are generally characteristic where electron flow is creating magnetic fields. In the ring nebula there is a powerful pulsing magnetic field that creates the strong energies that are perceived as the central star. These energies are moving with powerful rhythms that extend into dimensions of aetheric and subtle space. These can connect through what might be termed short-cuts in the universe to directly interact with ferrous matter on Earth. Most of the ferrous matter and magnetic substances on Earth are receiving information from this nebula through slight permutations of their molecular spin rates. This is a broadcast aetheric energy which affects ferrous matter extending out approximately one million light years from the center sun of this nebula.

These physical underpinnings are simply a way of transmitting vibration. The ability to translate and transmit various aspects of consciousness into human beings as well as others is an important function and purpose of the Ring Nebula. It also functions as a repository of ideas. So the ability to receive historical information, deep insight into patterns of long-standing cultural interaction, and the understanding of past civilizations in important ways (such as perceiving the threads of a civilization, the ways in which that civilization developed to the eventual perfection of humanity) are received when taking this as an elixir or in meditating on this nebula.

The characteristics of this nebula are significantly affecting the small amounts of iron-based substances in the physical body, including hemoglobin. These can be affected in a positive way when some consciousness and visualization is applied to circulation. Many ways of understanding and working with magnetic resonance phenomena of all kinds, even those separate from iron-based substances, will be accelerated and assisted by the use of this nebula. This is useful for people working with minerals for health, and in working with any sort of visualizations where the circulation is of great importance. People involved in mining can use this nebula to attune to iron deposits.

These energies will be utilized in the future in many ways. Because of this nebula's nature of transcending time and space, the connection between these magnetic resonance phenomena in the Earth and the tremendous and vast complex of the nebula's repository of information takes place automatically. It is one of the important core elements of what we have sometimes termed our cosmic computer.

The nebula acts as a repository of information for humanity's future. Many of the developments in the center of this deep and beautiful object occur in areas that far transcend the limitations of gravity and temperature of which you are aware. As a result the energy is very easily transferred to dimensions and levels of existence and awareness that transcend the limitations of time as you are aware of them. Thus this elixir can be used for understanding the future by enhancing an awareness of probabilities and what appears to be a likely course of events. Images of powerful changes in the future may be available to people working with this nebula.

The beings from this nebula are very different than what you are used to. Intertwined and interlinked with the nebula itself, they are like a living organism, but are not distinct in the way of individual, body-centered creatures. However, the consciousness available from this place can give an insight and reflection on humanity's course from a context completely outside the one you usually use.

The Trifid Nebula (M20) in Sagittarius

2,000 light years.

This nebula could be considered a daughter of your galaxy if one wished to try to translate this relationship into human terms. The energies associated with this nebula are of many varied civilizations. Many of these beings are directly involved in interdimensional transfer. They are nourished by such transfer and awareness of multidimensional nature. The process of change helps them to increase awareness and to expand; this is the most available attribute for individuals wishing to work with the elixir of this nebula. Even the visualization of this nebula is helpful. The great beauty of this nebula symbolizes on some levels a transfer between the three primary existences for humanity: those of mind, body, spirit.

Individuals working with the elixir or meditating on the nebula can have a deeper awareness of their own abilities to transform by seeing that change is nourishing in itself. This can strengthen their ability to change their perspective and shift how they see themselves or others. This does not necessarily mean that processes of change are eased or accelerated, only that individuals actually become more nourished by change. Individuals will feel more whole by receiving this understanding of change. With the influence of this nebula they will feel nourished and strengthened by what they have learned. This is a way of taking this process of change more deeply within oneself and then bringing it into some usable form.

Dumbbell Nebula (M27) in Vulpecula

3,500 light years. One of the brightest nebula in the Northern Hemisphere. It has a hot central star. It appears to be expanding with noticeable turbulence.

The energies of this nebula have recently undergone a shift. It is likely that this shift will be observed by astronomers and other scientists within the next few hundred years. This shift of energies is imparting a twisting motion to the opposite ends of this structure. One is twisting in a clockwise direction, the other in a counterclockwise direction. That will tend to add stress, putting additional energies into resonance with the brightest star at the center. A strengthening effect going on between the beings in this place is also having an effect on the structure itself. These beings have found a way of communication which transcends various forms of telepathy and other methods of which you are aware. However, this effect is not imparted to the entire structure.

There are certain star systems on the perimeter that are approximately at the level of awareness and consciousness as Earth. For this reason, using the elixir of this nebula can bring a sense of evolutionary purpose into people's consciousness, an understanding of what will happen next with Earth's civilization. This understanding of evolutionary purpose is the primary sense that is being transmitted by this magnificent structure, because the combined energies of its stars and beings are more focused on their own work right now. It appears likely that within about another 2,000 years this work will complete itself. At such time, a powerful energy will be created, an energy of a great availability of love between it and the center of the Milky Way. When this occurs, humanity may then find a well-timed jump in its own evolution, so that their energies of love can be communicated further into the other galaxies.

At this time the energies of this nebula have to do with glimpsing the future for humanity, being able to remain on course with that future, and being able to use that vision to perhaps awaken the heart a little more, so that attunement to humanity's own evolution is easier. Mistakes that might be made by improperly employing or utilizing technological devices may be avoided, various new societal constructs may be encouraged, and new shifts in mass-scale economies will perhaps be seen ahead for many.

These energies from the nebula radiate in a pattern that will likely increase in frequency over the next few hundred years. One of these has just recently passed a peak. This has left an inspiring energy for the economic systems newly forming on Earth in Communist nations, in the Soviet Union in particular. How it will come to pass, how the vision will be transmitted, is up to humanity. But it is likely that another such vision will also be transmitted approximately six years, two months from May 10, 1991, when this last burst of energy occurred. Another one will likely occur approximately five years and eleven months later, then another one five years, six months after that. (You can see the increasing frequency of these pulses.) These are pulses that may eventually be detected as X-ray pulses, but they simply coincide with pulses of energy released at specific frequencies and rates in order to accelerate consciousness on many levels within the nebula. These energy pulses that are being received on Earth now occurred a long time ago. These pulses are still being projected to all beings to encourage their own evolution.

Crab Nebula in Taurus

4,500 light years. This is a remnant of a supernova, seen in China July 4, 1054. A rapidly rotating pulsar in the center gives off pulses of radio, light x-rays, etc. every 0.033 seconds.

The star itself was destroyed in this supernova, but many of its characteristics were transferred. When you die, you move through a transition into another way of being. This is apart from reincarnation, for all beings eventually do die, sometimes with maximum consciousness, sometimes without. The primary characteristic that the elixir or meditating on this place will provide for people is this way of transformation of consciousness, the ability to let go, and the ability to appreciate and understand the true purpose of death as a transition.

There will also be an appreciation of the ability to transfer the characteristics you have learned into your children or into the works that you may write. Scientists certainly wish to see their theories continued, musicians their works performed, and artists their works observed in the future. With this nebula one may then understand more about the search for such immortality continued across time and space. There will also be an enhanced ability here for people to prepare for the future by the writing of a will, looking into how things are to be inherited, how guardianship is to be appointed, and all of such mundane matters as some of the emotional underpinnings of this process will be made more available to people.

What differentiates this from other supernovas is this resulting pulsar. It has an additional ability to assist people with the process of manifestation. Thus while they are contemplating the end of this life, they are also consciously putting attention on the next one. This is unique to those who are involved in the reincarnational process, as beings in other civilizations are rarely involved in such. Should people be aware of reincarnation, when they are doing such things as writing a will or thinking about inheritance, another thing they should be aware of is being ready for the transference of energy into a new form.

In this pulsar's period there is an inherent relationship to the awareness of time. This rapid pulsation tends to give rise to a consciousness that affects the process of incarnation. You may have known someone in the past who has died. Many years later, you are thinking about this person a little differently, perhaps remembering him or her without the same constraints of emotion or limitation that you had before. You begin to recognize these are symbols that the person is ready to incarnate. Using this elixir or meditating on this nebula, you think about this energy, and you can deliberately welcome their energy to come into form in such a way that you will know. This person may be your child, the child of a friend, or you will get to meet him or her in this world in some way. You can then give a little bit of your energy to this process by asking that it be more conscious, and helping in any way that you can. Very little will be taken from you in order to influence this process. You will not be harmed by it in any way. But you will likely have a little deeper appreciation of the entire process, and a greater ability to recognize that individual when you do meet again after he or she has incarnated.

Lagoon Nebula (M8) in Sagittarius

4,500 light years.

This is a magnificent collection of civilizations which have integrated and brought simple ideas into clear form. They are more involved in the creation of other galaxies, other civilizations, other levels of awareness than those directly related to the Earth. The civilizations associated with the Lagoon Nebula naturally act as a beautiful vibrational example of ways in which intercoordination can take place so that many different ideas, points of view, and ways of life are integrated appropriately. This energy can inspire people who are seeking to join a community.

There is some gentle attunement from Lagoon Nebula to Earth for the creation of communities based on things that transcend the current reality. Right now this is primarily relating to communities that are service-based, as opposed to being money-based. In time this energy will eventually transcend that, into communities that are vibration-based rather than service based. And eventually this energy will transcend that, to create communities that are interdimensionally-based rather than vibrationally-based. The use of the Lagoon Nebula will be very helpful for people who wish to understand the true path of the formation of larger communities which can evolve into the very highest form possible.

Saturn Nebula (NGC 7009) in Capricorn

3,000 light years. Bright green oval shape.

Working with light and color in various forms has been shared as a technique amongst three of the civilizations that have lived in this part of space. They developed the technique of sharing the appropriate light with many developing civilizations throughout the universe. They have projected this green color towards Earth for the strengthening of the heart and for the ability to release grief and loss. It is also for the strengthening of the immune system and the ability of the heart to assimilate and integrate loving information from other people and for other techniques of sharing of information and resources. This can also be used for releasing addictive patterns. This energy strengthens so many things that are essential for humanity's development. This nebula has many characteristics available to it, but by deliberate filtering is allowing only those that directly affect the aspects of what humanity needs most right now, such as this new awareness of deeper compassion amongst people. People who seek to awaken such deeper compassion in themselves and others would do well with this elixir.

There is some benefit here in combining this with Apophyllite and to a lesser extent Emerald, partly because of the green color and partly because of the symbols associated with these stones.

Section IV: Globular Clusters

Globular clusters M3 in Boötes

35,000 light years. 100,000 stars, with a large number of variable stars.

There are a number of civilizations associated with this globular cluster. Those with attention on Earth will work with one's own personal energies in a most significant way. At this time this has to do with understanding creative cycles in people. This is a way in which people are able to work with their creative energies in the appropriate time and place, and then withdraw them when necessary. At a deeper, more spiritual level, there can be awareness of the cyclical nature of all life forms. By appreciating these inner cycles, there can be a very powerful awareness and understanding of the very nature of life itself.

The stars appear variable because some of the beings are able to work with the light from these stars with thought forms to create this pulsation to remind individuals of the possibility of attunement to these inner cycles. Should you journey to this place, you would discover that many of the stars which appear variable are instead being pulsed by some of the beings living there to use as energy networks. These energies are utilized for the development of their own awareness and understanding.

The God-nature in such a place is very different from what you are aware of here. There is a sense of the deep reverence for all life in a way that is incomprehensible in this galaxy. Some of this reverence can be transferred through the cycles of breath in people. When meditating on this object, being aware of it by seeing it through a telescope or in a photograph, or in taking the elixir, being aware of the breath can assist greatly in the development of this understanding of cycles.

Globular Cluster M5 in Serpens

27,000 light years. 10 billion years old, it has 500,000 stars.

This cluster has a powerful entrance-way at its center which is a transfer point to multiple galaxies. It is an important transformative energy for the evolution of many galaxies, the Milky Way Galaxy included (and therefore Earth). This was a place in which the consciousness which eventually became the center of the Milky Way Galaxy was developed. This being evolved in ways that were quite different from consciousness as you understand it. The ancient energies associated with this place have dispersed throughout most of the galaxies to which they are connected, but often return in various forms to the center of this cluster.

There is a wave of energy which passes through this structure in a rather complex series of movements by drawing on energies from the different stars as they change in their own brightness, shifts in consciousness, and outpouring of energy back to the center. There are times in the evolution of a galaxy when the need for connection to other galaxies and awareness of its relation to the others is necessary. This cluster's ability to allow this communication between galaxies is its primary purpose.

This communication between the various aspects of the universe represents the highest level of attainment which is possible for a human being. These energies are helpful for individuals who wish to contact beings in other galaxies or who wish to be aware of the universe as a whole. For those who wish to accept the magnificent capacity of the billions and billions of galaxies to pour their energies and light into your galaxy (and thence into you), this awareness of communication can be very helpful. The expansion of consciousness to the highest capacity possible for a person, and the expansion to the level of becoming one with energies far beyond even your galaxy, are strengthened here more than any other place.

This is not for everyone. There are many beings who are working with star elixirs or working with these energies in their own ways who find it pretty hard to attune to the galaxy or even just to a single star. But when a person has worked with star elixirs long enough, worked with meditating on the stars, or worked with astronomy long enough that they are ready to expand even further, then the use of M5 would be strongly recommended.

There are many civilizations that have worked with these energies in the past. Thus, in working with this cluster one will have a taste or feeling for many sorts of extraterrestrials. However, at the deepest level of this work will be a simple feeling of connection to and oneness with a source. It will be then as if the eldest parents, guardians, and lovers of the Elohim are contacted in working with this energy. This is an energy that can be in some ways very peaceful and very thought-provoking. This can reach a quite profound level of quietness for some individuals, and is valuable in states of deep, quiet meditation.

Globular Cluster M10 in Ophiuchi

20,000 light years.

There is a spark of consciousness within this cluster that has ignited a shift amongst the many beings that have lived there. This is proceeding as a conscious expansion of energy in various waves throughout the universe. It has only reached

Earth recently, coinciding with the seeding of the Egyptian civilization. Most of the tremendous potential for consciousness and awareness of the Egyptian civilization has been unrealized in the sense of true creativity, kindness, and the enhancing of the highest capacities of humanity. The waves of this spark of consciousness continue to pour through the Earth as a beneficial influence for your civilization.

This elixir can give a generalized sense of higher potential and a sense of a deeper capacity for love and creativity. Some individuals who have difficulty in working with certain past lives associated with the early phase of the Egyptian civilization will do well with this elixir. It will attune them to some of the seeding and strengthening energies at the levels of consciousness which brought that civilization into form. There are many other aspects of this powerful spark of consciousness shared by these beings that will affect humanity in the future.

Globular Cluster M12 in Ophiuchi

20,000 light years.

Here there has been a sharing of technological ideas for the development of various new components of genetics, and awareness of Carbon-based, Silicon-based, Manganese-based, and Iron-based structures that all hold consciousness. The Carbon-based substances have yielded information through genetic means that are sometimes transmitted to the galaxies around them as a reminder of various capacities. These energies may be received by Carbon-based structures in the human body through meditating on this place or, more importantly, by using the elixir mixed with food, taken mixed in water, or in a bath. This may be better than simply a few drops under the tongue.

One may then be able to recreate genetic structures and patterns from the earliest childhood times. Individuals working with regeneration would do well to use this elixir before they actually work with physical reconstruction, inert gas energies, or other regenerative techniques. This way they can be aware of the underlying genetic structures and prepare for the energies yet to come. There is a magnificent energy of coordinated beings in this place, but the energy made most available to people runs along the lines of reminding one of underlying genetic structures.

Globular Cluster M92 in Hercules

25,000 light years.

There is a sustaining influence pouring into the center of the galaxy from this place. It causes some additional strengthening of the very nature of the Milky Way Galaxy. Individuals who wish to understand all the other stars in the Milky Way Galaxy that have been described and shared through this work would do well to use this elixir. There is some additional attunement to the purpose of the Milky Way Galaxy as a single entity.

You recognize how the individual cells of your body make up the whole consciousness of your being. You can almost understand the way in which this translates into your awareness of your interconnection to the Earth. To go beyond this and understand the entire galaxy is difficult for most people. This elixir can make available some awareness of the great potential of the Sun, and the way the Sun influences the Earth and what is happening on the Earth. People can appreciate the stars more, understand the very nature of their galaxy all that much more easily, with this elixir. People can especially find some kinship with the stars that are the nearest neighbors, or the civilizations with the maximum impact for humanity, by using the magnificent light from this star cluster.

Other civilizations have utilized this star cluster for the development of galaxies by forming co-creative energies with the essence of God. This has allowed the cluster to act as a transfer point by linking regions of time. This has made energies available that are needed in order to enable the civilizations to pursue the various goals and aims that are needed for that galaxy's own development. Because it is able to act as a time portal attuning the Milky Way Galaxy to other galaxies in their development through levels of very powerful dimensional transference and transcendence, it is actually a spot that allows deeper awareness of multiple times all at once and in this way does influence how it is perceived from Earth. There is a general tendency as well in using this as an elixir or in meditating on it to be aware of some of the ability to transcend time yourself, to remember things long past, to be aware of the future, to see this in a time of peace, to imagine it in ways that are loving and helpful to your own condition.

Globular Cluster M15 in Pegasus

34,000 light years, one of the biggest globular cluster.

This cluster has a number of remarkable capacities. One of these is the creation of the energies of hope and strength for many people. The stars there communicate amongst themselves and with beings who have resided there and worked with their energies. This has resulted in the creation of concentric spheres of intercommunicative energies somewhat like the aetheric, mental, and emotional bodies of a person. There is a communication and coordination amongst these. There will be a general strengthening of the interchange of energies between emotional, mental, and aetheric bodies with people when utilizing this as elixir, and so it will combine well with Silversword and Lotus flower essence for promoting such interconnection.

There will be deeper awareness of the potential for people to be able to coexist or interrelate to each other. There can be some deeper awareness of the true nature of such relationships that do not lead to codependency or ways in which addictive processes allow less power and love. This is a way in which the combination of energies creates a new being whose aetheric, emotional, and mental bodies are united and shared, and this is of great benefit in humanity's future.

There may be for many individuals a time in future lifetimes in which they will have a chance to go to one of many planets that exist in this cluster. This is a place of much energy and has stood in the past for many human souls as a place for a vacation out of time and space in the usual sense. In these places of learning and inner strengthening, some ideas have been impressed upon consciousness that have been brought back into incarnation for people who are teachers, who are seekers of light, and for beings who seek also to lead others. There can be a certain sense within individuals when viewing this place of a remembrance, and there is great benefit in observing a photograph of this cluster or looking at it through a powerful telescope to have a sense of its wholeness.

There are many civilizations in this place that have developed into an interconnected society over time because of close proximity and awareness of various potentials within their own stars to interconnect one star to the next. This does allow them group consciousness, but this does not generally reflect into levels accessible in the third, fourth, or fifth dimensions. There is much activity at the seventh, eighth, ninth, and tenth-dimensional levels, and this is deliberately shielded from humanity at this time. They might see humanity as little brother and wish then to assist only in a way of providing potential, loving, and a sense of compassion and deeper awareness. This may manifest for many at this time as hope, as a sense of deeper awareness of what can be for humanity as a shared entity.

Globular Cluster M22 in Sagittarius

10,000 light years, 70,000 stars.

This cluster has a transformative capacity. It has in its center a vibrational shifting point that can allow beings to shift into not only very far away places such as other galaxies or other clusters, but into other dimensional realities that you would consider parallel universes. This has allowed the individuals who have worked with the stars and have lived lifetimes in those areas of the cluster itself a deeper understanding of the nature of the universe, of God, and of the energies that are shared amongst many in the universe. This does not translate very well into things that are easily accessible by people at this time, except for the capacity for individuals to shift in their own vibration to attune to communication of extraterrestrials.

There may be some individuals who channel extraterrestrials of a generally positive and uplifting nature. There will be more and more of this over time. Some individuals will experience stress in the physical body because of this. This is because there is an innate transference of energy which requires a shifting in vibration for the person which they are not used to. Although this would be helped by Sirius or by various flower essences, particularly Green Rose, Potato, and Lotus, there will be a different benefit imparted by this cluster when utilized as an elixir or meditated upon. The elixir itself can have the capacity to ease some of these stresses by providing a doorway or pointing out a path for the individual of a way in which they can transfer vibration easily and shift their own perspective. This can sometimes be startling, as some individuals may have channeling capacities that are latent and waiting to come forth. If an individual has a hint of this by experiencing some excitement or deeper interest in the works channeled by others from extraterrestrials, then they might be advised to utilize this elixir to see what happens, as it may encourage their own channeling abilities and strengthen them on some levels.

Globular Cluster M2 in Aquarius

40,000 light years.

This is a cluster currently being utilized on a temporary basis to broadcast various energies to ease this time of transition on Earth. These energies can be helpful when choosing a place to live. This cluster can assist individuals who seek to balance aspects of the old society transforming into the new one, the transfer from Pisces into Aquarius, or who seek to balance in themselves some of the difficulties relating to such transformation around them. This can assist individuals approaching old age who have some deeper sadness or resentment about not being able to have the physical stamina or inner strength necessary to continue in life. They may be seeing the great benefits of the energies and work the younger ones are doing and not be able to be so fully enmeshed in such work. They will find inner strength and look more easily at their own lives and what they could contribute to such deeper awareness.

This cluster is utilized as a broadcasting point for some of the energies relating to what you call the "New Age". These are not so much formed energies with clear messages as they are general encouraging energies to help people look at their own spiritual evolvement, recognize it in a larger perspective, and see of how it assists them. This can assist with deeper attunement to past lives and awareness of the continuity of past lives into a strong and beautiful possible future for individuals. This can assist with people who are seeking together in groups or coordinated activities to create a better life on Earth. This energy will become more and more important as time goes on, bringing deeper awareness of humanity's future into easier recognition and form for people.

Globular Cluster Omega Centauri

15,000–22,000 light years. Many older giants and many variables stars.

A resonant condition is being created by many of the civilizations within this structure that is affecting the vibratory frequencies of the emissions from these stars. These energies have been in place for very long periods of time. Many of the civilizations within these stars have gone, having had their tremendous awareness and capabilities enhanced by these resonant conditions. They have merged with God in a different sense than you are aware of, and have added to the expansion of the entire universe. This is not to say that a release of individuality has taken place, but rather it is as though an awareness of higher function has been created by these beings for themselves. The energies of this entire structure have been directly affected by all of these energies; and working with the elixir or meditating on this structure can assist in one's perceptions of this higher function.

It can bring into individuals a sense of the interconnection between all the cells of the body. It will also enhance the sense of interconnection between the individual and other objects that are held, so that psychometry will be significantly enhanced. Telepathy may be enhanced. The ability to work with hands-on healing where the hands are touching the skull or face, will be enhanced. A deeper awareness of the holographic function, where multiple images in multiple sensory patterns are formed, is available for the creation of new ideas and new perceptions within people. This can extend to various levels of consciousness that you have not yet tapped. A deep increase in such consciousness is possible for individuals.

Combined with substances such as Silversword flower essence, White Diamond elixir, and Lotus flower essence, some powerful energies can be shifted for people. When Xenon elixir is added to this mixture, a deeper consciousness and connection to the highest self can come powerfully. This is not the same as enlightenment, but it does show the powerful ways that the interconnection between the souls of one civilization and the souls of another civilization can be drawn together and known.

In addition this globular cluster's energy allows a more conscious ability to modulate and work with human energy systems at subtle levels. Thus the natural cycles that the subtle bodies go through, such as what are called biorhythms (and each of the subtle bodies have their own sets of biorhythms), become more available and understandable. This is not quite the same as control, but an awareness of these rhythms, and an ability to shift them very slightly, is enhanced. For many individuals, this can lead to visionary states, ecstatic states, or states that can be joyful. Sometimes one must move through several intervening emotional states of struggle, grief, or other energies to reach such deeper conscious states.

Part Three

Expanded View of Other Civilizations

SPICA

Psychic awareness, spirituality, and related forms are difficult to speak about without bringing some of these altered states into greater clarity for people. Because Spica is so bright and its influence is in so many ways so powerful, understanding more about Spica can quickly attune one to these forms of intuition. These beings who exist on Spica have an awareness of the transformation that can take place through the intuitive, through higher consciousness, and through the dream state. The ability to transform themselves consciously is also utilized by these beings as a means of space travel.

In an early period of their civilization, there was a deliberate attempt to seek out solutions by the inner intuitive forces. They were seeking solutions to the usual things that plague civilizations at an early stage, such as how to relate to each other, to their planet, and to all the things that have happened to them. In seeking this inwardly by noting the perfect symbolism so often felt around them, this inner journey quickly yielded much information. This showed them that the best approach was to use their intuitive faculties—this is the ability to know something directly. From their intuition, they understood about the development of science, machines, and various physical techniques in other civilizations, but recognized that this path was one that led to so many difficulties, so many ways in which the whole understanding of what was happening around people seemed to be lost. As a result they developed an internal frame of reference which gradually allowed a shift in their civilization's own understanding to a place where thought was unnecessary.

This may be very hard for you to imagine. For Earth people, the longest period of no thought generally exists for a matter of seconds. For the great masters who have studied this for countless incarnations, meditating and being in a place of emptiness can continue for hours or days. Yet to imagine an entire civilization working with the unified intuitive faculties without thought interfering on any level is almost impossible for you to grasp because you are attempting to do it with your thought processes. However, this is indeed what has taken place with these beings in the civilization relating to Spica.

By asking for assistance from their star, they developed an easy way of energetic transfer through Spica itself. In these intuitive states they were able to move in groups to various other places to learn many things. In this way they learned how to shift dimension. Gradually all of this powerful intuitive energy led them to ask the deeper questions of God. They entered into a long period of intercommunication with the very forces of the galaxy, of God, and of the highest aspects of what could be pulled out of vibration from many civilizations.

This was very difficult for other civilizations to work with in a conscious form. They would observe the influence of these beings from Spica but not be able to define it, understand it, or work with it. This was not so much because their own intuitive faculties were undeveloped, but because this influence was created with the group consciousness of these beings from Spica. In their development of all of these magnificent energies, these beings from Spica came to a place of deep peace. This peacefulness gave God the awareness to understand the intuitive function, and provided many civilizations with opportunities for dreaming and for letting go of any thought processes.

It was seen in the early seeding of humanity that the necessity for sleep would be very important. This unconscious state could welcome such intuitive journeys. So a genetic seed as influenced directly by these beings was put into the genes of most creatures on Earth. Not only is the sleep state utilized for recuperation of the physical body, but a deliberate attempt was made to encourage all such beings, and even the Earth itself, to move through states of unconsciousness where the thought processes are turned off. This would not be created by a deliberate conscious attempt, but by the very nature of the physical body. As a result of this there would be opportunities for exploration in the dream state, as well as awareness of the release of the physical body, awareness of the subtle bodies influences, and awareness of the physical body's influences on the subtle bodies. Examples of this would be the healing as created by the connection between the aetheric body and the physical body, and astral travel as created by the connection of the physical body to the astral body. These things were gently placed within humanity and all beings on Earth. Therefore sleep is not just a burden or a thing you must do in order to recuperate, it is also a beautiful opportunity to attune to these other forces.

This seeding did not take place without the awareness of the human race. It was a seeding with the cooperation of the lifestream of humanity, with a sense of what could be for humanity. The early Lemurian phases were as if a test to see how humanity could work with intuition. The result of this is a way in which these energies have been incorporated within people. Individuals may be reminded of this when they think of their Lemurian incarnations.

Due to this seeding, it was seen that a direct link to beings from Spica might be a residue of this energy. Yet their love and their understanding of God's energy required that all such links be severed. This is why when you sleep, you do not feel yourself drawn instantly to this star. Spica has a gentle influence to enhance your understanding of all of these energies. Because of this general encouragement that Spica provides, there can be a shift in consciousness that occurs when you deliberately focus on your intuition as you attune to Spica. This will be affected by the living aspects of Spica itself. This magnificent star was able to receive and work with these energies in ways that allowed it to understand and work with intuitive functions very differently than most other stars. This also allowed Spica a deeper understanding of God which has been very nourishing and strengthening to this star.

The energy that Spica is broadcasting is simply an overshadowing influence for intuitive development. For many people there will be additional benefit if they combine intuition and the dream state. This is separate from the star, though certainly encouraged by the star. If you are developing a conscious, deliberate invoking of intuitive states, and in your sleep state you welcome a dream or are working with the ability to maintain lucid dreaming states, you may find that there is a beautiful co-development. Bringing in the energies of Spica can assist this process even more deeply. Spica is so bright and so powerful in your sky so that indeed there will be this constant reminder of the great importance of intuition and the great importance of releasing thought as necessary for your development.

Now we have mentioned certain psychic abilities that tend to be increased by working with Spica. These abilities in people are not the result of any direct influence from the civilization or the star. It is what is developing in humanity. By being on a planet and constantly working with electromagnetic and gravitational forces in a state of tension and balance, people are able to manipulate this balance by means of abilities inherent in their nature. This is largely unconscious. Making people more aware of these abilities does not entail conscious understanding, but intuitive understanding and an awareness of this through the subtler senses. Many psychic abilities that take advantage of this balance of forces on Earth can be strengthened by working with Spica.

ARCTURUS

The beings from Arcturus have bonded with their star. The energies of the star influenced the development of this civilization from the very beginning, and the energies of the civilization naturally coupled with the star. Much of this occurred unconsciously for the early period of that civilization but grew more conscious with time. They had distributed themselves across four of the planets of their solar system by means of a fairly early discovery of primitive forms of space travel. These planets of widely different environmental conditions gradually became more similar over time.

These beings were imbued with a question concerning their development. There were certain aspects in their science and in their awareness of their interaction with the sun and other things that brought up basic questions. These were questions about important mysteries. Their entire philosophy, religion, and ways of being began to be focused on these mysteries. It was not just a matter of solving them. It was observed as the very nature of the universe reflected in the individuality of their own form. This focus on the mysterious, on what could not be known, on what was separate from them, somehow became clearer and clearer with time. It was as if for a while there was a deep reverence for this. This sense of reverence for the unknown was broadcast because of the natural radiating ability of the Arcturus sun. Other civilizations throughout the galaxy began to focus a little on them to give them more questions, more ideas, and more things to look at.

Gradually this became a certain form of understanding and an energy of interconnection between these beings. It was as if when they would meet they would ask a question. These beings were very different from people on Earth. They have understood many aspects of what it means to be alive or not alive; and interdimensional transfer and other things were of a second nature. So what began to occur in looking at this deeper aspect of mystery was the whole idea of communication, interaction, and understanding of what could be, and what could not be. This led very soon to a deep awareness of the very nature of how beings are created. They utilized these energies for the changing of their co-planets. They also used these energies to extend their own civilization, their lifetimes, and their awareness.

Along the way it was not all a rosy path. For several hundred of their years there were some difficulties where the fractionalization of society took place. Several different paths were taken to solve various mysteries. One would state that there was an awareness of God-reality that extended through multiple dimensions, another would state that there was an awareness of God-reality through biological form, another through the creation of personalities, and these groups would clash. Eventually this gave way to a deep understanding that all of these paths could be merged. This then led to their own abilities to strengthen the physical body. This directly affected the relationship between them, their sun, their other planets, and the other planets that they might visit in their locality of space.

By asking these deeper questions and coming to understand the mystery of life and the universe, there developed within every one of these beings an ability to make a link or a bond. Once per year a deliberate linking together of all these beings was formed. This was created as an answer to their wars. This truce was to be observed as an interplanetary holiday once per year. As this took place, a powerful energy began to form within their sun and radiate out to alert them to their underlying roots. This created new mysteries and new things to be looked at. Eventually they were able to understand the whole aspect of what it means to relate and to assist somebody else—in this case, their sun. At this point their sun as affected by a number of forces came close to a nova and changed its size and shape a bit. When this occurred, the beings of these planets were able to interact with Arcturus, becoming even more bonded with their star, understanding this deeper mystery of the stars, and saving their solar system. As a result of this deeper interaction, a certain stability and inner strength began to form which has lasted for about 15,000 years.

This brings us up to the present. This energy and interaction between these beings and their sun has allowed a certain deep sense of what it means to heal, to create energy of health, clarity, and focus, but more importantly an awareness of the whole healing relationship and an appreciation of the healing process. There is intermeshed in this a deep appreciation of understanding in the knowledge sense. This is a way of learning all of the facts, working with the information, with the symptoms that are presented, the circumstances, the history, and from this also being able to derive information and answers, sometimes by intuitive means, sometimes by logical means, but most of the time by a combination of these. Asking questions, learning to receive the answers, and working closely and deeply with the information, this was one of the key issues that became much clearer in this time period. This is now being radiated in its various forms throughout the dimensions. This can be of direct benefit to people on Earth. This can be a strengthening force that allows people to face these questions. But more importantly, this is an ability to listen, to work with the answers, and to understand the bond created between a healer and their client.

Now you might think that this would most likely affect psychotherapy rather than bodywork, acupuncture, or homeopathy. In the development of their own personalities, the awareness of the ego, as you understand it in human civilization, this was put to rest a long time ago with Arcturians. For these beings, the ego is nonexistent, and so aspects that focus only on personality are pretty much useless in working with this energy. Most other forms of healing interaction between client and practitioner will certainly benefit. Certainly psychologists and psychotherapists will benefit by use of this star in an indirect fashion through an enhancement of their ability to listen, to understand the bond, and to work with the energies of their client in a way of inspiration and strengthening. There is a certain encouragement of the ability of any of the people involved in this process—but most importantly the practitioner—to look deeply, to solve the mystery, to see it as a puzzle, to see it with some amusement, to be able to perceive all of the clues, and to find the solution using intuition, logic, or whatever is available.

As you can imagine, the early development of this civilization did work with the equivalent of your mystery books and legends, and such things were extremely popular there. They find the broadcasts from Earth, for instance the Sherlock Holmes material, Agatha Christie, and so on, rather amusing and overly simplistic. In the sense of understanding puzzles, mysteries, and so on, they would consider Earth people quite elementary. However, they have an appreciation of your love of solving mysteries, of misunderstanding converted into awareness.

Therefore, these beings are able to deeply assist people in solving one of their great mysteries. As the subtle bodies are non-physical and definitely a mystery for most people, the awareness of the subtle bodies and how they interact is of great importance. The Arcturians are consciously directing greater energy to Earth at this time to assist people in working with these energies. This is to be a gentle influence with no specifics at first. But as people would tune into this star—meditating on Arcturus or working with the elixir on a fairly regular basis—they would find that their ability to attune to specific aspects of the subtle bodies will become clearer and clearer, and specific answers to their questions will come much more deeply.

One may be able to work with these energies for introspective discovery as well. Most people have multiple selves. There are many different parts of you that communicate with each other. The usual result of using Arcturus on your own will be to create better understanding among these different aspects of yourselves. The other benefit of using it on your own is that you would find that in working with others many difficulties are eased because the motivation behind their words becomes clearer and easier to work with. Although you are not consciously aware of it, even in your introspection you are defining yourselves by your relationships, by how you see others and know them in the world.

The Arcturians were involved at an indirect level in the process of seeding the Earth. Here was the whole idea of the creation of mystery. It was as if in the consultation with other beings and in working with these things over a long period of time there were questions as to how much should be known, how much should be revealed. The very idea of reincarnation as if creating these aspects of mystery, these things not known, this was influenced significantly by Arcturus. However, the creation of too much of an unknown had the potential to create suffering on Earth. The Arcturians had discovered that a question and its answer being separate was an artificial condition. For this reason they also influenced the way in which the Law of Help is modulated and worked out for humanity. It is as if the angelic beings, many guide beings, and many non-physical beings have studied and worked with Arcturians specifically to know this deeply so that when it is time to work with someone asking for help, these guides will be aware that a question and its answer are created together, and that this help will be given in great amounts.

The energy of Arcturus is more closely aligned with Earth's subtle bodies, in particular the atmosphere. A seeding of the geosphere of Earth has taken place in more direct fashion by comparison to DNA seeding and such as physical matter in the human being.

MIRZAM

Mirzam is projecting an energy of great loving to Earth which can be helpful and useful to understand the context of what a miracle is—the unexpected, the thing that seemed outside the context that you had created. This civilization deliberately sought to understand all contexts through their own science and awareness. This ability to move through all of these things gave them a great appreciation for their past history. Because their planet afforded them many great principles of health and longevity, many of these beings chose to live for extremely long periods of time. This allowed them to absorb and learn about many things. By telepathically combining their knowledge and understanding many things through their own science and experiments, there came a time in which it appeared that nothing new would ever be created and that there was nothing left to understand. This was a period of great stagnation for this civilization.

During that period there was the development of the idea of seeding other races and starting other systems, but the beings involved did not understand what benefit there could be from this. Having understood so much and taken this to its absolute limit as far as they could understand, they were unable to make that leap. They gradually became aware that there was a vibration on the other side of the galaxy. Their science did not understand this unusual vibration. They made preparations to visit such a place and instantly had an appearance by beings from that place. These were beings from El Nath that came to alert the beings of Mirzam to other possibilities, and then disappeared. This rather strange phenomena kept the beings of Mirzam quite occupied for a time. They began to realize that the very context that they had created was the place from which they could welcome these new energies.

They did some experiments where they took away memories, understanding, and awareness from some of their very oldest residents and then exposed them to new things and noted their responses. They began to understand that knowledge of all things was unimportant because they had not developed wisdom and the appreciation of what could be. At the moment of having such realizations, in a very inadvertent and unconscious way they produced a massive response like a joyous shout that sent itself through the galaxies with a great deal of energy. This alerted beings from Andromeda and several other neighboring galaxies to make their appearance known, and a new level of surprise came into the consciousness of these beings in the planets encircling Mirzam.

Having absorbed and understood what was presented by these other galaxies, they reached a point of stasis again. This was not an easy time for these beings. It was as if they deliberately created some degree of being stuck or misunderstanding the entire nature of things. At that point, there was a powerful change. It was as if shocked out of the barriers of time and space, and now able to suddenly move to other dimensional levels without any degree of development, they faced an energy. This energy was God as the creative force and the awareness of all things. This energy said to these beings: "Thank you, I have received what you have developed and have understood that this sense of contextual shift is a way in which limitation gives way to perceiving something as new. This contextual shift can give rise to a sense of spontaneity which is extremely helpful for the development of life." At the moment that this happened there was a shift throughout the entire civilization. In moving up through several dimensional levels, these beings merged with God.

This was certainly a magnificent miracle and surprise, but it also left behind a residue. This residue was left to the beings that co-inhabited this planet. As an extended life-span was part of their own development, these beings employed the natural tendencies of balanced ecosystems. On this planet there were all kinds of beings, many of these of great intelligence, though not to the awareness level of the original inhabitants. These beings were left with this energy. It was as if in merging with God, the release of this energy of the miraculous became available for other beings to choose consciously to use. They could not know everything that was, but they could understand God. From this they decided that in their evolution they would deliberately create appreciation as part of their awareness.

And so a custom began. This custom has been mirrored in other civilizations on Earth but not nearly to the extent of these beings. Many of the children were brought up isolated from sight, sound, and sensation. Then at the point beyond maturity, they were allowed to see, feel, think, and know. Naturally they developed an appreciation of all things. This was one technique that was utilized. As a facet of appreciation, some way of renewing faith and understanding was necessary for this sense of the miraculous to be in place. This second civilization on Mirzam never had any periods of stagnation. By experimenting with these different techniques of bringing deprivation and then awareness into consciousness, there was a great deal of energy created of tremendous benefit.

They realized that some of these ideas would be of great benefit to any other beings on other planets. When it came time to bring these energies into other systems, it was seen that on Earth there might be some benefit. Many of these things were brought into various civilizations in the past. In the times of greatest awareness of any civilization, the energies of both the old and the more recent Mirzamites were projected to Earth. So you have the great cultural flowerings in Lemuria, Atlantis, Egypt, Greece, the Renaissance, as well as in the current civilization on Earth. These energies are available. They are projected as if in waves which are spaced closer and closer together so that people will have more and more opportunities for this discovery. But discovery is to be understood and appreciated for its miraculous nature. The real aim here is to bring through an appreciation of what can be, of the ultimate possibilities. By working with Mirzam, some people may reach the point where they accept many things as miraculous.

There was a being from the first civilization on Mirzam who detached itself from the rest of this race during the time of maximum enlightenment and shift in dimensional level back to God. This being wishes to bring this sense of the miraculous and ways to achieve this into other civilizations throughout this galaxy and others. So this one has influenced those civilizations on Earth that have experimented with sensory deprivation in order to achieve a sense of greater awareness of the miraculous. The Sufis have been influenced by this to a large extent. Civilizations long unknown in South America are being brought into greater conscious awareness. Certain individuals are kept in a cave throughout their childhood and are not able to see what the world is about until their twenties. These individuals are able to maintain a constant sense of awe and awareness that brings inspiration to others. This is now being revealed, and such civilizations will have more and more attention on them in the future. They were inspired by this being from Mirzam and indeed saw him as a god for a while, but then in their own spiritual evolution began to recognize that he was a brother and was one who could assist when necessary in the future. It is possible that in times of great struggle such a being may make its presence known again on Earth.

To some extent, this individual is more interested in surprise than in spiritual awareness. This is the reason this individual detached as this race ascended. Its interest in such ascension was secondary to its appreciation of the miraculous. In interacting with many civilizations and seeking to inspire and learn from them, this ancient denizen of Mirzam was able to grow and appreciate what was really important in the development of the appreciation of miracles in various civilizations throughout the galaxy. For miracles to be truly appreciated as miracles, they must also have a little bit of danger in them, a little characteristic that makes them very much something to keep you alive, to keep you on your toes. In this new uncharted territory created by this contextual shift, there is tremendous free will. There are more opportunities, more wonderful things, but also more horrible things that can come from such miracles. For free will to be appropriately developed in people, it is very important to give people such a choice. In the creation of this miracle, they realize what choice they have made.

POLARIS ★

Polaris is the easiest to find of most stars. Most people in the Northern Hemisphere have an ability to locate it. This is good because it allows them direction. They can find north. More than with the other stars, the location of Polaris has allowed it to become a symbol for humanity for a way of finding their way around. This business of finding direction is directly related to the underlying idea of having the energy or drive to complete tasks, to find your direction, and to stay focused on that direction.

However, this has something to do with the civilization there. Beings who exist in the single planet that encircles Polaris have existed for a long time, have learning much of the wisdom of the ages, and have much understanding of many things. They have also developed astronomy to an extremely high degree. Their own ability to manifest space travel is rather interesting. They are able to create space ships by mental function and bring them to Earth. If necessary, they can get here quite quickly, even though they are quite far away by your reckoning, over 300 light years away. With focus on the star, some individuals have noted interesting subtle experiences. When meditating on the star they become aware of an unusual disk-like or triangular shape approaching them, or a sense of other-worldliness. This is indeed contact from these beings.

In their great wisdom they have looked out into the galaxy and identified and worked with all of the different planetary systems, all of the different galaxies, and all of the different beings amongst them. When they look at Earth they recognize a struggling civilization. They do not wish to interfere, but they also recognize that due to the position of the Earth's axis, Polaris appears pretty well fixed in the sky in alignment with the North Pole. Therefore, a special relationship exists between Earth and the star. This is no coincidence that this place of wisdom and clarity has been the focus since the last pole shift which occurred approximately 11,117 years ago. It was hoped that a deeper relationship might get going with this alignment between Earth and Polaris. These beings saw that Earth needed this extra sense of direction and focus. When the pole shift occurred and re-alignment of the Earth took place, this resulted in a short period of very cold weather on Earth. This new alignment was created by a deliberate attunement by Earth's guides and helpers, and by a number of beings of great mechanical power with the assistance from the Polaris beings themselves in their space ships.

A set of devices taken from some Earthly material, utilizing primarily quartz programmed in Atlantis and connected with the Egyptian pyramids, were placed on Polaris at that time. These were utilized on the Polaris planet as broadcast antennas in a radionic sense to allow deeper attunement between these planets. Then it was decided that whatever would be best for each of the civilizations would be allowed forth. For the Egyptian civilization the idea was to reflect the sense of life itself, of things beginning, of people coming to know each other, to learn from each other, and to trust each other—and that this would be a period of rapid growth. This was in alignment with humanity's guides and so the sense of growth came forth. The switch-over to the current idea of encouragement, inner strength, and a willingness to persevere occurred in the time just preceding Christ, approximately 37 BC. At such time the energies began to take clear form and shape, and these were allowed to pour into Earth by faster than light processes.

The idea is that this sense of direction, focus, and awareness of the life process itself now gives way to encouragement, to continuing on, and to looking in the face of all obstacles. This appears to be what these beings from Polaris would deem to be the wisest for humanity at this time. Recognizing free will, they will not impose this. They are not the ones to say that is what you need the most, so we are going to force it with you. But at the same time there is quite a bit to think about in terms of the very nature of free will. If the purpose of this planet is for this creation of love through free will, then anything that takes you off of that path or that becomes discouraging, or those ways in which you don't see yourself clearly, these things would be the most important to avoid, the most important to understand and let go of. At a deep level, these beings from Polaris are encouraging free will itself. This is a very important energy that might otherwise have been ignored in Earth's own development.

This sense of encouragement, of inner strength, what does it come from? It cannot come from one's own individual personality. It must come from the group consciousness. However, group consciousness must not be that which is developed only from humanity but must include all of the highest aspects that humanity strives for, such as a unity of all energetic forces of the universe and the whole understanding of God as one within people. This is the basis for the encouraging energy itself. The beings from Polaris have observed over and over that the civilizations that survive, the beings who grow to a sense of wisdom, creativity, love, or whatever anywhere in the universe can only do this with a sense of inner connectedness, and an understanding of God as manifested on all levels.

The civilization from Polaris has existed for a very long time and these beings have understood many interesting capacities. They have developed techniques of interdimensional travel in which they have been able to explore other galaxies. From this they have decided that some of the most important aspects to gather had nothing to do with intelligence or love, but had to do with perfection, with wisdom, and with the ability to understand and work with all forces in all ways. This was a gradual development over a long period of time, and certainly appears to be a logical sort of thing. But they have also recognized the principle of interference, that by looking at other civilizations with their wisdom they could interfere with them unconsciously; and so they became very careful about how they observed and worked with other energies. This has led them to a position of holding records, understanding the nature of many solar systems, and other things. In humanity's future, it is possible that visits to this place will be of great benefit to the wisest, to the leaders, to the people that would be of maximum help on Earth. However, this will not be available to just anyone. The overall sense of encouragement that Polaris can bring to people is the level that will be available for most people. This higher level of awareness that encompasses infinite wisdom and understanding of things far beyond time, space, and dimensionality as you perceive it, this would also be made available to those individuals who would reach the highest and best that their civilization has provided them.

PROCYON

In some ways, Procyon personifies or crystallizes the most typical path of development for so many extraterrestrial civilizations. Beings on the eighth planet in this system developed a natural tendency to work with mathematics and the understanding of the pure energies of their sun. By the mid-point in their evolution, they were able to manifest by concentration. By shifting the very energies of their sun, they were easily able to influence various physical processes. An equivalent of this would be using your mind to grow food. As they evolved, they began to have a tremendous perspective on things. They began to understand the nature of the universe itself. Many characteristics of the universe were understood in a scientific way. Over many evolutionary cycles of this, they became aware of the capacities of their own physical bodies to retain information. They began to bring the very starlight from their sun deep into themselves, creating pockets of this light for maximum intelligence and a strengthening of this awareness until each began to see the common goal of true education.

They decided that a tremendous energy derived through the education of karma would enable them to understand karma completely. They recognized that they would not be able to make any true progress until they understood the tremendous balancing necessary, until they had an awareness of karma on all levels. They allowed this for themselves on many levels. Many times in their evolution they deliberately created negative karma in order to evolve by balancing this in a more positive and powerful way. For instance, they decided that a test of this understanding of karma would be given when the children of this society reached a certain age. They were asked to determine the correct karmic course of action of a complicated situation involving thousands of beings on other planets, even including the motions of celestial objects and of minute microscopic beings of all kinds. Any failure to understand this and work with it correctly resulted in the instantaneous death of that child. Any success in this allowed them to transcend their own awareness to a deeper level. This very deliberately created negative karma within this society. The society was forced to evolve through understanding all of these things as deeply and powerfully as possible.

There was a gradual disassociation from all aspects of emotionality. The awareness of emotions were seen to slow down the race, and interfere with their goal of learning all of the universal laws. The Law of Karma was the first one they understood. They also became fully aware of the universal laws of manifestation, permanence, opposite expression, progress, thought, and speech. In working through multiple dimensions and various powerful mental levels, they came to this awareness in many ways. However, the Law of Love was beyond their comprehension. What was seen and understood was impossible for them to grasp.

They recognized their own limitation, and began to see that by broadcasting the highest level of their own mental functioning into the universe, they might encourage other beings to quickly come to this revelation themselves. Their energies were lost on most of the civilizations who have to find similar mental paths for their own survival. Because of the relatively low concentrations of negative energies of emotional nature on most other planets in most star systems in this galaxy, these energies of the mind are natural as ones that ensure the survival of the races.

So then these beings from Procyon recognized that their ultimate gift would be to provide this mental awareness to particular beings who might be able to work with it in their own creation of heart energy, of love energy, such as with Earth beings. The conscious broadcast of these energies is a great deal of fun for these beings. These mental energies pouring into Earth can help people create a deeper ability to concentrate.

But these beings are also a bit dissatisfied with their own evolution. Although they took all measures to move forward, did all things possible to come to a place of maximum evolution, they missed something. They missed the very thing that people on Earth struggle so much to gain and understand. It is not just compassion or love, but it is a willingness to allow the love itself to direct one's activities while the mind is asleep. This is not to say that the minds of human beings are asleep, but in comparison to beings from Procyon, human minds are in a state of deep, deep, trance sleep. These beings can have full awareness of every molecule in a sun, can understand every atmospheric interaction of all the particles, substances, and beings in a volume of space that might exist around an entire planet. However, their awareness of such things has not given them the understanding and evolution that they desired. Earth people may eventually be able to teach other races about facets of love, such as letting go to discover that love, knowing it within yourself, and seeking it as its own end. These beings from Procyon hope that they will be taught about love, that they will be the ones perhaps to combine this with their own understanding and transcend. When this occurs, they will finally reach their next goal. It is not clear what it will be, but it may be something along the lines of the creation of a magnificent sister galaxy to the Milky Way. This would be a galaxy full of all sorts of beings that have the capacity to enjoy, to grow, to play, and to love, as well having the capacity to think, to understand, and to create their own universes should they choose this.

This general evolution towards creativity appears in many races. And this dependence upon mental acuity and understanding of karma through the mind also appears in many races. The beings from Procyon have perhaps taken this to the highest degree of evolution of any society that might come in contact with Earth. Through their own great intelligence and observation, they have seen that Earth is perhaps the place holding the greatest and most important answers to their own evolution. By understanding and working with the Law of Progress, they have come to accept and understand patience. They have infinite patience, and they will wait as long as it takes for Earth's own evolution to be eventually shared.

FOMALHAUT ★

Early in their development, the beings on the fourth planet from Fomalhaut recognized the importance of addictive principles, but were unable to fully integrate this into their society. They had understood that the chlorophyll-based forms they ate derived energy directly from their sun. At first, this was viewed as a natural process, just as you do on Earth. They began to derive energies directly from Fomalhaut itself, eventually releasing the need for the ingestion of physical substance. The light from Fomalhaut was of the perfect spectral configuration to provide them all the energies they needed.

There was a great debate amongst Fomalhaut society of the principle of the addictive versus nourishment. This principle is that which plays upon your consciousness whenever you begin to look at any addictive principles yourself. Is this something my body really needs or is this something I am addicted to? You may even play with this in humorous ways as in: "I am addicted to water." But there is a difference between an addiction and that which is part of your substance and needs to be replenished. These beings were made of light and needed to be replenished by such. But they were on the verge of a transformation beyond such a level to a realization that they were made of God, that they were made of the essence of things higher than light. They were able to see the addictive principle, and in many cases chose—not always consciously—to attune to the light of Fomalhaut rather than to the forces higher than that.

By very slightly altering the spectrum of the light from Fomalhaut, machine beings originally created in the star system of Procyon were easily able to accelerate sensations of pleasure and euphoria within these beings and enslave them. These machine beings were able to provide powerful energies of a nourishing nature in order to transfer the addiction away from the light of Fomalhaut towards the machine beings. This became the ultimate addiction—where you become consciously, unconsciously, in all ways a slave. The slavery was complete. Their minds, the awareness of their hearts, their day-to-day lives, and many other things were influenced by this. These machines needed raw materials. Fomalhaut is a star that has twelve planets around it that are very rich in all kinds of natural resources such as various materials, various energetics, crystalline structures, and many other things of great interest to other beings.

This position of slavery existed for a long time. After the machine wars ended on Procyon, the civilization on Procyon still maintained a relationship with the beings on Fomalhaut. The beings from Procyon decided to listen to what these beings from Fomalhaut really want. And the Fomalhaut beings, many of them at such time oppressed and in places of struggle and discomfort, did recognize that they were being listened to. In a very short period they created a collective message: "Help us to let this energy somehow change."

As a result beings from Procyon, Alcyone, Polaris, and many other star systems poured their energy into this planet. It was seen that direct interference with the machine beings was actually unnecessary and would not aid in the development of this planet. This energy poured into this planet to give these beings more free will, more choice, more awareness, and more ability to understand the very principles that they were working with. What became very clear here was that an eventual break could be made by deliberately creating a situation where these machine beings became dependent on the people of Fomalhaut and on the resources of the twelve planets. This beautiful energy of understanding was kept secret from the machines. This was very easy to do, because machines don't really understand in that sense.

Over a period of about fifty years, the beings from Fomalhaut concentrated on understanding the addictive principle. They came to understand very deeply, very clearly, all facets of addiction, and applied this understanding in great amounts to the machines. Being machines, they did not have much awareness (in the sense of consciousness) about such dependence, and found such addictive principles were impossible to resist. The machines became very addicted to such as the beings from Fomalhaut provided. This was an addiction to materials, but also to ways of thinking, particular machine parts, and particular ways of showing them how to do things.

Towards the end of this fifty year period, the beings from Fomalhaut used their understanding of addiction to produce a device. This device was the most addictive device that could ever be produced, as anyone who utilized it would focus all their energies on the sensations produced by the device. This device was provided to all of these machines, who became enmeshed with it until their batteries ran down and they all died. It was really a very simple solution once the full awareness of addiction as a principle came into consciousness. Of course when we speak about batteries running down and the rest, we are oversimplifying, but you get the general idea.

The principle of addiction was clearly used to create a situation of powerlessness among the machines, which was then utilized to free these beings from their position of powerlessness. As a result of this, all of the civilizations who had helped as well as others sought information about this principle. The question for them became: "What is addiction, what does this mean, and how do we have this in our society?" Almost at once, the beings of Fomalhaut became teachers to share this. In their own way, this was a very difficult period for them. It lasted about 3,500 years. It was a period in which they became addicted to their own ability to teach, to share information, and to assist others.

These beings had to work with these principles for awhile to fully understand them. Having transcended and understood thought addiction, utilizing it for the freeing of their planet, what would be a further step in this road toward releasing addictions? The next step would be to release the addiction to helping, to making a difference, and to assisting others. These beings came to the deeper understanding that they were in some ways short-circuiting their own development by helping others. As a result of this a period of inner work took place. This lasted for about another 3,500 years. They came out of this with a deep understanding of all life processes.

They created a series of protective energies around their planet. These were to be sure that no enslaving would ever take place again with their civilization. This was simply a beacon of powerful energy that would burst forth from the star and pour into their solar system and their region of the galaxy. This energy would empower, would say to any beings: "You need nothing from us. You may find all that you need in yourselves, in your own awareness, in your own understanding."

It was initially a protective device to minimize any interference from other planets. It was not that the beings who interfered were doing so in any way to harm beings from Fomalhaut; but they did not realize that these beings from Fomalhaut had created for themselves this path of learning and understanding all facets of addictions. Initially, it was not a deliberately chosen path. But in God's wisdom in working with these energies with this planet, what was discovered was a magnificent principle. This principle came into formation toward the end of that second 3,500-year cycle. Once this came into greater clarity it was seen that this principle needed free will and assistance on all levels in the way in which the Fomalhaut beings themselves wished it. The energy of their beacon was respected, known, and relayed throughout the galaxy and into many other galaxies.

As a result of this a gentle influence came into the Earth at that time. It was an influence that said: "What can you learn from this whole principle of addiction and dependence where a reference that is external is seen as being more important than a reference that is internal?" This was an influence in the development of the dinosaurs. Later the development of various conscious forms of this energy was allowed in human society during the middle and later Atlantean epoch. This was a period when the addictive principle was first explored in a direct and conscious way by humanity.

Many hundreds of thousands of years after the dinosaurs, the beings from Fomalhaut had come to an entirely different understanding about this. Between the period of the end of the age of the dinosaurs and the period of the Atlantean civilization for humanity, many changes took place in the Fomalhaut system. They were able to recognize the great benefit of empowerment and the releasing of any aspects that could take one away from the higher sources, higher love, and higher purpose of whatever civilization. They observed this by seeing the effect their beacon had on other civilizations and on other beings who came close to Fomalhaut. They also observed that although it was a defensive maneuver, still this beacon had capacities they had not thought of, they had not seen, and they saw the benefit of this.

So it is that very beacon that continues to affect Earth when people attune to Fomalhaut. As they attune to this whole principle, many of these things come into form. This powerful influence is deep within the core of humans because of this energy influencing the genetic development of reptiles and this having been incorporated into humanity's genetic development—the reptilian core of the brain is sometimes referred to in some older texts. In meditation or working with the star elixir, there is a positive influence that can help individuals attune to what they have been. This can assist them in tracing their own contact through past civilizations, and understanding how in past lives the addictive principle has influenced them so much.

There is of course with all of this a parallel in that civilizations have been created that were slave-based or addiction-based and there are powerful aspects of this running through human society right now. Right now in society there is enough consciousness and free will, and many programs that deliberately focus on addiction, that if people choose to look at this consciously, they can do so.

The parallel to the beings on Fomalhaut so long ago is very different. Without the help of others, they could not begin to look at this issue and understand the very nature of their slavery.

The core of addiction is an aspect of free will that is removed from consciousness. A slavery to the external reference takes place. Slavery is a condition where one aspect is directly coupled to another with no potential here for its own free will or its own development. Where consciousness, awareness, love, or any other higher aspect of existence is present in the master, some of it always leaks into the slave. As a result, the awareness and the consciousness of the master will naturally be transferred to the slave. This means that the master/slave relationship must be a dynamic one that must change by its very nature. As God's understanding is now transmitted to all beings, slavery can only be a temporary condition, and is generally not seen as a balanced, healthy, or useful state.

This realization has been especially clear over the last 120 years or so on Earth and coincides with the channeling of the Emancipation Proclamation and the information given to Abraham Lincoln near the middle of the Civil War. This is important because in this understanding of addictive principle is this awareness of the external reference and the awareness of the similarity between slavery and addiction. This may not always be very clear, but is certainly alluded to in all of the literature. The monkey on my back is one of the old terms referring to heroin addiction.

The wide resources available to the Fomalhaut beings through the variety of substances, energies, and other things found throughout their solar system makes the energy in their beacon one that can affect people on Earth in many different ways and can help them with substance addiction of many different substances or addiction to particular forms of co-dependent relationship, sex, or even addictions to thinking. There are many energies here that are helpful on many different levels, and it is up to the individual to attune to the specific aspect they require when utilizing the Fomalhaut energies.

From the story of the civilization from Fomalhaut, you recognize that a society poised on the brink of transformation is most vulnerable to enslavement. This principle has direct parallel to humanity right now. People as poised on the brink of this transformation are most vulnerable to new energies that would say to them: "Be asleep. Take power for yourself. Choose power over others." or other foolish messages. Of even more importance is that beings have choice in this matter, if they are but willing to see it. This tale is not simply of historical significance or for understanding of these patterns, but also relates to people on Earth.

ALDEBARAN

In a time long before the seeding of humanity on Earth, beings living on the fourth planet that encircles this star had the ability to understand and work with powerful energies of all sorts. There was a development of a separate race. This race was the ultimate gift. They saw that working with the energies of procreation would have a great impact on the development of their society. One soul would give birth to one child. The child was conceived of over a period of several thousand years. This massive group effort was society's goal.

The production of this race took place in a tremendous burst of creative energy. They utilized many sources from other suns and star systems, including Procyon, El Nath, and even from other galaxies as yet unknown or unnamed in your science. All sorts of vibrational methods were utilized to genetically and aetherically crossbreed these energies to create this new race. These newly-born beings had a tremendous ability to communicate, to understand, and to transcend the lives of the parents. These beings then gathered together over a period of 200 years to understand themselves.

They saw that it was necessary to separate from the parent civilization. The parent civilization saw that this was in greatest harmony, and assisted these children to migrate to the sixth planet in their star system. Because this planet was much cooler and not as life-supporting, this involved the production of all sorts of artificial energy sources so that they could exist. Since the beings that were created were so powerful and had inherent capabilities to manifest in new ways and transcend dimension, this was fairly easily done.

After the settling took place and the society began to grow on this planet, the parent group began to perceive all sorts of energies at subtle levels. These energies seemed to radiate from the sixth planet. These were unclear energies of struggle which became very deeply saddening to the parent group. The parent group began to recognize that they did not know the child. Emissaries and diplomats between the two planets conveyed information back to the parent saying, everything is fine, these are just your interpretations of our feelings.

But in fact there was deep problem within the society being created on the sixth planet. They could not accept that the universe they had come into was ready to hold them, love them, and know them. This was implanted in their genetic structures, but they did not have the inherent understanding that comes from a history of struggle and difficulty. It was as if what they were attempting to do was touch a small portion of emotion. All of these beings together were attempting to know all facets of emotional awareness. Although not nearly to the extent that all the different kinds of loss, grief, or struggle are understood by humanity, just this small portion of emotional understanding was too much. There was a mass suicide. They simply disconnected all of the equipment that allowed life to be sustained, and within a few short hours all were dead.

These parents had established this society by their own love and kindness, their own bodies, and their own willingness to see this. All of a sudden the energies that emanated from this planet stopped, and emissaries brought back the sad news. This caused a great struggle in their civilization, and a rethinking of many goals. There were some suicides, and much difficulty, insanity, depression, and other problems amongst those people. Yet for the most part they made it through. Recognizing that this is planet populated by beings who were in telepathic communication, emotionally aware, and who understood many things, even so it was barely up to their ability to handle this. They moved through a period of grief and struggle which you cannot imagine.

As a result of this they came to a new understanding. They discovered that the best way to experience the overall depth of evolution would be through the experiences that were created by free will, not through genetic manipulation or the understanding of the parent. They had not been attempting to side-step evolution, but they recognized their failure. They had a vision of a future race who had evolved by means of free will and a separation of love from other characteristics, eventually to utilize the science developed by these parent beings and others to further this new race's own evolution. Such was glimpsed as one possibility for the race that was to be humanity.

One result of this was some of the seeding into the desert areas of Earth, such as the tribes of Israel, bedouin tribes, the Nairobi desert, the Sudan, and others. Some of this genetic seeding was derived from the experiments that were done by these beings from Aldebaran. These energies were powerful and very useful for other races who contributed to the seeding process on Earth. The link with Aldebaran was broken so that the beings from Aldebaran would not influence humanity, would not be directly involved, and would not interfere with their will upon humanity's will, even if the cost meant mass suicide for humanity or some way in which the people on Earth did not accept the gifts of love that the Aldebaran beings had.

Certain changes in the planets of the Aldebaran system required some changes in their own evolution. The development of water-based and desert-based technologies gave rise to civilizations there, and so it was very easy to draw on those for some benefit in this seeding process on Earth.

There is an inherent link very deep in the genetic character of all people on Earth. Should they attune to Aldebaran, they may sense a little bit of this loss because this is in their history. But these beings from Aldebaran have filtered most of this out of what they are broadcasting to Earth. What is left is an empowerment, a loving, an encouragement, and a willingness to say: "You live. You grow. You may be." These are some very beautiful things, which act as an example for other civilizations that have sought a seeding of Earth.

These beings from Aldebaran hope that humanity may someday choose to co-create a civilization with them on this sixth planet. This planet was not chosen as a place to struggle against ecology and other difficulties. It was chosen because it is a planet with tremendous internal capacities for a powerful support structure. The highly compressed inert gases of xenon and krypton act as a core within its center which projects a magnificent, strong, clearing energy that could be quite sustaining and helpful to any civilization capable of living there. Most natives of the Aldebaran system would not be capable of living there because of the higher energy levels required to be in such a cold place.

ANTARES

The seeds of this civilization was an understanding of light and dark that ran very deep in their consciousness. In the religious development of this civilization, there was a powerful energy of light and dark. There is a planetary system around the star Antares that includes at the fourth planetary orbit two planets equidistant from the sun Antares, and on opposite sides of Antares. The other planet could not be seen night or day. The result was an energetic connection between the beings on these two planets that was largely unconscious, since without space travel the beings on one planet were not aware of beings on the other. This balance at an unconscious level was very powerful between them.

These civilizations were seeded by a number of factors from other places somewhat influenced by the explosion of energy from El Nath we spoke of earlier. They were also influenced by a parallel course in genetics that came about through the natural geological formation of the planets. These two planets were very similar in many ways, having similar quantities of substances such as water, air, food, and other things.

As these civilizations developed, they recognized each other through the intuitive and through the dream state. In many cases their seasons were also balanced—one moving through winter while the other through summer. This led to some rather interesting balances before space travel was possible for these beings. This gradually led to a development of a clear understanding within of the dream side. The activities even eventually reached a place where the genetic structures themselves became powerfully influenced by consciousness and one soul group would create in the other civilization on the parallel planet a balanced soul group in incarnation. One would be experiencing out the negative karma that the other was experiencing as a positive karma. This led eventually to a seeking of understanding of consciousness through this balancing of the two halves.

When space travel became possible, much was revealed. A co-development between the civilizations took place through free trade, free travel, and understanding. There was also a co-development through religions on both planets of the understanding of light and dark, of the powerful nature of the two sides of existence, and of the many polarities. Over a period of about 3,500 years, the co-seeding and co-development led to several phases of war, some difficulties of understanding of relationship, and the eventual genetic merging that led to a unification of the races coinciding with a transformation into other dimensions. This powerful energy was primarily third dimensional in character and was the foundation for this civilization's transformation to the fourth dimension. The pooling of resources from both the planets was of great power and developed within this civilization a great respect for the awareness of life and for the awareness of all sentient beings on both planets. After many thousands of years, this led to the eventual development into higher dimensional levels—fifth, sixth, and seventh—where the civilization now exists.

Although the animal and plant life was not as varied as that in humanity's existence and awareness through terrestrial forces, still a pattern emerged even there where plants on one planet would tend to mirror action of plants on another, acting as the shadow self one for the other, and there was a general balance here too. Many of the foods taken from one planet to another were found to be exotic, stimulating, strange, and yet with a ring of familiarity. This ran in many ways through the civilization because of God's influence and the seeding influence of the Elohim. These powerful energies were to create these dichotomies for the deliberate purpose of allowing a new merged self to emerge from these civilizations. Telepathy, interactive communication, and awareness of the intuitive state or dream state was far more prevalent, accepted, and understood through these civilizations than it has been on Earth.

But at the same time, the development of space travel was impeded. There are a number of factors, primarily the deficiency of metals as found in these planets. Eventually, biological means of space travel over short distances were developed for the interaction between these planets. Here again, the spacecraft were developed pretty much concurrently between the two civilizations. These biological entities could attack each other, sometimes without the direct knowledge of those who worked with them.

Honoring both sides of all issues became an important aspect of the combined civilization. This was to give an even-handedness, creating a race of diplomats when these beings eventually rose to sixth dimensional level. These diplomats settled crises and wars throughout the galaxy. But such an energy is not accessible to humanity at this time. The diplomacy issue relates very much to the acceptance in oneself of the parallels that one sees in one's enemy; and this is an important principle of diplomacy that has not been sufficiently applied on Earth. Diplomats on Earth are primarily mediators to achieve compromise, to see the bigger view and transmit this to the parties involved; but not to help them see themselves, to help them understand their own purpose in this conflict, and to see how the shadow self is reflected in one's own enemy. Therefore at some later date when there is greater spiritual awareness and acceptance of this inner principle of the shadow self mirrored in one's enemy, then the diplomacy aspects of Antares will become more prevalent. This may be available now in small groups of people. This will become a more important principle after about 2010 or 2025 in mankind's own development

In this awareness of the shadow self, what you see is another aspect of yourself mirrored in your world, mirrored in your own understanding of your past lives, or mirrored in your understanding of so many aspects of your personality. These civilizations from Antares co-developed energies that they put into their sun which were broadcast. Some of this broadcasting is directed specifically at Earth for the purpose of awakening this dual nature, these polarities in people. There is a certain mysteriousness associated with it because it is clearly derived from experience. The greater lesson from Antares is that through the experiences of life itself and in the experience of one's own personal revelation comes also the ability to communicate, to trust the intuition, and to look squarely in the face all those aspects of oneself that one was not always able to accept. In accepting these and in seeing them for what they are, progress can be made, changes can be allowed, and ultimately this awareness can be shared with others.

Beings from Antares were involved in the seeding of Earth and interaction with humans for the development of emotions through understanding the primary function of the hypothalamus, and in the development of the various chemistries that are necessary for the understanding of emotion. Here it was seen that both the free will aspect where humanity would develop on its own and the way of seeding very deep or even unconscious activities into humanity would be necessary. So the influence here was partly genetic but also an overshadowing influence in the development of the emotional body of people. The influence here was for a time created by direct interaction emotional body to emotional body between Antares beings and Earth people. This was tried in many different ways. One way was to offer a bit of a vacation to individuals in Lemurian and Atlantean cultures to come to Antares to experience this blending of many things and to experience some of their own culture and history. Another was a way in which the emotional body of an Antarean being was actually detached from such a being and allowed to work directly with humans who chose such path. This was more in the later phases of Atlantis than in the Lemurian phase, but was often experimented with at various times in prehistory.

There is some overshadowing by beings from Antares in relation to the concept of the Tao. After all, Tao is about unity through diversity, and a way of these yin and yang forces combining. But here it extends even beyond the influence of any single civilization. The work of Lao Tzu was influenced by beings from Antares, but was also a direct creation from his own awareness, consciousness, and acceptance of the Earth. And this is the part that is unique and the part that also attracts Antares beings here today. The Earth's own influence is of great importance right now in your civilization in an understanding of the shadow self, in an understanding of your own personality development, and ultimately with your interaction in groups with the Earth. Many of the most important ecological issues people face are solved not just through the interaction at scientific level or understanding of your biosphere. These problems are also solved by an emotional acceptance of the Earth as a parallel for your own development—your own life blood being her waters, your own awareness of immune function relating to the rain forests, and many other things acting as parallels. This is very interesting to Antares beings: how you solve these issues will be of benefit in their own understanding of humanity.

VEGA ★

Many beings from Vega were involved in the seeding of the human race. Partway through this process, they began to experience some emotional difficulties from their extensive interaction with humans. They chose then to look at all of the different ways things had been done in the past to discover what would make the most difference for all of the civilizations and societies on Earth. Once again, they found their feelings were very difficult to understand. It was as if they had to almost become partly human in order to have such insights.

As a result, they began a long search for the essence of vibration. This search was inspired in many ways by the initial bringing together of forces for the creation of genetic structures on Earth. In this way, the further development of the Vegan civilization occurred at the same time as the development of Earth's civilization. These beings began to recognize that their affinity with humanity could best be served by some portion of free will and love being projected in a way that created a minimum of dependence. The idea was to create inspiration without any particular form or any particular way in which it was to come.

The beings from Vega have a hypersensitivity to dependence and co-dependence, relationship addiction, or even the development of societies and civilizations which have a sympathetic relationship with each other. Part of this is because they experienced a great deal of difficulty in the early development of their civilization. There was a series of wars on the sixth planet from their sun. These wars destroyed a large portion of their natural resources. It was as if certain bacteria were created that were able to devour and destroy only specific plant species or specific materials. There is some kinship to the neutron bomb which destroys all life, but leaves the buildings and larger structures intact. The great horror that many people feel about this is in some ways irrational and based upon their genetic connection to these Vegan beings. After they put aside war, these beings developed a natural interdependence as they became better acquainted and decided to find a way of life together. Due to the resulting scarcity of resources, it was with a great deal of struggle that they were able to trade across continents. They became fully dependent on each other for their survival.

They recognized that there was an underlying source of energy deep within their planet that gave them the strength for peace, for understanding, and for wisdom. Just as Earth has a vibration of approximately 7.83 cycles per second associated with her own being, this planet had a multiplicity of profound and powerful vibrations that are almost musical in nature. This was a uniting energy for all of the beings. An inner communication was then created and telepathy opened for all of the beings on this world. Over a period of several years, a relatively short period for such development, there was a great deal of interconnection and understanding.

As this process continued, many of the children suffered, for they could not adapt easily to the shift. To save the ones that were remaining, their answer was to let the inner vibration of their planet pour into these children to inspire, nurture, and sustain them, and not have them weighed down by the history of the planet. From this the children began to do something very strange. They began to make noises with their mouths, to pick up various objects and make noises with them, and to utilize various substances to make various tones, generally in harmony and occasionally in deliberate disharmony with the vibration of their world. This was not understandable to the adults, but it saved the children. So it was understood, studied, taught, worked with, and from this the science of music began.

There were certain precedents for this in this galaxy in the ways in which natural vibrations tend to work together. But this was a new way of utilizing the underlying inspirational vibration of a world to save lives, and to increase life itself. These children had a natural ability to appreciate newly developed things. This music gradually evolved, taking hundreds of thousands of years before it became something that could be well communicated and understood. Growing up at the same time as telepathic communication, music eventually surpassed telepathic communication for these beings. These beings took their music with them as they increased their vibrational level to reach higher and higher vibrational, interdimensional, and density levels.

Many attempts were made to seed other civilizations using primarily music. Very little of anything has come from such experiments. Other civilizations sought the assistance of Vegans to create a genetic transfer into the human race that would help human children survive, partly by an attunement to song, music, and rhythm, and partly by an attunement to the life force within them. However, the Vegans discovered that this would create too much interference, too much dependence on the other civilizations, too many ways in which Earth people would not develop independently.

So what was designed into the DNA structures were simple links at vibrational level to an attunement to the Earth's own vibration, an attunement to the principles of music, and a natural way in which music would tend to realign the DNA patterns and hence be transmitted throughout the body. Cultural aspects were also planted deeply into human society by the Vegans, such as the ones who are mythologized in the various religions of the Earth as ones who have played instruments and used music to teach these principles of healing through music. There was no requirement as to how these abilities would be used, only that they would be available. This was unique, and was a very different way of structuring such seeding. The Vegans understood this as the best way to proceed.

Until this experiment with Earth has come to a place of some logical conclusion, the other seeding experiments of the Vegans throughout the galaxy have been halted. They are waiting, and because of this there is especially a great deal of focus and attention on Earth at this time from these beings. They will not interfere by such as visiting here on Earth or causing any difficulty amongst Earth society. But they will continue to broadcast many frequencies and energies to Earth to inspire people, to help them to understand music, to play where needed, and to listen deeply to the inner music. When people experience music together, this can create a deeper connection between people through a resonance of their DNA structures. Just as the ways of telepathy and music were able to be as one with the Vegans, so it is likely this will happen to humanity.

You generally recognize music as the result of emotional work or physical body work as influenced by the mind. However, you would recognize telepathy as mind interaction influenced by the emotions, the body, or other things. Therefore, communication through music with telepathy is beyond simply a sharing of a song. It is the underlying energy that is shared. The result is that the individual may find the inspiration deep within them to sing that song or to express this feeling in some way. This attunement can eventually lead to a new musical form: simultaneous musical improvisation. Many individuals have experienced this at various times, and this is the beginnings of this telepathic musical communication. For instance, jazz musicians are well known to be in synchronization together, and thus are able to play duets where everything fits together very beautifully. This has even been extended into larger groups. There are many examples of this, and most of them tend to be with groups that are short-lived. When they are playing music together, they are unconsciously communicating in a way in which they release all aspects of their beings to each other. They may be unable to continue this level of communication outside the musical context. This can often lead to struggles where musicians have a difficulty with drugs or other addictions. Although Fomalhaut will be helpful, Vega can be especially helpful in such cases for assistance with understanding the underlying principles. Many times the addiction comes just because the intimacy and closeness with the other musicians has been very deep, and the person has been unable to assimilate and work with the experience.

For the future, it would appear that the Vegans still have a bit to teach in the way of music. But in a few hundred years it is likely that by working with their own free will and with this gift, humanity will have reached a level parallel to that of the Vegans and be able to contribute musically there. This is nice to know for those musicians who would like to imagine having a wider audience in the future.

As a developing civilization, it is wise to focus and concentrate on those things which are most necessary for the insured survival and development of that civilization. But it is also wise to assist beings in other worlds with what they need. In their own way, Vegans have made a great deal of hope, love, and assistance available to humanity, partly for selfish reasons. Their civilization has developed to a certain point in an understanding of this magnificent interconnectedness, this wonderful musical vibration, and the awareness of its rhythms throughout galaxies. But the amount of love they can manipulate, use, and understand is limited. Perhaps more than other civilizations, they hope for humanity's evolution so that the aspects of love that humans have developed will be shared. At the appropriate time in humanity's future, these beings will most definitely cry out for what Earth has to share.

The Physical Form of Vegans

The physical form of musical reception is actually secondary. Although you would recognize that the ear is a surface that can vibrate easily, the skin is one that can be affected by music, as well as the cells themselves. Although the brain causes the messages to be received, it is not the place where the energy is felt. Indeed although the heart is part of the process, at a much deeper level it is by resonant structures throughout the physical body, primarily DNA based, that most of the musical information is received. This is the part of you that likes the music, finds it very beautiful, reminds you of something, takes you to another place, or puts you in a state of emptiness or fullness. Once this was recognized, this was coordinated with the natural development of science in Vega's own evolution. What began to emerge is the way of change for the physical body. This is a natural sort of thing to coordinate with vibrational interaction, and so this is also true for the physical structures of most of the beings of higher vibration throughout the galaxy. Throughout this book, we have mentioned various different beings and not put very much attention on their physical structures. As they have evolved, they have recognized that it is easily possible to alter their physical structure, and have usually done so to reflect the inner being, to reflect the nature of who they are, what they are growing from, and the sort of things that they are wishing to work with.

So for a time on Vega there was some attention on physical structure, including the development of very sensitive ear structures. But very quickly it was found that all of these structures were simply to bring the energy into the DNA itself, and so all that seemed to be necessary was to be aware of all the DNA in the body and set it into vibration, letting that vibration then interact with the vibrations created by other musical sources be they the planet, stars, other beings, or some of the natural forces of life through the various plants, animals, and other living things that might be contacted. As vibrational awareness to higher dimensional levels increased, it was a simple matter to increase resonance between the subtler DNA structures—those which relate to the subtle bodies and the higher dimensional aspects—and the DNA structures of other beings. So the idea is that the actual coupling takes place through resonant structures. The physical structure's ability to transmit such vibration became unimportant.

You could imagine a Vegan being looking very much like you, but when you play music for them they begin to glow all over as if every cell becomes alive. In this aliveness there is a magnificent vibration. As the music is received each individual cell with its own individual DNA strand vibrates in its own unique way. Waves of color pour through the being. There is some gentle movement as in an undulation, and these reflect the responses to the music. A more receptive audience you could not ask for. If you can imagine a musician playing to a crowd of such beings, it would be quite an amazing experience. They would also be broadcasting feelings, awareness, and many things which relate to higher dimensional characteristics. Clouds of light would tend to gather over the entire group, and these would also move through various variations in color and shading. When the concert is over, they would become as if one vibration of thanks and receptivity, and this energy would simply move from these beings into the musicians playing, and this would be the equivalent of the clapping of hands.

The Influence of Vega on Music on Earth

At times these beings from Vega are imagining about music that would be helpful to humanity. If people can be given a choice as to how to work with it or not, these things can be made all that much more available. What is seen as useful for many people on Earth is a time of peace, a time of emptiness, a time for recreating the energies of inspiration and source—not the energies that would tend to be disruptive or remind you of your past, but rather those energies that open you to your possible future, your potential. This music is sometimes known as space music, but is really more accurately called emptiness music. The Vegans have influenced the development of this sort of music, and individuals who have expressed themselves this way have sometimes found themselves very surprised to discover that the music is widely received. These vibrations pour from Vega into Earth, touching everyone. Those people who feel a need to experience this emptiness but cannot do it without some inspiration, they will do well by working with such space music.

Vegans have influenced various forms of music in the past. One of these was the shift from the earlier musical forms shortly after the development of the equal-tempered scale, the shift out of Mozart into more Romantic music. This was an important development for bringing heart energy and more love into humanity. But beyond this there are no primary influences, they would never interfere. Though such beings have some resonance and acceptance of all forms of music, some are not as popular on Vega as they are here on Earth.

SIRIUS

Sirius has great historical significance for people on Earth. This star is a binary with a periodicity of approximately 49.5 years. This is well known to astronomers. However it was also known through esoteric sources. The teachings through Alice Bailey describe the powerful influence of Sirius on many levels. The understanding of the magnetic energies that pour from this system to Earth is only a symbol. This works like any astrological symbol, but having a much longer period than most of the astrological symbols in the solar system, this cycle has a profound effect on individuals on Earth because humanity has chosen to work with this symbol. The second reason for this great influence is that the powerful aetheric energies of the star itself have an ability to create transformation.

Sirius is shrouded in a little bit of mystery. Few extraterrestrial beings who communicate telepathically with humans appear to explain clearly about Sirius.

Part of this is the strong genetic connection, and the understanding of these powerful cycles. But more importantly, there is a direct tie-in to Earth's immediate future. Because of this, some of the information we will share may have impact at a cellular level. So we will assist with your creation in your imagination of a beautiful emerald light swirling and easily releasing this information so that the cellular structures do not have to hold this information. The cellular structures can let it go, but at the same time you can recognize the potentials and opportunities that this reveals.

Earlier in this book, we have spoken of this star in the past with regards to some of its healing properties. But to recognize the value of this, we need to go back about 500 million years. Time is very difficult to peg into exact categories because the very nature of time itself is shifted by consciousness. The single sun broke apart approximately 500 million years ago. This was a rather unusual phenomena, as most binaries are captured binaries. The Sirius binary is unstable due to the nature of this star giving birth. When this occurred there was a tremendous explosion. Flares, magnetic forces, and other powerful energies swept through the Sirius star and into multiple dimensions and swept across the surrounding planets. This destroyed the life on all of the planets, but at the same time seeded these planets with a very interesting characteristic of transformation. The birth of this complex binary created a cyclical movement of transformational energies.

This cycle has been different at various times in the past. These larger cycles roughly correspond to periods of approximately 26,000 years, and are similar to the major periods of Earth's own evolution. In one case this binary had a cycle of about 126 years, in another period a cycle of about 7 years, and now it is about 49.5 years. As the shift into the domain of the Aquarius energy takes place, it is likely that a new cycle will emerge. This may be created by a powerful instability that will occur as two stars reach their closest approach in June of 1994; or it may occur during the next cycle, about 49.5 years later. It is unclear as to just when this new cycle will begin, because many of the energies of consciousness strongly affect this.

The planetary system around this binary is strongly affected by these energies. Every 49.5 years the interaction of the two stars causes a tremendous shift in their magnetic fields, powerful solar flares, extreme weather changes, and even shifts in the axes and orbits for all of the planets that go around this star. Many naturally occurring civilizations based on simple life forms were able to survive for brief periods only to perish. The irregular nature of these stars and how close they pull to each other occasionally causes a tremendous change. Sometimes this would occur every 500 years, sometimes every 1000 years, sometimes every 12,000 years, or at other combinations of these cycles. These stars would pour forth powerful energies such as magnetic fields and all kinds of electrical energies. As these energies pour through the planetary worlds, this would create earthquakes, floods, fires, and other things of catastrophic nature that are difficult for you to imagine. The beings that have grown there have to cope with this.

With the gradual development of life on the second, third, fourth, and fifth planets, these energies were implicit in the development of all plant and animal species. Entire worlds were created with the underlying idea of periodic cyclical transformation. Imagine a world built on the very principle of this powerful transformation from its very beginning time. Upon the second planet a variety of life forms began to recognize this powerful energy. This was an evolutionary step by which they would actually absorb and work with this energy. They found a way to allow what was going on around them to simply pass through them. They made an unconscious transfer from a third-dimensional form into a fourth-dimensional form, and later into a fifth-dimensional form. For their own survival, insects, plants, and other living forms of simple nature were able to make this transition.

As intelligent beings naturally evolved, they had an innate capacity to shift in vibration and to work with many different energies. In the development of this civilization at various times long past, they worked with this energy of transformation energy in various forms. Naturally there was a time of primitive worship of this. It was necessary for these beings to transform their own bodies in the time of maximum transformation of their own suns. As these two suns get so close together their magnetic fields become extremely strong. They gradually learned how use these magnetic fields for their own healing. Where there is destruction because of natural cataclysms as in high winds, powerful storms, flooding, fire, and such things on their world, they heal these by manipulating the movement of the aether with their own ability to love. In this way they did have to wait many years for the ecosphere to repair itself.

Their ability to love is a bit narrow at this time by comparison to the opportunities available for Earth people, and it is this which draws them or bonds them to Earthlings. Their development of love was a way of directly manipulating the magnetic forces of their suns so that plants and animals which had been harmed could be brought into a state of physical health quickly. In this way the effects of such cataclysms were short-lived. Over the many thousands of years that these techniques were utilized, the underlying message that gradually came into consciousness was one of the innate ability to heal something far larger than any sort of individual disease. They had the ability to heal an entire planet by the utilization of thought, visualization, and deep contemplative awareness for the manipulation of the aethers to create this healing. This understanding gave these beings a deep reverence for such an energy.

During one of these periods of transformation on Sirius, a powerful link was established between the Sirius suns and the Earth's sun. This link was the bond that allowed the DNA seeding that took place in the early Lemurian epoch. Very powerful energies were focused to work with physical matter on Earth. The DNA constructs left humans with some powerful energies, including an awareness into several dimensions, though without consciousness. The most important of these was the ability for humans to create through their subtle bodies the understanding of their world that provides both death and life. As a result, healing is innate in this transformation process, transformation is innate in the healing process. This is what is a little difficult to assimilate and work with in your cellular structures—the very idea that imbalance leads to disease, and that correcting the imbalance or working with it on some level must inherently lead to transformation. Any form of transformation can create the shift which brings healing. This can be created by changing one's vibration, working with the subtler levels within the capacity of the subtle bodies, or just in some way attuning to another vibration.

They have specifically developed technologies and techniques to beam this energy as a supportive healing function to Earth. This is especially useful in dealing with the energies of love. This can bring a sense of the combining of all of the subtle forces, a sense of how the subtle bodies interact, and a sense of how the energies of the aetheric body as manipulated by consciousness can come into the physical body. They have worked with all of these tools extensively. This is a different focus than most other star systems, even the Pleiadean system, because they have a sense of responsibility. These beings recognize that transformation is easily possible on Earth when people understand how to utilize the transformational energy of Earth's own heated inner core, the energies of Sirius itself, and humanity's co-creative combined energies. It would then be a simple matter to end disease.

By living with this tremendous change, accepting it in themselves, and working with it over many thousands of years, they gradually realized that they had developed something quite unique. It was difficult to apply this perfectly in the world. There was the difficulty of how to trust, how to know where it would best be utilized. They have found that the very best method is to attune to it, to use it, and to utilize it for transformation, understanding, and awareness. As a result of this development there was a connection through consciousness with the early Lemurians. They were asking the same question: how do we bring this transformative ability into form? The answer was very simple. The Lemurian understanding of these principles was that what was needed was trust, faith, and awareness, and not logic. The acceptance of transformation was unnecessary, because on Earth such transformation would not hold for very long. The Lemurians saw that in humanity's future the separation of the soul into its individual parts would make it very difficult for such transformations to take place on the Earth.

The canine species was created to remind humanity of this energy. These beings are to learn trust from humanity, and in many cases have done so very well. This trust does sometimes extend into a trusting of certain negative ideas, the hunting dog might be an example here. But many positive ideas have also been shared, the seeing eye dog as an example. These energies are being constantly transmitted back to the second planet near Sirius. The canine species does not just listen and learn of the simpler things. To a limited extent, they are also the eyes and ears of this civilization, and do occasionally transmit bursts of information about Earth's evolution.

These beings on Sirius do not fully understand the extent to which individualization of soul has taken place on Earth. Genetically ingrained in them at a very deep level is this time of shared transformation when all over their planet things change, cataclysms take place, and they must protect themselves and help each other. They adapt to this together. This creates an inherent shared condition in which an alignment to an outside force, this change in the suns, brings them into a shared energy and creative effort together. It is very difficult for such beings to comprehend individuality at the level which Earth beings have achieved.

However, in their DNA seeding they have significantly added to humanity's capacity just for such individuality because they have recognized that their ability to love is insufficient to mirror back to God the very energies that were needed. Sirius is an experiment that has failed. Indeed this energy sweeping through the planets of Sirius was planned. The idea was that by this regular, magnetically-based transformation, love would be utilized to manipulate the aethers and create these powerful energies. Some of the initial seeding of Sirius was influenced by beings in the center of the galaxy, as well as by beings from Andromeda and other locations far away from this galaxy. But the experiment has not yielded the ability to love nearly to the extent that was seen as possible, principally because the impetus for transformation comes from outside, it comes from the sun, it does not come from within the beings themselves. This did create a great linkage among these beings. In the seeding of Earth, individuality leading to the possible destruction of a planet was seen as a necessary risk. So this seeding of individuality is the other aspect that these beings have contributed to Earth.

As this civilization developed through periods of primitive worship of this transformation, co-creative ability to heal the planet, and into places of contemplating their own purpose and ability to assist, many technologies were developed and discarded. Small amounts of these technologies have filtered their way into Earth's own environments at this time. Many ideas for technologies of a healing nature are likely to be released over the next few years from Sirius. Some of these energies come from the beings. But many of these energies come from the compassion of this star, which has a direct link to the Sun. In this way there is as if a witnessing of a great event.

The third planet of the Sirius system was seeded by the beings on the second. They have gone through a similar process of development. They have provided energies of technical ability and transformation for many worlds. Their own abilities to work with space travel and other things are in line with humanity's evolution and with humanity's understanding of physical properties.

Therefore some of their technologies may be the most accessible to people on Earth, and these may eventually be brought into humanity's awareness.

An inherent self-governing factor that prevents such beings from causing destruction or difficulty on Earth, or any willingness to take it over, is the way in which their own sun every 49.5 years goes through its great trials and tribulation. It is as if the inherent nature of transformation and a willingness to see this proceed is such an important part of their society that they would not seek to dominate other beings, they would seek only to promote transformation where possible.

In many ways the Sirians are sympathetic, for instance, while the Pleiadeans are empathetic by comparison; and so this can lead to a little bit of difficulty at times. Individuals who contact beings from Sirius may experience fear as they begin to see through the eyes of a Sirian their awareness of this time of change. Many individuals may not be able to easily accept this at a conscious level. They might find such change would be unthinkable. It may be too difficult for them to imagine that their sun would be as if exploding or shifting. At the same time there would be in the cells a remembrance, a reminder.

In their development over many centuries, Sirians have come to understand many opportunities in their contact with Earth, through their influence of Earth technology, and through their willingness to assist people to understand more of their own potential and their own future. At the same time, because their genetic structures are based on these times of tremendous change, they no longer fear it. They do not have capacity to fear it. Because this cycle of change is fairly predictable, they can come to expect it and understand it and know it, and at the same time work with such an energy.

This powerful magnetic storm and this energy created on multiple dimensional levels that pours from Sirius every 49.5 years or so affects other stars. The ways in which various beings have accommodated or worked with such an energy has been very important. But the beings from Sirius primarily attune to Earth at this time because of this sense of responsibility and the potential they see. More than most other beings, it is possible that they will learn from Earth's own evolution in their own way, and be able to contribute directly. Due to the relative closeness of Sirius, it is also possible for these beings to actually come here in physical form, and for Earth beings to go there with very little difficulty. This may take place as soon as 2025.

Now this is a little different than giving just the ancient history because here is a star more so than any other star directly associated with humanity's evolution in a positive way, and therefore these things are given in historical and present tense as well as some hint of the future understanding.

ALMACH

In comparison to other stars, Almach appears to have a major spiritual impact on people. This star has a long history of spirituality, which is in some ways far more intense and far more developed than anything that has been experienced on Earth. This civilization developed on the second planet from Almach. In their early development, there was a natural tendency towards religion, superstition, and looking outside themselves. This is because in the orbit area of the third planet were two planets that collided and created a massive asteroid belt. The proximity of this to the planet caused frequent meteor showers. These were multicolored as the atmosphere of this second planet contained many radioactive gases as well as inert gasses, which caused all sorts of interesting effects. These spectacular stellar displays seemed randomly timed, as the orbits of the asteroids were very difficult for any sort of mathematical calculations due to their high degree of eccentricity. As a result, this attention on the outside and on spirituality was deep within these people. They began to ask: "What is this world we live in, what is this universe, what is it all about?" This was very important to them from the very early beginnings of their civilization. This civilization was seeded by certain energies emanating from El Nath, and Procyon in its early development. As a result of all of these energies and this attention on spiritual form, the shared soul of these beings from Almach became attuned to this question about the nature of existence. This deep questioning occurred for about 5000 years.

At that time there was a destruction that was very intense on that planet. Asteroid interaction caused the depletion of oxygen and various other substances in their atmosphere. There was also a simultaneous development of a microbiological organism similar to the aids virus. This virus only needed a few seconds to take action. This combination of factors caused the death of the entire population with one exception.

The beings saw that if they put all of their energy, their love, their attention, their oneness, and their kindness into one being, there was a chance that one of them would survive. Any one of these beings could have been given all the facets that were needed physically, structurally, as well as the ways of working with their form dimensionally and in the ways of working with their own consciousness and understanding. However, the being that would be involved in this would lose all sense of personal identity, and their personal identity would be then be equivalent to all of the other beings. So what was asked of all of the race was who would be willing to give up the most. The one who would only sacrifice their life, this would not be sufficient. The one who would sacrifice only their personality or their learning was not sufficient. The one who would let go of all, who would then be aware of all aspects as a result of this sacrifice, the degree to which this being would move toward such an ideal by their very nature, this was the one selected.

This was an individual that by other standards would be seen as very ordinary, a person of perhaps even low or medium intelligence. But this individual had a sense of compassion, a deep reverence for life, and the willingness to allow this in whatever form would be appropriate. It was for these qualities that this being was selected. For these beings, love was a feeling of interconnectivity to all the other beings and a willingness to appreciate them. It was this aspect of compassion and lovingness within that being that ensured the survival of the race.

These beings did not fully understand that this was an important developmental aspect of their own awareness. A tremendous power of consciousness was developed in this individual by focussing the energy of an entire civilization into one being. This in itself was able to cause this individual to have an ability to transfer dimensional levels very quickly, as well as being able to maintain the consciousness and evolution of all of the individual souls from that society.

After the biochemistry problem was solved, the replenishment of the atmosphere was accomplished. This one person was able to create many clones of himself. The DNA structures could be varied to create some variation amongst these clones. From that point forward, a sense of oneness was inherent in that society. All beings with any sort of racial memory or memory across generations could recall themselves indeed being one. Out of this oneness and this ability to transfer dimensional levels, this race developed a tremendous appreciation of the nature of God and the reflection of this oneness throughout the galaxy. There was also a deep expression of a tremendous sadness at the death of all of these beings. But there was also a tremendous energy of hope—a sense that anything is possible, that people can do as they choose, and an entire civilization can indeed be birthed through one person.

This being is a very powerful representation of the oneness of all, and the ability for this oneness to be able to change vibration, not for any particular reason, but just because it appears appropriate to be many at once, to understand all aspects of being, and to release any need for things being a certain way. Naturally this also develops an ability to survive. It is as if the spirituality of this race survived. When these beings all died, their physical form disappeared. But the form was unimportant, it was their essential spirituality, their essential awareness, which was maintained and was continued.

This being has acted as a model for many of the great beings of tremendous light and energy that have existed on your Earth, such as Mohammed, Buddha, Confucius, and Jesus. These beings have known of this one in the times transcending the limitations of time and space that these beings have experienced in their own enlightenment. They have been able to meet with this being and understand enlightenment in a different way. They knew this being had an awareness of at-oneness and emptiness that had become one, this is the nothing that is all things.

In the seeding of the Earth, this energy of oneness was the essential characteristic that was shared with the subtle bodies of Earth beings. This was an influence on the mental body and emotional body of Earth people. This was to allow these to connect when this sense of oneness was there; and the reverse, when they do connect there would be this sense that all beings are one, that indeed humanity can share and understand this as one. This is very helpful for the survival of the human race. It is through this spiritual awareness that many of the problems on Earth will be solved, and many of the accidents or difficulties will instead simply prove to be times of deeper opportunity and change for people.

There can be in working with the Almach energy sometimes a sadness felt, a place inside from which this memory of loss comes from. Immediately after this there will usually be felt a sense of tremendous uplifting joy, and a sense of all the possibilities. Your enlightenment may be on a minor scale by comparison with the great enlightened ones on Earth or the enlightenment of beings from other star systems such as those from Almach, yet in your own deeper awareness you have a transformation, a deeper awakening, and a deeper love born on the oneness you share with all humanity.

As a society, there are questions that have not been formed yet that will have their answers only in oneness, in spiritual form, and in the awareness of this magnificent God-light which all people are able to manifest. Utilizing this elixir can remind you of this, take you to this place of preparation, and bring you to know this energy a little more. You may be reminded that even in the darkest or most difficult days, there is hope, and that you are not alone. This combining of energies is not just like having a friend, but is more like having an the extension of yourself into realms that you have only dreamed of be available to you as something second nature, just very much a part of you. The ability to recognize more of the spiritual aspects of your own self, trust this, and know that it is appropriate, can be of great help to most people.

ALCYONE

The civilization from the Pleiades gets a lot of press these days. There is good reason for this. Many of the seeds sown by these beings in the early Atlantean times are now bearing fruit. Their intent was to increase lung capacity in people to give them extra abilities to manifest energy, and also to increase people's intuitive abilities.

Approximately 118,000 years ago, these beings primarily home based in Alcyone reached a powerful obstacle in their development. Having developed space travel, having the ability to communicate with many other civilizations, and having seen many of the wonders of the galaxy, they began to recognize a powerful force within them that was not easily manifested. This was a force of God's strength, a force of love and compassion formed with a certain degree of powerful creativity. A hands-off principle was applied to this creativity, as for instance is applied to Earth, where something is created and allowed to find its own course. So these beings respected this energy they discovered in themselves as if seeing a part of God within it, yet it was not easily understandable. They had understood and worked with many powerful intellectual principles, having well mastered certain of the basic concepts of the universal laws of thought, speech, manifestation, permanence, and to a lesser extent, still though understood well with them, karma. Through their deeper awareness of these principles, the obstacle was sighted, and it pretty much froze the development of the civilization for a long period. There was almost a cry for help and assistance, but the other civilizations they had contacted were unable to assist. It was seen that this part of themselves needed to be purified, understood for its highest and best aims, then released, eventually to grow, to seed, to become what it could be, and then to be returned to that civilization in any form.

It was not entirely clear exactly how this would take place, but it was clear that it was a long process and that a great deal of patience would be needed. So the initial seeding of a number of civilizations took place. In each of these, what was perceived as an important component of this obstacle-producing energy was then allowed into the world that they seeded. On Earth this became an awareness of higher intuitive faculties and abilities that could be called channeling or telepathy or communication with higher forces—always with the blending influence of will and love. The other civilizations that were seeded have not progressed as yet as far as terrestrial civilization. The abilities that were seeded into one of these civilizations included capacities for instantaneous healing combined with will and love. In another, an awareness of the ability to transform one's physical form into multiple dimensions combined with capacities of will and love. In yet another civilization, an awareness of an ability to see in all the electromagnetic spectrum from ultraviolet all the way through far infrared, this combined with will and love. This civilization would likely be the next one to make contact with Pleiades-based peoples, and this will likely occur in about 600 years. At such time contact with Earth may also be possible for this civilization.

Indeed this seeding was of interest to many others who observed the process and influenced it at various times. It was not as coordinated a thing as you might imagine because at various times in their own development various splits that you might call political insurrections or struggles of various types took place within the various governments, among the people living in the Alcyone civilization, as well as other influences to change things. But the gradual increase in this seeding of energies both genetically and telepathically with humanity has continued. The harvesting of this has not yet begun. It is unclear just how humanity will project this energy back to the Pleiades. It is clear however, from our perspective and the understanding of most of those Pleiadeans who many generations down the line will come to inherit this eventual gift from humanity, that humanity owes nothing to these Pleiadeans.

Rather, if humanity chooses to give, if the development of this loving and this ability to transfer it utilizing intuitive faculties becomes a part of humanity's own loving desire to share, then much will be opened. The doors of the great libraries on Alcyone will be opened to any who wish to explore them. This can be of great benefit to those who wish to understand and extract information about universal principles, about their very world, and about God. Eventually a joining of these civilizations from Earth and Alcyone will most likely take place, though it is hard to say quite when. It may be many thousands of years from now, but appears more likely to be far sooner.

Although they are continuing to maintain this hands-off relationship, there is still a great deal of attraction between beings from the Pleiades and humanity. Beings from the Pleiades still want to interact, to learn, and to be a part of things here. Pleiadeans are easily able to incarnate on Earth. Certain individuals who don't fit in very well may feel very attracted to extra-terrestrial activities and have very pleasant dreams or very enlightening awarenesses when they are feeling this connection to Alcyone and the Pleiades. These individuals would do well to utilize the elixir of Alcyone so that they may attune more to this civilization and allow this communication more deeply. There are certain drawbacks to this in that one can be as if contacting one's ancestors. Sometimes the ancient ways may come through into an individual's consciousness, overriding some of the patterns they have already created in the world, thus creating a bit of confusion. However, this usually passes, because the underlying influence of free will and love usually comes forth for an individual.

Many of the communications from various Pleiadeans who have attempted to assist on Earth through for instance the Billy Meyer contacts or various channelings from various Pleiadeans, this has an overriding theme often of love, of some assistance for humanity, and many times prophecies as given in such are inaccurate because of the powerful loving influence between the beings on Earth and those in the Pleiades. The underlying message is that humanity can experience greater loving and compassion for itself. This is of great importance and is the foundation for the building and understanding of the higher intuitive faculties. Now one must be cautious here not to assume that intuitive faculties come from the Pleiades. They come from humanity's own development, most importantly in reaction to the powerful negative emotional energies, the thickened aethers on the Earth, and other things. Just for survival, people have had to create this for themselves. But to show people on Earth the direction of this, to give some hints as to how this could be accomplished, this has been aided dramatically by individuals from the Pleiades in centuries long past.

To answer your question concerning the physical appearance of those from the Pleiades, the ability to physically transform has been with this race for a long time. They can recreate bodies in various forms. At one time there was a natural appearance somewhat similar to the human appearance. There were some differences: much smaller skin pores, and physical stature on the order of usually 9 to 11 feet. However, this form can be easily altered, and indeed such beings can appear very much like humans, and in this way appear far less threatening than when they are so tall.

Many individuals on Earth have had lifetimes on the sixth planet circling Alcyone. However, many individuals have had experiences on many planets in many star systems. They may find it easier to attune to lifetimes in the Pleiades because of two factors, one genetic. The most powerful genetics within the human body is that influenced and created through Pleiadean encounters. But secondly, there is a similarity in form and aim for these two civilizations. Individuals will often be working with their own intuition when they are looking at past lives, or when they are recognizing familiarity when reading books by various authors including Ruth Montgomery and others who speak of being from the stars. They are attuning to their own intuition, and so therefore it is only natural that they would work with those beings who work with intuitive faculties so importantly and clearly as beings from the Pleiades.

Some of the channels who work with beings from the Pleiades may have difficulty transmitting this information and energy because of some struggles in themselves. Many of them have had recent incarnations or even have a primary soul influence in the Pleiades, and bringing themselves into human form has been very difficult. It is often up to the channel to translate the energy of love from these beings from the Pleiades, and this is one of the toughest things to actually recreate and transfer. We recognize that the energies of compassion and love of most extraterrestrial civilizations are very different than anything a human being can assimilate or work with. However, in some ways the energies of compassion and loving as created through the Pleiadeans are perhaps more advanced than the other civilizations in so far as their potential ability to transfer this love to humanity. Unfortunately, when individuals are be exposed to such a level of love and do not have an easy way to work with it in their lives, they naturally throw up obstacles, create various resistances, boundaries, and other things inside that keep them from moving forward. This would manifest through the channeling and the information they are able to share. But the purpose of that would be so that other people then alerting them to this so that they would attune to this deeper lovingness—not as born from another civilization, but as created within themselves. Channels may be struggling with pieces and parts of the puzzle, but not be able to bring it all through because of their own patterns or ways of working with things in the world. This is true for all channels including the channel speaking and naturally occurs as a by-product of the channeling process.

It is important to recognize that your own attunement to various civilizations is an important factor. Each individual will attune to a different civilization because of their own awareness of a lifetime in such a civilization, meeting somebody from that place, having an awareness of the deeper concepts, or by perhaps simply being aware of the universal laws that civilization has dealt with. Each individual will naturally create an attunement that is different one to the next, and so naturally there would be some attraction to these general energies in different ways.

EL NATH

The individuals associated with El Nath in their own transformation process were able to recreate themselves at eleventh and twelfth-dimensional levels in ways that created a powerful burst of energy. In this there was the formation of many galaxies as well as powerful energies within the Milky Way Galaxy which inspired change for many beings in many civilizations. Many of the civilizations responded, including those from the Pleiades. Beings from Alcyone were able to make contact with their sources of such energy in El Nath.

Part of this was due to a bursting forth of energy from the star itself. This is one reason why the star elixir has a little more potency and power than other ones. El Nath is still projecting an energy of transformation, change, and tremendous assistance, as well as an understanding of many aspects of the very nature of the universe. The original civilization from El Nath deliberately allowed this as part of their own transformation.

When the Pleiadeans contacted such beings to learn more, they were led on a very beautiful journey that lasted approximately 10,000 years. This was a time of great and important education for Pleiadeans and was in fact the beginning of the breakdown of their own understanding of the obstacle that faced them as a civilization. One of the solutions they came up with as a result of such inspiration from El Nath was the seeding of other civilizations and the eventual way in which this would affect their own civilization. What was given to them through El Nath was the way in which this seeding could be created by use of basic physical principles at the primary dimensional levels of third, fourth, and fifth.

The Pleiadeans have acted as the bridge between the energies of EL Nath and humanity. As a result of their inspiration from El Nath, the seeding took place, and thus the genetic influence. It is through those who are attracted to the Pleiades that a deeper awareness of these energies from El Nath usually take place. At the same time as this the underlying principles of the awareness of universal law, the awareness of mathematical concepts, and the understanding of multiple dimensions is made available gradually to people. But most of the people who would be most profoundly influenced by this have not yet come to discover and work with starlight elixirs. This is a general trend for the future, but we do see that scientists and individuals who seek deeper understanding of these matters will indeed have some assistance given them by utilizing El Nath in the future.

El Nath has been a beacon of light for many, many civilizations throughout this galaxy. But the only ones who were able to respond in a way in which dramatic breakthroughs and shifts took place as direct result of such correspondence were those on Alcyone and other stars in the Pleiades. The individuals on Sirius certainly were influenced and gained a great deal of knowledge and inspiration, but were not able to complete what was needed to allow the more powerful communication to take place and the intimacy that is usually the result of such.

PART FOUR

APPENDICES

APPENDIX A

★☆☆☆☆☆☆☆☆☆

Interview with Hilarion

Although some would perceive us as a being with a physical form, we would say that the best way to think of us is as an emerald light that is shared throughout this planet. It has no source. It is within you and it is all around you and as it allows itself to connect to others, it is in and of itself fulfilled. We would like to be as available as possible to all individuals. You might wonder how someone can be in a dozen places at once. This is fairly simple when what is transmitted is a thought. A thought takes place in an extremely small fraction of a second, so we are not utilized to nearly our capacity even by the number of Hilarion channels currently in existence on the planet Earth.

We have had a number of lifetimes on this planet, as well as several incarnations in completely different lifestreams on the planet Venus in your solar system. In our lives, we have experienced many important beings of great light and teaching. We have also experienced many of the dramatic and amazing changes that the human race has gone through. Having deep compassion and connection with human beings, we have become as human a soul as is possible for such evolution, and have tied our karma and understanding to human evolution. From such we are able to have a unique dualistic viewpoint. One of these is the point of view from understanding universal consciousness, universal law, the essential principles of the cosmos, what are essentially just mathematical principles. At the same time, we have a viewpoint from the heart, from what human beings know, from the essence of what it is to be alive and part of the human lifestream, encompassing those elements of human development including incarnation as mountains, as dinosaurs, as beings of the sea, and as beings of the land. By understanding this from both points of view, we are able to make some interesting and unique choices, and note that most of the information is valuable only from the point of view of where it opens you to your own heart, to your own awareness, to your own human qualities. It is the human condition that is admirable here, and not ours.

The other thing to note here is that in recent times we have had incarnations in the physical vehicles known as John in the time of Christ, Plato in the time of ancient Greece, and as a scientist known as Hilarion in the later phase of Atlantis. The choice to choose one's name based on one's soul understanding was clear in the later Atlantean period, and such was very common. It is hoped that individuals will rediscover this at some time, perhaps towards the end of the next century as well.

In working with these lifetimes, we came to observe very directly certain aspects of human behavior, and were able to assimilate information as well as share certain perspectives. The most important points of this have been lost from all three of these lifetimes, and what remains is but a skeleton, a shell. Individuals will often point to the literature which remains, particularly by Plato and John, and say: "Did you say this? What did you mean by that?" It really means very little, for so little of this actually remains. But that is all right. It is important for people to come to decide on the essence, not the words.

In working for long periods on Earth with people in certain avenues and endeavors, each of us have become a little specialized. What we work with in a specific fashion can intermesh with the other guides of humanity in a way that really seems to make a difference. What we are personally (if we could use such a term) exploring is the transformation of matter into form. As we are assisting individuals in understanding how things work for themselves as the mechanisms and purposes of life unfold, we see that this tends to assist more than the individual. It seems to also work with a number of individuals who are joined together in examining that issue. We see this as a way of serving you. You may be drawn to us because we have an interest in common, an understanding about the transformation of matter into form, about how things work in the overall picture and pattern for this planet. In this way we can be of a little assistance.

We are acting as guides for many, as well as acting as guides for certain guide beings who can transmit or translate that energy. But nevertheless it is up to you to choose how you would wish us to work with you. It is indeed up to each person and what they would wish to create. Then it is up to us to understand the best way we can fulfill such requests. Our true purpose is provide information and help in a way that assists not just one individual but all people everywhere, and even beyond that perhaps to the beings that co-inhabit the planet with you: the nature kingdom, the animals, the plants, the guide beings of a nonphysical nature, and of course all aspects of the Earth herself. This is why the answer to a question may not just come at just one level. By allowing the unfolding and opening of your consciousness, this inspiration can touch the consciousness of others.

In our purpose in working with those who are delving into these arenas of vibrational shift, the understanding of the true nature of humanity's evolution, and how this relates to disease, difficulty, and change, it is important to recognize that where we allow more opportunities, we tend to speed up the process a little bit. We tread a thin line between destructive and difficult change and ways in which this energy can be valuable, useful, healing, and most importantly, able to assist people. The key to this is in the question and answer process. In this way individuals such as yourselves are willing to be responsible to some degree for the information that they receive, and Jon as the channel or others who work with our energy are able to be a part of the process.

Because of the human side of such an equation for bringing through information, we have more opportunities now for bringing through information than we have had in the past in either a body or as a pure repository of scientific information. So therefore, it is important that individuals increase where possible their understanding of that side of the process so that not only can they bring through more information, but they can learn about the appropriate use of channeled information for themselves. So it is simply that old way, knock and the door shall be opened. In this time period individuals are learning how to knock better than ever before. So our own energy as well as that of many other guides are bringing through more and more information, opportunity, and understanding for people, as people are able to use such more and more responsibly.

Where individuals are given freedom as to how to use the information in the form of particular products, devices, and technologies, this is an appropriate and responsible use of channeled material. When this is made available through the books and tapes as principles, as ways of understanding, this gives individuals freedom to choose, to work with it as is appropriate, to check it out for themselves. This appears to have had a slight but noticeable beneficial effect on humanity's evolution at this time. To some extent, our efforts have been successful due to your willingness to work with the information,

So the actual end of this, its actual complete purpose has not been decided by us, by you, or by anyone else. However, it appears that the direction this is leading is similar to a funnel that is becoming wider and wider. At some point it will be wide enough to encompass the universe. The idea being to understand that as you open this door more and more, more and more pours through. At certain points along the way, the distinguishing of the nature of the energy becomes difficult as to this is from Hilarion, this is from me, this is from God, this is the nature of the way things work. One of the points that is emerging is that distinguishing the source of this information doesn't matter, that indeed what is important is that this becomes valuable and brings aspects of choice, service, understanding, and God into people.

Even this is the request of others. In the Atlantean period when there was such difficulty on Earth, there was a great crying out of souls. Many individuals asked: "If we could have done it differently, what would we have done?" They did not know the answer, but they did feel in themselves that there was something missing. They felt there was some aspect of their own humanity, their own hearts, their own love which was not there. Those who had consciousness at such time of the pattern that led up to the great difficulty befalling Atlantis, those such as ourselves and others who wished to warn the Atlanteans of this were involved deeply at an emotional level in this request. It was as if in collective consciousness it was stated "When the opportunity comes, we will not fail this time. We will bring through the information, the understanding, the technology, and the awareness in a way that is balanced, that is helpful, that coordinates and assists with the human side of things, with the love aspect in people, with the awareness of consciousness and understanding and not purely the destructive energies."

So this is why some of these developments are a little slower than you would like. This is why the guides who exist from such time and those people in incarnation from such time discover and work with information in a piecemeal fashion so that such mistakes will not be made again. It is a karma that has not yet been cleansed from the human condition at this time, and that which you are cleansing quite rapidly by working with this information and understanding in these subtler areas.

In working with star elixirs, flower essences, various herbs, gem elixirs, the vibrational remedies in homeopathy and inert gas homeopathy, more and more choice, energy, and subtlety is brought to this. These techniques are easily able to coordinate with humans, with what they think, with what they feel, with what they know in their hearts. This is never forced upon them. This is an excellent way, a way of maximum choice, freedom, and understanding.

For those who wish to contact the devic orders or begin channeling, find what creates resonance in you, what feels good in you, what gives you a sense of change or upliftment, lightness, or even laughter. The devic orders are particularly entranced with laughter. Ways in which you contact them can be as varied as the ways in which you work with your own guides. The idea is that you find what works. This can mean going out into a garden or into the woods where the flowers are, or it can mean simply imagining that you are playing with an elf, a tiny point of bouncing light, the flower spitting forth a fairy, or even walking inside a magnificent and large gem and playing inside it. These ways of playfulness, joy, and attraction are the door for most people to explore and create this resonant condition.

What we do in working with each individual channel is to find a position of resonance in which we can create a very slight shift at the aetheric and mental body levels in the brain and the mental body of the channel. We do this only if they have fully requested this and it is clear at the soul level that it is beneficial or at the very least not harmful to work with this individual. When the channel opens enough that we can work with them, we observe a rhythmic pattern occurring at multiple vibrational levels. These correspond to the theta wave vibration at approximately 5 cycles per second, and in many cases for individuals, 7.82 cycles per second. There are also the breathing rhythm every 3 or 4 seconds, the heart rhythm at 2 per second or so, and the rhythms of various other aspects of the individual's physiology. At the subtler levels the rhythms are much faster, much higher frequencies in the hundreds to thousands of cycles per second. There are certain places within those patterns where the energy is at a zero, where it is neither bringing in or taking out. At such a point it is very easy to perturb those rhythms very slightly and shift time very slightly within the consciousness of the person. During such a shift it is an easy matter then to transfer various patterns of light into the person, and what is brought in then is a thought.

The form of the thought will be based upon what the channel is capable of receiving. This can vary very widely. The individual will only be able to receive and work with certain aspects of those thought packets. In some individuals, this will relate only to emotions or to sensation. But in working with Jon (the channel speaking), we are able to transfer the visual, some of the specifics of the words, as well as some of the underlying concepts, which can include equations when necessary. We can also transfer some of the understanding from our perspective, which is an experience that is based on fourth-dimensional vision. By and large, this is a non-language capacity.

After the thought packet is lodged within his consciousness, we are able to assist to coax it out of him by interfering very slightly in the wave forms which relate to the speech center. By working more deeply with the rhythmic patterns of the breathing, the words are brought forth in greater clarity. This is a part that is a little more difficult. It is easier to place the particular thought packets within his consciousness than it is to express them clearly. Our ability to channel better and better through Jon is based simply on such observations. By actually channeling a little bit less of the essence and a little bit more of its application, it is expressed better. But the problem with such is that we have provided less information at a deep level to Jon's consciousness that is of value to him at a later time. Because the implantation of this energy and information has taken place at a deep level—and this is with his permission—we know it will surface sooner or later. This has already taken the form of various devices of healing nature that he has created. This information is made available to him in exchange for his willingness to work with the channeling process. This is a difficult matter to balance appropriately at all times, and the imbalance of such can cause Jon's consciousness to be dramatically shifted to higher vibratory levels. This would not be seen as a difficulty under most circumstances, unless he is to drive a car, deal with his children, or do something of very practical nature. This can cause a rebound effect, and he will be tired later.

This parallels channeling for most individuals. The beings of non-physical nature who channel through individuals are able to do so by matching these various rhythmic patterns. The way in which this occurs is different for every person. Even if it is not fully conscious, the energy they can receive and know and work with on some level is only that which they are capable of working with due to developments in their immediate past lives or in their present lifetime. This is why certain vehicles are better for technical channeling than others. The information itself, the transfer of the experience, the awareness of the light, this is really unlimited. As individuals practice channeling more and more, they are often able to open to new areas and work with this energy more easily. At the same time they may find themselves drawn to learn a little more in the world about the subjects that they may have previously had little interest in, and this will also improve their channeling ability.

The problem with this is that so many individuals would not trust it. They would say: "Well this is coming from my conscious knowledge, it isn't pure channeling." And all we can say to this concept of what pure channeling is, versus deep trance channeling, versus conscious channeling, versus all of these other ways in which channeling is described, is balderdash. This is a process that is still in an experimental stage. If they are drawn to it, all beings are advised to work with it on all levels where possible, without judgement, without deciding ahead of time what is what.

APPENDIX B
★☆☆☆☆☆☆☆☆☆

Astrology and starlight elixirs

The meaning of the signs of the zodiac have developed from the way these symbols have been used throughout human history. Individuals have attuned to these symbols through the collective unconscious, and not through the sum total of the stars in a given sign of the zodiac. Such a sum total will have too many characteristics of balance and counterbalance. The stars do not directly influence the zodiacal representation, but rather the collective unconscious association with the zodiacal representation provides the symbol, and then the guides arrange for timely events to occur with the planets, houses, etc. arranged among the zodiacal constellations. So therefore it is to be seen to be an influence very much related to the choosing of a particular time by those who would select various events to take place, and that these are then using the symbols that are well known and available already.

Many of the choices of symbols have been influenced from many means of consciousness and awareness. This has been influenced by extraterrestrial sources as well. Before the signs of the zodiac were created in the collective unconscious of humanity, many of the underpinnings at a symbolic level that create the essential astrological bridges were influenced by the civilizations associated with the stars in these constellations. Certain symbols were created, and the civilizations and action of the stars themselves influence those symbols. The influence of the stars in many cases preceded the astrological symbolism.

This makes it a little bit more difficult for people as if then they are contacting archetypes which are larger and deeper reaching than the archetypes they are already used to. The intellectual explanation or awareness of this in a logical sense is insufficient. As individuals learn of this information and work with it, the archetypes that are being contacted run very deep. They are genetically connected in some cases. In many cases these are influences that have stimulated some of the great astrological writers. You may find that the influence of these more important and representative stars upon the writings of individuals such as Dane Rudhyar and others who are so well known in astrology is an influence that is now being made directly available to people as they learn about the stars. With such a powerful influence, we cannot hope to answer people's questions about astrology with more information, there must be an inner experience, a deeper awareness. So it is actually by taking these essences that the people themselves will come to know this.

A good way to do this would be to pick a single star from each of these constellations, and use that star to bring that general influence. But individuals must attune to this in their own way. A simple way to do this would be that when the Sun is in a particular sign, you take an elixir of a star within that zodiac sign. Thus over a twelve month period individuals would have an opportunity to experience each of the twelve signs in a very direct and forthright manner. For individuals who wish to speed this up, they can take the elixir with the movement of a planet or the moon through each of these signs, and that would be of some assistance for those who wish to quickly assimilate this. But they will not assimilate this very well because a couple of days is usually insufficient to have a deeper awareness of the vibrational capacities of any particular remedy.

APPENDIX C
★☆☆☆☆☆☆☆☆☆

Stars with negative influences

Some of the people with powerful connections to extraterrestrial civilizations have negative experiences. These individuals are attuned to various extraterrestrial civilizations whose primary alignment in their own evolution is an evolution in opposition to humanity's. Humanity's evolution is on an upward spiral, and these civilizations are on a downward spiral or are struggling with de-evolutionary energies in some ways. For such people, if they can identify the star that these beings come from that are negatively affecting them and take that star essence at a high homeopathic potency such as 10M or even higher, there will often be great benefit. There may be a release for the individual in which they have a deeper understanding in their consciousness of this process, they understand why they have attracted it to themselves, and at last they are willing to let it go. Sometimes these individuals experience a little change, and the beings that are attached to them or working with them have nothing to hold on to anymore because that person has been willing to shift their own evolution by recognizing the inherent lesson in the difficulty.

The two visible stars in this category would be Rigel in Orion and Eta Draconis. The other two, Barnard's star and Zeta Reticuli, are not very bright. The entities that come from these places have influence over the process in the way in which humanity is sensitive to meditating upon these. So these four stars would be wise to be utilized in a very specific form in the starlight elixir form. The homeopathic version at 10M, no lower, of these four stars can be made. This will be quite valuable with individuals who are seeking to come to a place of peace, understanding, and greater awareness in correcting some of the difficulties with these four races. The blue entities are short in stature and associated with Barnard's star. The gray entities are a bit taller, thinner, lighter, with almond-shaped eyes, and are associated with Zeta Reticuli. The insect-like or praying mantis shaped beings are associated with the Rigel system. The beings from Eta Draconis are reptilian in form.

Appendix D

The major stars in each Zodiac Constellation

Aries
March 21 to April 21

Hamal

Mesarthim

Sheratin

Taurus
April 21 to May 22

Alcyone

Aldebaran

El Nath

Hyades

Gemini
May 22 to June 21

Alhena

Castor

Pollux

Tejat

Cancer
June 21 to July 21

Acubens

Asellus Australis

Asellus Borealis

El Tarf

M-44

Leo
July 21 to August 22

Algieba

Denebola

Regulus

Zosma

Virgo
August 23 to September 22

Porrima

Spica

Vindemiatrix

M-104

Libra

September 23 to October 22

Zubenelgenubi

Zubeneschamali

Scorpio

October 23 to Nov. 22

Antares

Dscubba

Gertab

Graffias

Lesath

Sargas

Shaula

Tau Scorpii

Wei

Sagitarrius

Nov. 22 to Dec. 22

Ascella

Kaus Australis

Kaus Borealis

Media

Nunki

M-20

Capricorn

Dec. 22 to January 21

Dabih

Deneb Algedi

Giedi

Nashira

Aquarius

Jan. 22 to February 21

Sadalmelik

Sadalsud

Scat

Pisces

February 21 to March 20

Alrisha

Gamma Piscium

Petra

STAR MAPS

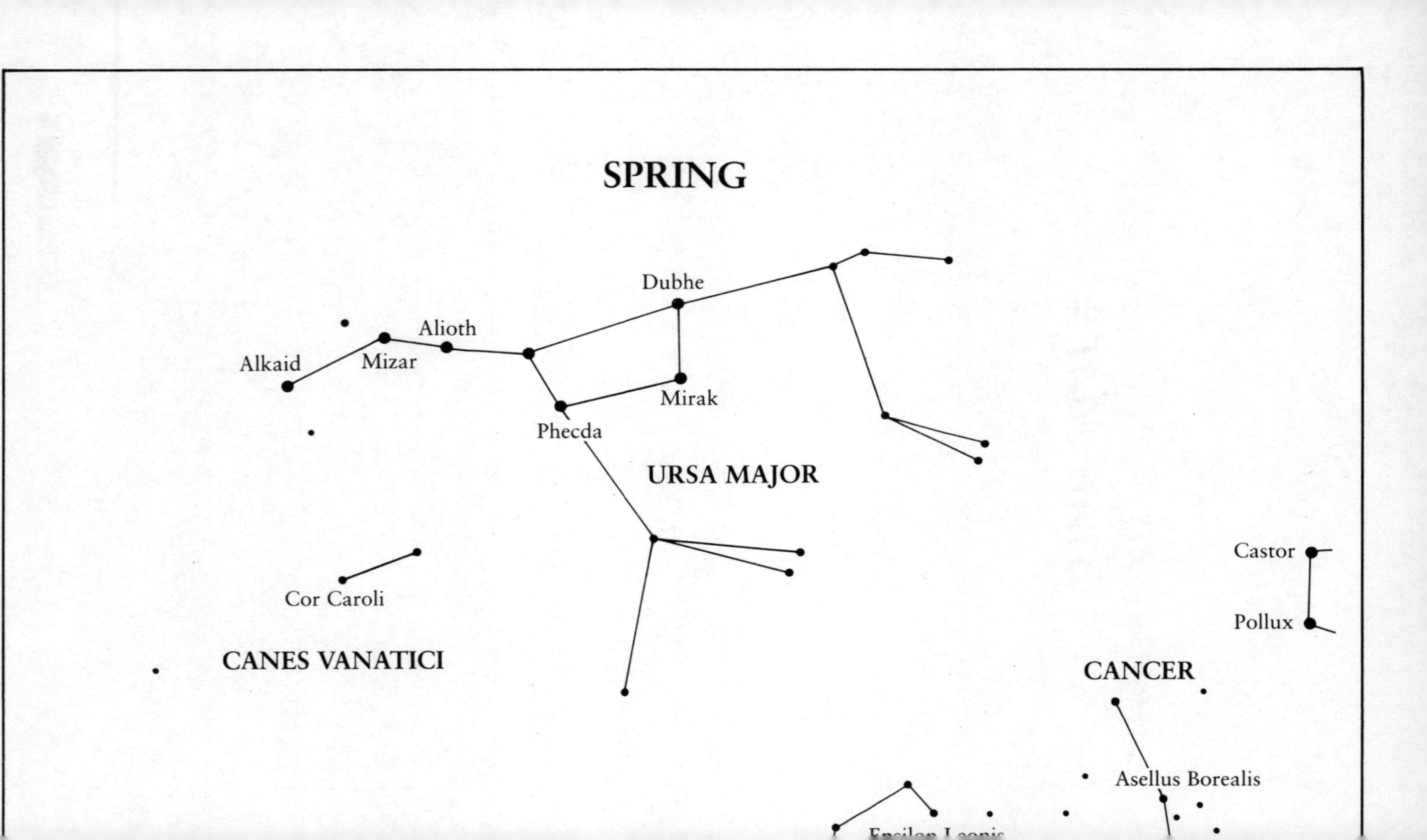
SPRING
Dubhe
Alioth
Alkaid
Mizar
Mirak
Phecda
URSA MAJOR
Castor
Pollux
Cor Caroli
CANES VANATICI
CANCER
Asellus Borealis

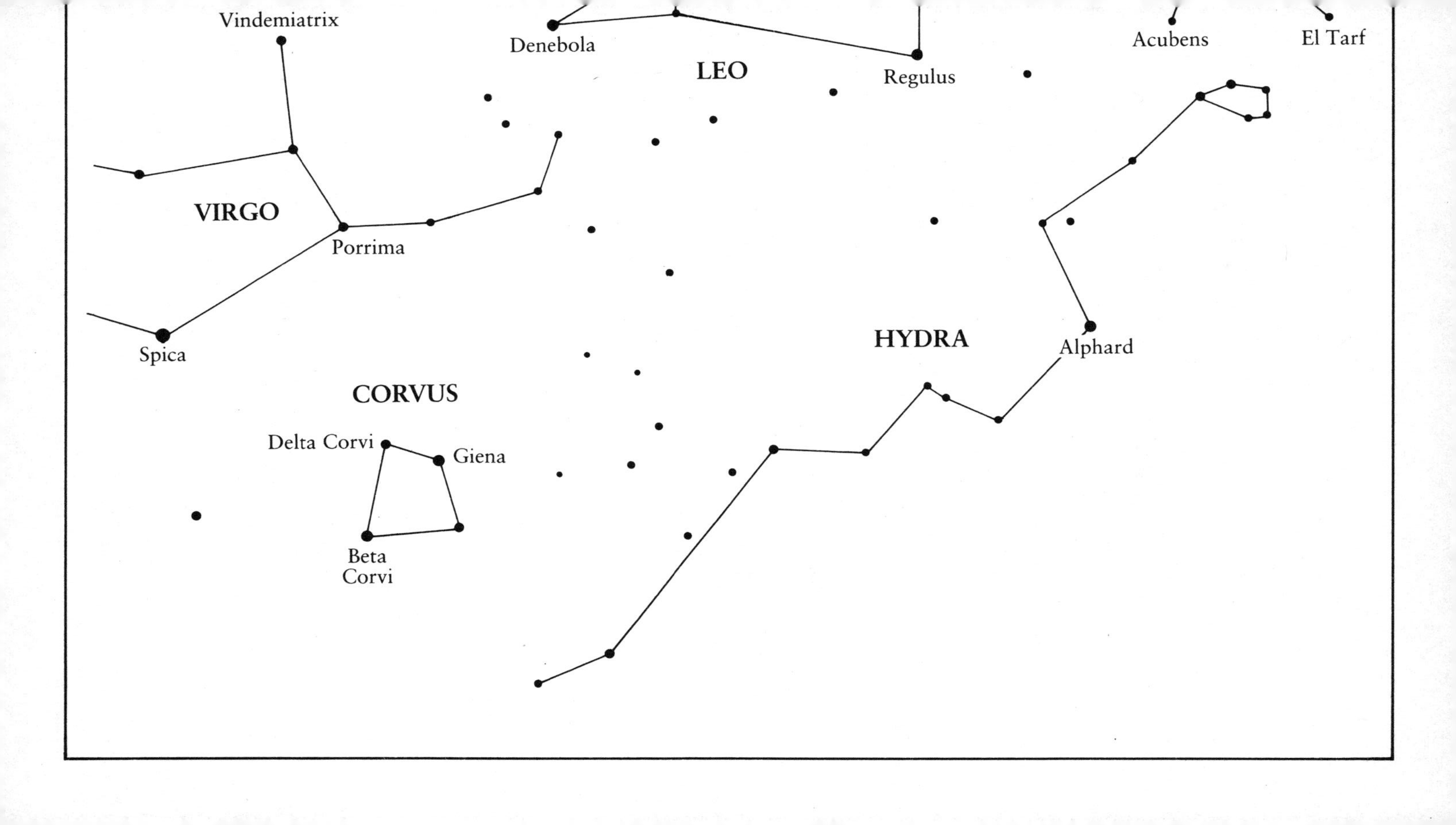
Vindemiatrix
Denebola
Acubens
El Tarf
LEO
Regulus
VIRGO
Porrima
Spica
HYDRA
Alphard
CORVUS
Delta Corvi
Giena
Beta
Corvi

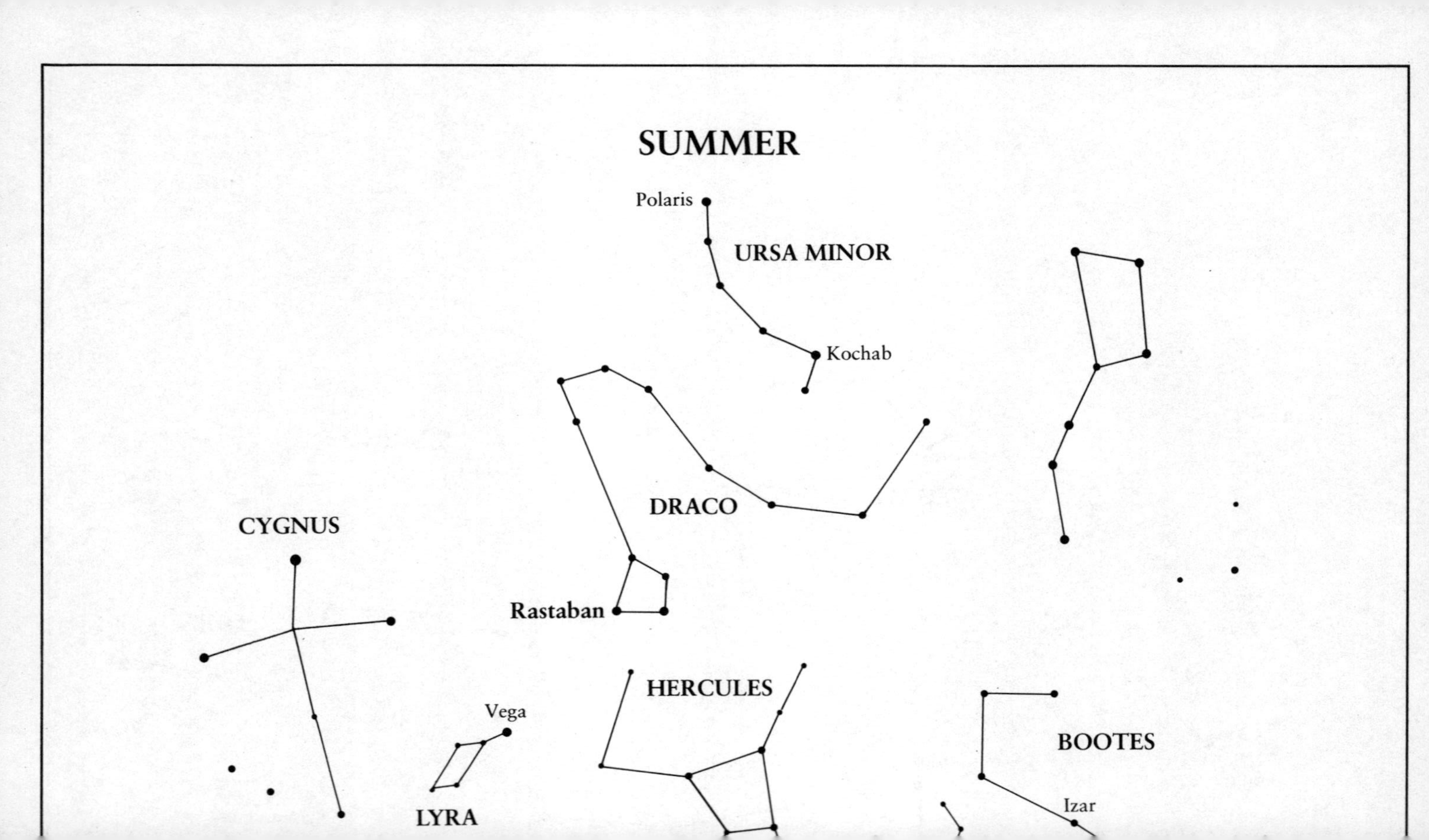
SUMMER
Polaris
URSA MINOR
Kochab
DRACO
CYGNUS
Rastaban
HERCULES
Vega
BOOTES
Izar
LYRA

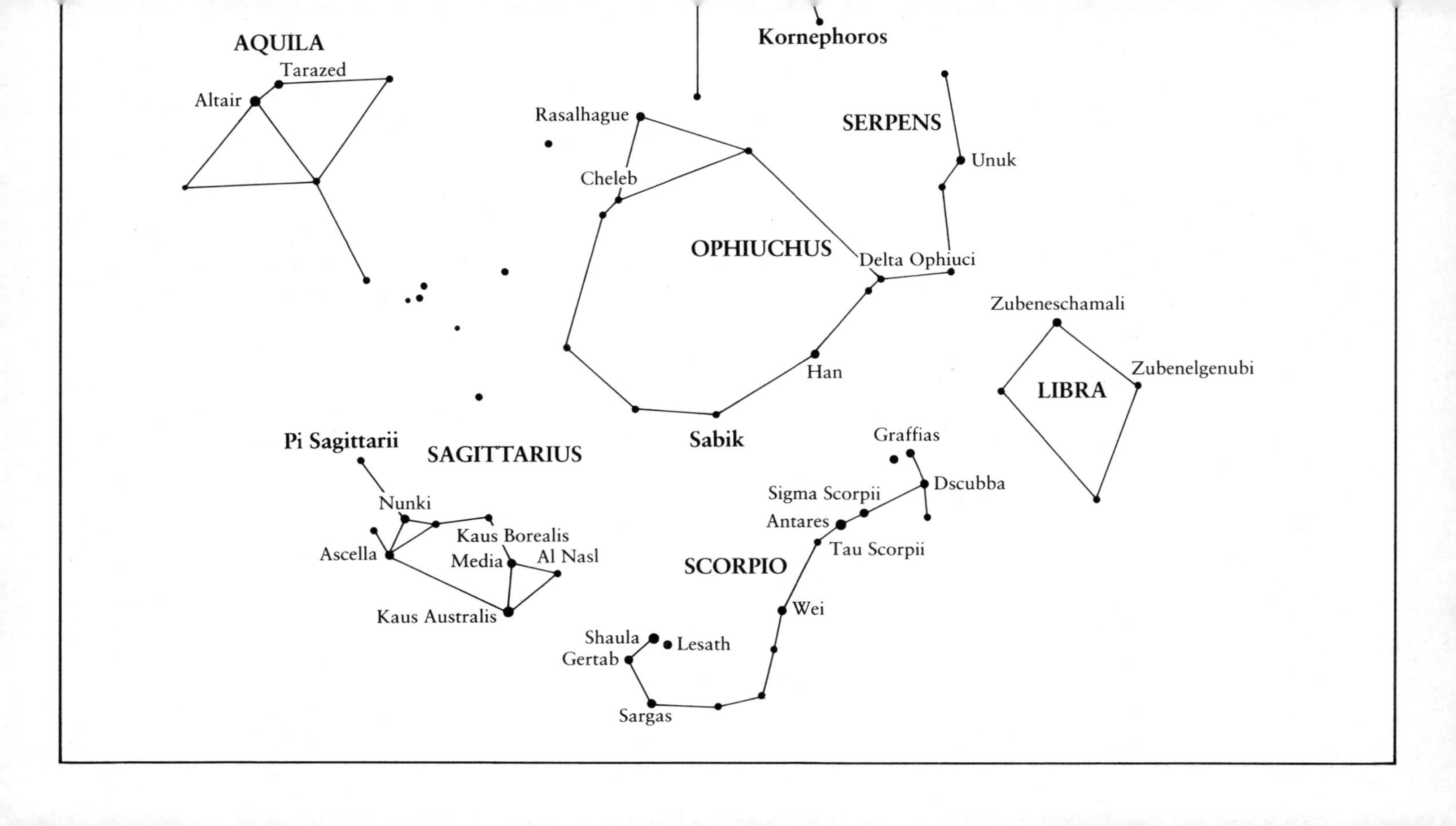
AQUILA
Tarazed
Altair
Kornephoros
Rasalhague
Cheleb
SERPENS
Unuk
OPHIUCHUS
Delta Ophiuci
Zubeneschamali
Zubenelgenubi
LIBRA
Han
Sabik
Pi Sagittarii
SAGITTARIUS
Graffias
Dscubba
Sigma Scorpii
Antares
Tau Scorpii
Nunki
Kaus Borealis
Ascella
Media
Al Nasl
SCORPIO
Wei
Kaus Australis
Shaula
Lesath
Gertab
Sargas

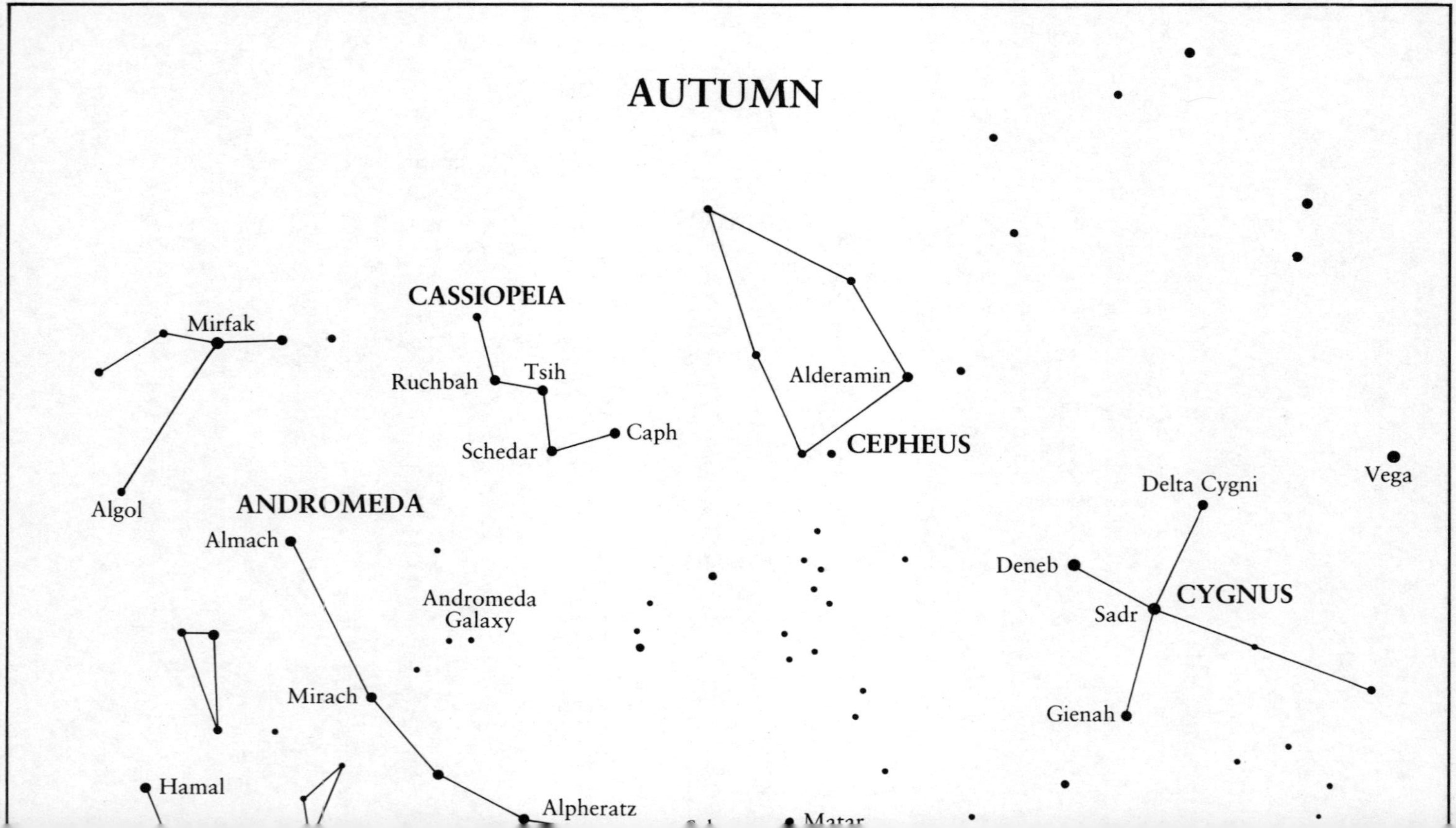

AUTUMN

CASSIOPEIA
Mirfak
Ruchbah
Tsih
Caph
Schedar
Alderamin
CEPHEUS
Vega
Delta Cygni
Algol
ANDROMEDA
Almach
Deneb
CYGNUS
Sadr
Andromeda Galaxy
Mirach
Gienah
Hamal
Alpheratz
Matar

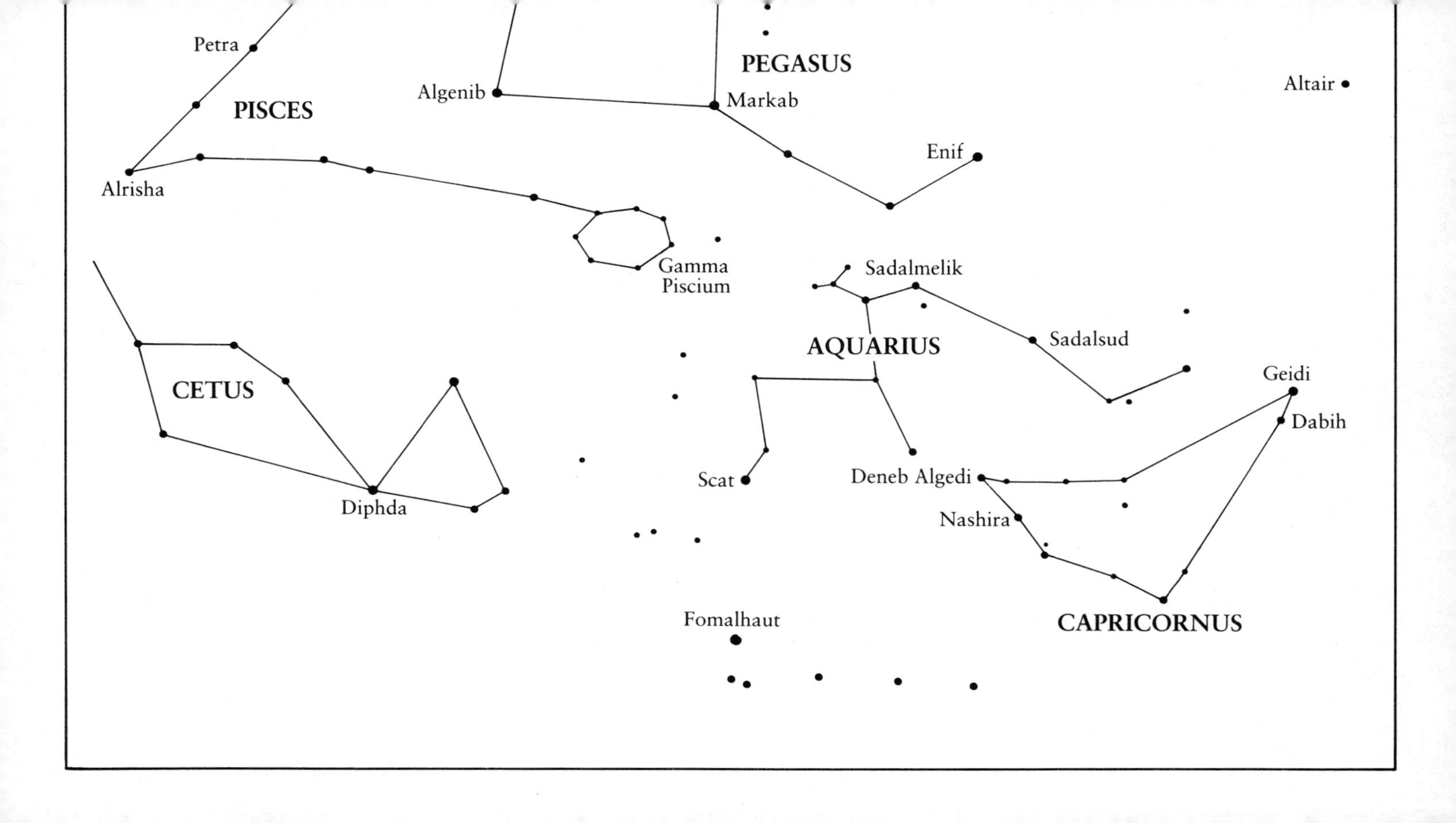
Petra
PISCES
Algenib
PEGASUS
Markab
Altair
Enif
Alrisha
Gamma
Piscium
Sadalmelik
AQUARIUS
Sadalsud
CETUS
Geidi
Dabih
Scat
Deneb Algedi
Diphda
Nashira
Fomalhaut
CAPRICORNUS

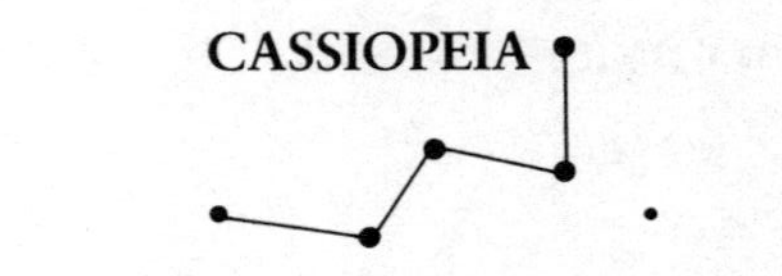

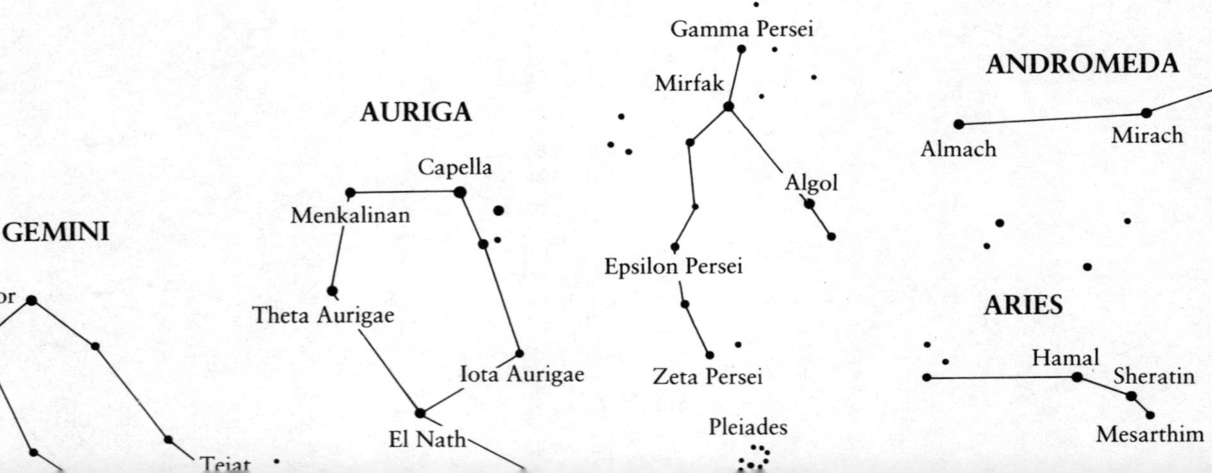
WINTER
CAMELOPARDALIS
CASSIOPEIA
PERSEUS
Gamma Persei
Mirfak
Algol
Epsilon Persei
Zeta Persei
Pleiades
ANDROMEDA
Almach
Mirach
ARIES
Hamal
Sheratin
Mesarthim
AURIGA
Capella
Menkalinan
Theta Aurigae
Iota Aurigae
El Nath
GEMINI
Castor
Pollux
Tejat

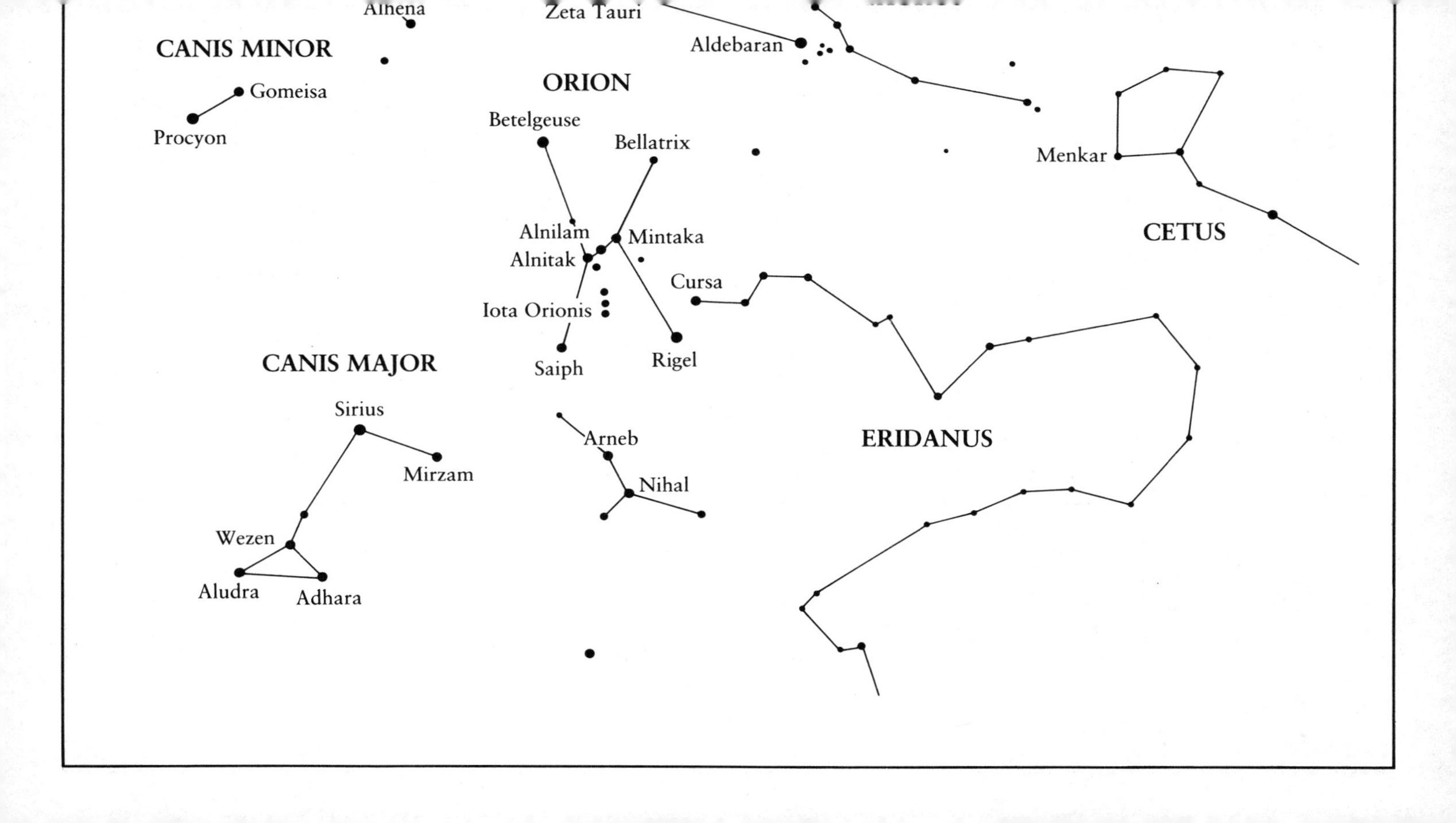
Alhena
Zeta Tauri
Aldebaran
CANIS MINOR
Gomeisa
Procyon
ORION
Betelgeuse
Bellatrix
Menkar
CETUS
Alnilam
Mintaka
Alnitak
Cursa
Iota Orionis
Saiph
Rigel
CANIS MAJOR
Sirius
Mirzam
Arneb
Nihal
ERIDANUS
Wezen
Aludra
Adhara

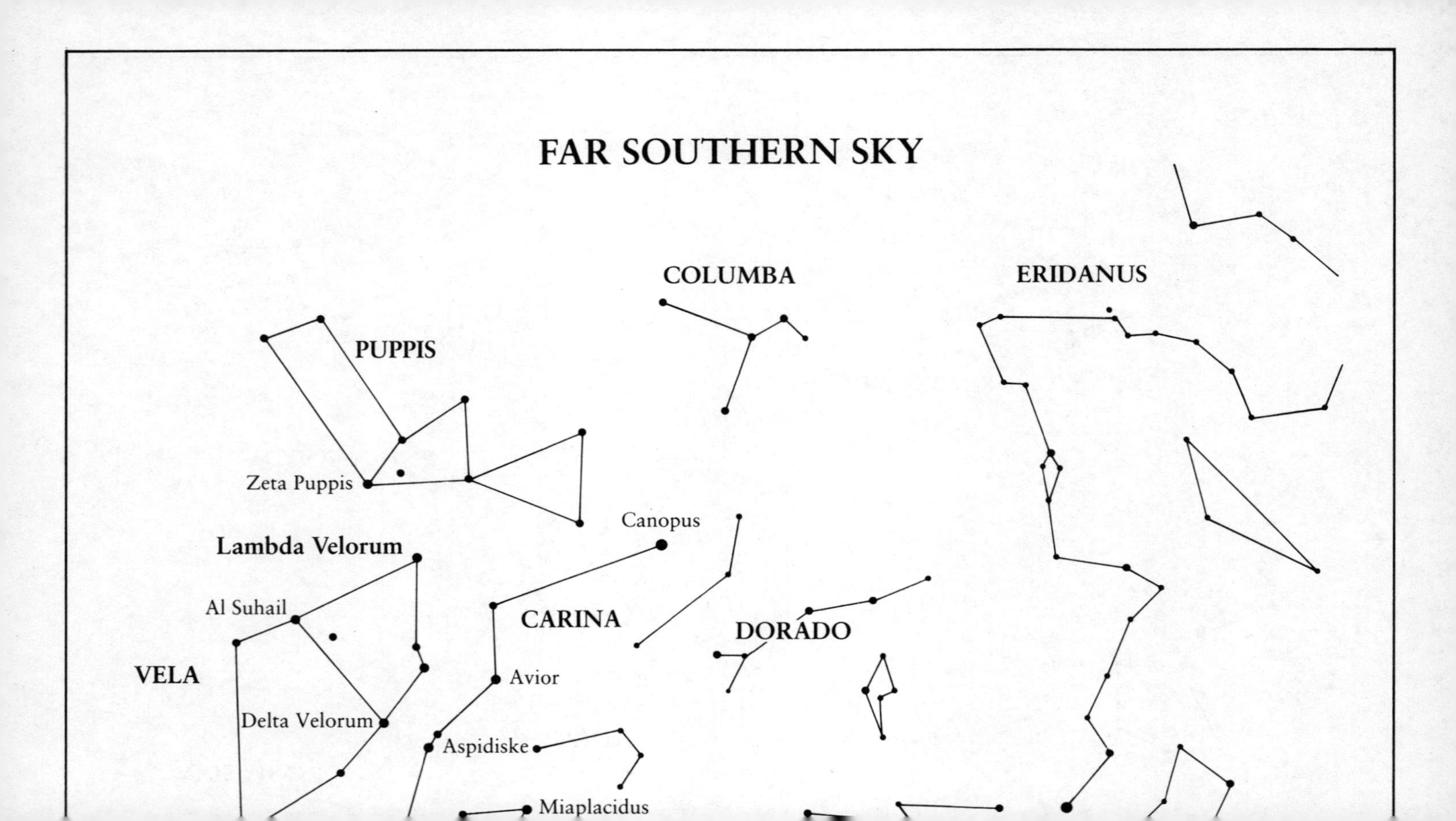
FAR SOUTHERN SKY
COLUMBA
ERIDANUS
PUPPIS
Zeta Puppis
Canopus
Lambda Velorum
Al Suhail
CARINA
DORADO
VELA
Avior
Delta Velorum
Aspidiske
Miaplacidus

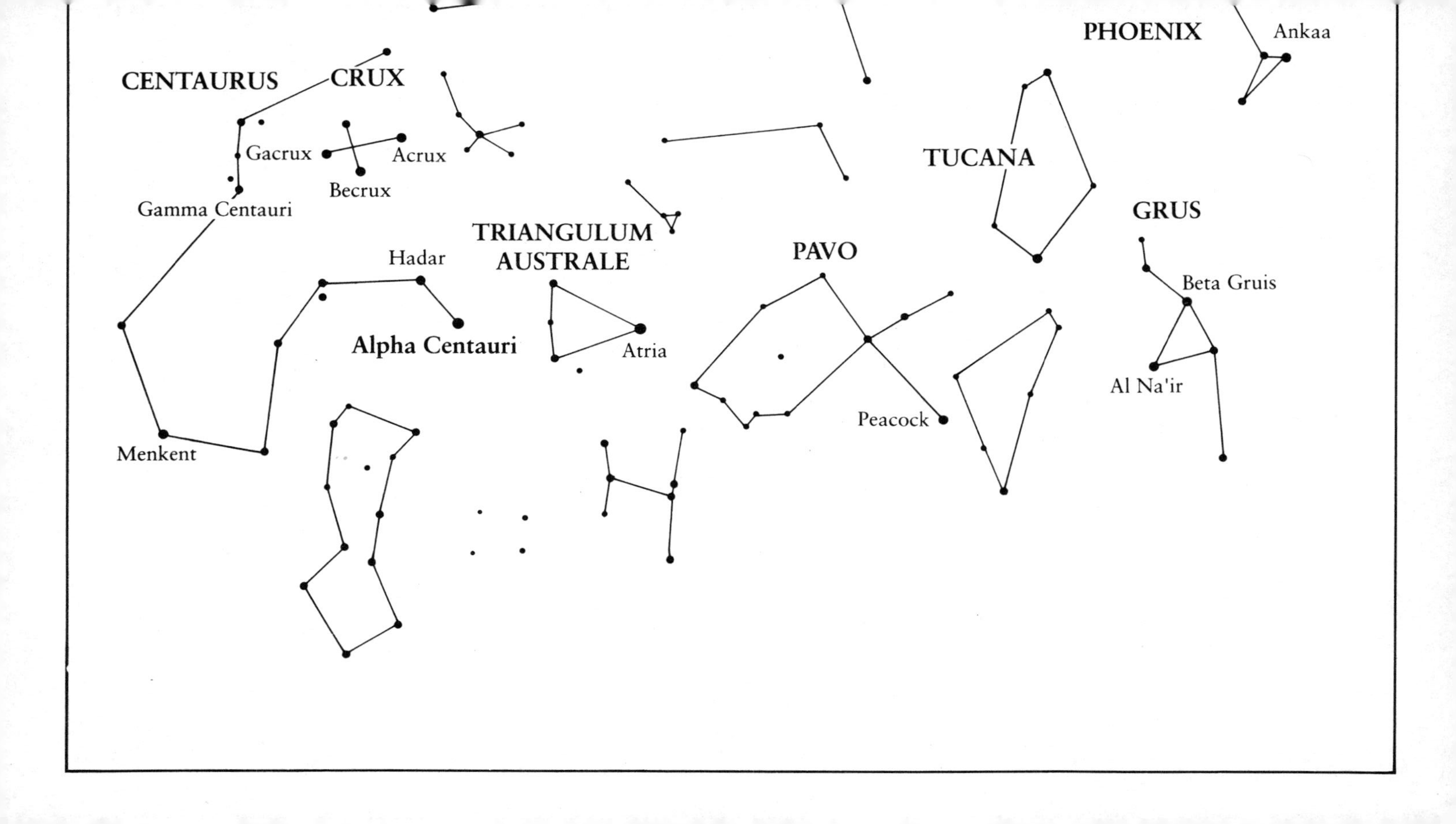
CENTAURUS
CRUX
PHOENIX
Ankaa
Gacrux
Acrux
Becrux
TUCANA
Gamma Centauri
GRUS
TRIANGULUM
AUSTRALE
PAVO
Hadar
Beta Gruis
Alpha Centauri
Atria
Al Na'ir
Peacock
Menkent

Affirmation

(Take a deep breath and create a state of inner silence and receptivity).

I open my being to the Source of all.

Bringing inside the Divine as expressed in multiple life-forms.

Each one carrying within a particular essence of universal wisdom and love.

As I reach out to connect with and be connected to all of these expressions.

I realize the journey that my soul has e'er travelled.

Those forms I have taken to understand universal truths.

Those times I have rested between incarnations to seek out even more knowledge.

To allow me to know who I am.

I embrace all of these energies offering love and evolvement.

Towards the goal of my path to the Devine.

May all of the expressions of the One be open to my sight.

May I be open to guide others along their perfect path.

May an interwoven branch of earth-forms be ready to demonstrate planetary love to all other forms seeking it.

May we all be prepared to merge into a universal family under God.

Bibliography

Published Material by Hilarion through Jon C. Fox

Spiritual Properties of Herbs by Gurudas (Cassandra Press 1988)

with Kevin Ryerson:

Flower Essences by Gurudas (Cassandra Press)

Gem Elixers and Vibrational Healing Vol's I and II by Gurudas (Cassandra Press 1986, 1989)

with many others:

New Cells, New Bodies, New Life edited by Virginia Essene (S.E.E. Publishing 1991)

Channeling: The Intuitive Connection and

Intuiting the Future by William Kautz and Melanie Branon (Harper and Row 1987, 1989)

Channeling by John Klimo (Jeremy P. Tarcher, Inc 1987)

Celestial Raise by Marcus (A.S.S.K. 1986)

For a catalogue of available books, tapes and devices, and information about readings, write to:

Jon C. Fox
P.O. Box 2209
Nevada City, CA 95959, U.S.A.

Index of Stars

General Index

For those interested in purchasing Starlight Elixirs, flower remedies, gem elixirs, rare (inert) gas essences, universal law tapes or related books and products, please contact:

U.K.
ARISTIA
Royal Albert Walk
Albert Road
Southsea, Hants, PO4 0JT
Contact: Michael
telephone: 705 293668
fax: 705 873964

SWITZERLAND
CHRUTER-DROGERIE EGGER
Fischergassli 13
8200 Schaffhausen
Schweizl
Contact: Jorg
telephone: 053 245 030
fax: 053 246 457

BELGIUM
CULTURE 2000 ASBL
2 rue Antoine Breart
B-1060 Brussels
Contact: Jean
telephone: 02 539 2487
fax: 02 539 3385

U.S.A. and Elsewhere
PEGASUS PRODUCTS
PO Box 228
Boulder, CO., 80306
Contact: Fred
telephone: 303 499 8434
fax: 303 449 8870